New Directions in German Studies

Vol. 42

Series Editor:

IMKE MEYER
Professor of Germanic Studies, University of Illinois at Chicago

Editorial Board:

KATHERINE ARENS
Professor of Germanic Studies, University of Texas at Austin

ROSWITHA BURWICK
Distinguished Chair of Modern Foreign Languages Emerita, Scripps College

RICHARD ELDRIDGE
Charles and Harriett Cox McDowell Professor of Philosophy, Swarthmore College

ERIKA FISCHER-LICHTE
Professor Emerita of Theater Studies, Freie Universität Berlin

CATRIONA MACLEOD
Frank Curtis Springer and Gertrude Melcher Springer Professor in the College and the Department of Germanic Studies, University of Chicago

STEPHAN SCHINDLER
Professor of German and Chair, University of South Florida

HEIDI SCHLIPPHACKE
Professor of Germanic Studies, University of Illinois at Chicago

ANDREW J. WEBBER
Professor of Modern German and Comparative Culture, Cambridge University

SILKE-MARIA WEINECK
Grace Lee Boggs Collegiate Professor of Comparative Literature and German Studies, University of Michigan

DAVID WELLBERY
LeRoy T. and Margaret Deffenbaugh Carlson University Professor, University of Chicago

SABINE WILKE
Joff Hanauer Distinguished Professor for Western Civilization and Professor of German, University of Washington

JOHN ZILCOSKY
Professor of German and Comparative Literature, University of Toronto

A list of volumes in the series appears at the end of this book.

Writing the Mountains
The Alpine Form in German Fiction

Jens Klenner

BLOOMSBURY ACADEMIC
NEW YORK • LONDON • OXFORD • NEW DELHI • SYDNEY

BLOOMSBURY ACADEMIC
Bloomsbury Publishing Inc, 1359 Broadway, New York, NY 10018, USA
Bloomsbury Publishing Plc, 50 Bedford Square, London, WC1B 3DP, UK
Bloomsbury Publishing Ireland, 29 Earlsfort Terrace, Dublin 2, D02 AY28, Ireland

BLOOMSBURY, BLOOMSBURY ACADEMIC and the Diana logo are
trademarks of Bloomsbury Publishing Plc

First published in the United States of America 2024
Paperback edition published 2026

Copyright © Jens Klenner, 2024

For legal purposes the Acknowledgments on p. viii constitute
an extension of this copyright page.

Cover design: Andrea F. Busci
Cover image © Jens Klenner, 2006

All rights reserved. No part of this publication may be: i) reproduced or transmitted in any form, electronic or mechanical, including photocopying, recording or by means of any information storage or retrieval system without prior permission in writing from the publishers; or ii) used or reproduced in any way for the training, development or operation of artificial intelligence (AI) technologies, including generative AI technologies. The rights holders expressly reserve this publication from the text and data mining exception as per Article 4(3) of the Digital Single Market Directive (EU) 2019/790.

Bloomsbury Publishing Inc does not have any control over, or responsibility for, any third-party websites referred to or in this book. All internet addresses given in this book were correct at the time of going to press. The author and publisher regret any inconvenience caused if addresses have changed or sites have ceased to exist, but can accept no responsibility for any such changes.

A catalogue record for this book is available from the British Library.

Library of Congress Cataloging-in-Publication Data
Names: Klenner, Jens, author.
Title: Writing the mountains : the alpine form in German fiction / Jens Klenner.
Description: New York : Bloomsbury Academic, 2024. | Series: New directions in German studies ; vol. 42 | Includes bibliographical references and index.
Identifiers: LCCN 2023050013 (print) | LCCN 2023050014 (ebook) | ISBN 9798765106501 (hardback) | ISBN 9798765106518 (paperback) | ISBN 9798765106525 (ebook) | ISBN 9798765106532 (pdf)
Subjects: LCSH: Mountains in literature. | German literature—History and criticism. | Swiss literature—History and criticism. | Austrian literature—History and criticism. | LCGFT: Literary criticism.
Classification: LCC PN56.M7 K54 2024 (print) | LCC PN56.M7 (ebook) | DDC 830.936—dc23/eng/20231211
LC record available at https://lccn.loc.gov/2023050013
LC ebook record available at https://lccn.loc.gov/2023050014

ISBN: HB: 979-8-7651-0650-1
PB 979-8-7651-0651-8
ePDF: 979-8-7651-0653-2
eBook: 979-8-7651-0652-5

Series: New Directions in German Studies

Typeset by RefineCatch Limited, Bungay, Suffolk

For product safety related questions contact productsafety@bloomsbury.com.

To find out more about our authors and books visit www.bloomsbury.com
and sign up for our newsletters.

For Barbara, my home.

Contents

Acknowledgments — viii
Note on Translation — x

I Mountains Transformed—Towards an Alpine Aesthetic — 1
1779—No Human Eye Could Do it Justice • Mountains at Rest? • Kant and the Sublime • Georg Simmel and the Resistance of Mountains • Shifting Forms

II Figures from Mines—E. T. A. Hoffmann's "Die Bergwerke zu Falun" — 35
1720—Summer • Source Material • An Aesthetic Existence • A Task for Poets • An Empty Cipher • Inversions, Transformations, Transitions

III Lost in the Mountains—Perspective and Displacement in Georg Büchner's "Lenz" — 69
Arrivals • Windows to the World • Return to the Mountains • A Lethal Gaze • Medusa in the Mountains

IV Folded Mountains—Paul Celan's "Gespräch im Gebirg" — 103
Mountains Vanished • August 1959—Reading Leibniz • Leaving for the Mountains • Wordscapes • The Folded Eye

V Liquid Mountains—Elfriede Jelinek's *Die Kinder der Toten* — 135
Mountain Graves • Historical Matters • Into the Mountains • Metamorphoses—Die Murie. Die Furie

Coda—Mountains Immaterial — 163

Bibliography — 171
Index — 185

Acknowledgments

The sense of gratitude I have to those who helped me see this book to its completion is infinite. Juliane Vogel, Daniel Heller-Roazen, and Michael Wood read its earliest drafts. Their generous and demanding readings helped me see what I was writing about. Several institutions provided material support and an intellectual home for the book and its author throughout its writing: the Comparative Literature Department at Princeton University, the Graduiertenkolleg "Das Reale in der Kultur der Moderne" at the Universität Konstanz, the Netzwerk Transatlantische Kooperation at the Universität Konstanz, and the Department of German at Bowdoin College, where I was welcomed and supported by two generations of unfailing colleagues and Germanists: Otto Emersleben, Helen Cafferty, Steve Cerf, Jill Suzanne Smith, and Birgit Tautz.

Over many years, I benefited immensely from conversations short and long with friends and colleagues. Those who gave their precious time and generously commented on portions of this monograph at various stages are Sean Johnson Andrews, Luisa Banki, Katra Byram, Allan Doyle, Antonia Eder, Rachel Galvin, Leslie Geddes, Mladen Gladic, Karin Höpker, Sean Ireton, Antje Kley, Albrecht Koschorke, Joel Lande, Jeffrey Lawrence, Jonas Lüscher, Patrick Moran, Zakir Paul, Juliane Prade-Weiss, Kristin Rebien, Sandra Beate Reimann, Bastian Reinert, Caroline Schaumann, Kathrin Schönegg, Philipp Schönthaler, Mareike Stoll, Sarah Wasserman, and Dora Zhang. I thank Hali Han, Imke Meyer, Haaris Naqvi, and two readers at Bloomsbury for making this a better book.

An early version of chapter four, "Where the Earth Folded: Celan's Encounter with Leibniz, August 1959," was published in *New German Critique* 134 (August 2018). Select portions of chapters one, three, and five were published in "Suspended in the Archives—The Three Natures of the Miner of Falun" in *Colloquia Germanica* 52 (2–3) (2020), in "Georg Simmel, 'Alpine Journeys' (1895) and 'On the Aesthetics of the Alps' (1911)," in *Mountains and the German Mind: Translations from Gessner to Messner, 1541–2009*, eds. Sean Ireton and Caroline Schaumann (Rochester:

Camden House, 2020), and in "'Land der Berge'? Erhaben Unerhabenes in *Frost* und *Die Kinder der Toten*," in *Intertextualität – Korrelationen – Korrespondenzen. Elfriede Jelinek und Thomas Bernhard*, eds. Bastian Reinert and Clemens Götze (Berlin: De Gruyter, 2019). I thank the publishers for their permissions.

I am grateful to Dmitry Freitor, Oleg Horholyuk, and Sandra Beate Reimann for trusting me with both ends of the rope. I wish to thank my dear friends Sean Johnson Andrews, Meryem Belkaïd, Naydene Bowder, Allyson Casey, Allan Doyle, Ludy Grandas, Morten Hansen, Michael Kolster, Ingrid Nelson, Kristi Olson, Kristin Rebien, Christy Shake, and Maggie Solberg for shared meals, conversations, and company. Here, Allyson Casey and Ingrid Nelson deserve repeated mention. For her steadfast friendship and unfailing encouragement, I remain thankful to Karin Höpker. The pure, loving, and bighearted curiosity of Nathaniel and Gabriel is a daily reminder that life can be otherwise.

And what can I say to Barbara Elias except thank you again—and again and again.

Note on Translation

Wherever possible, I refer to English translations of works cited. On occasion, I have modified the translations to better reflect the original text. Unless otherwise noted, all translations are my own.

I Mountains Transformed—Towards an Alpine Aesthetic

1779—NO HUMAN EYE COULD DO IT JUSTICE

On October 24th of 1779, during his second journey through Switzerland, Goethe sees Mont Blanc for the first time. In the following days, the poet makes four attempts to describe the ice-capped mountain, each at a different time of day, in a different light, and from a different location. Just outside Geneva, the mountain appears for the first time: "Der Montblanc, der über alle Gebirge des Faucigni ragt, kam immer mehr hervor. Die Sonne ging klar unter, es war so ein großer Anblick, daß ein menschlich Auge nicht dazu hinreicht." [Mont Blanc, which towers high above all the mountains of the Faucigni, stood out more and more. It was a brilliant sunset, and the view was so grand, that no human eye could do it justice.][1] The following day, on October 25th, Goethe sees the mountain in bright morning light with only the highest peaks visible above a sea of clouds: "Nur die hohen Gebirgketten waren unter einem klaren und heitern Himmel sichtbar, alle niederen Gegenden mit einem weißen wolkigen Nebelmeer überdeckt [. . .] Daraus stieg ostwärts die ganze reine Reihe aller Schnee- und Eisgebirge, [. . .] Der Montblanc gegen uns über schien der höchste [. . .]." [Under a bright and clear sky nothing was visible but the high mountain chain. All the lower regions were covered with a white sea of cloudy mist [. . .] Mont Blanc, right opposite to us, seemed the highest [. . .].][2] And on October 26th, the poet grasps the mountain once more at the end of the day, bathed in the red hue of a melancholy sunset:

> Es sah fast ängstlich aus. Wie ein gewaltiger Körper von außen gegen das Herz zu abstirbt, so erblaßten alle langsam gegen den Montblanc zu, dessen weiter Busen noch immer rot herüber glänzte und auch zuletzt uns noch einen rötlichen Schein zu behalten schien, wie man den Tod des Geliebten nicht gleich bekennen, und den Augenblick wo der Puls zu schlagen aufhört, nicht abschneiden will.

> [There was something fearful in the sight. Like a powerful body gradually dies off from the extremities to the heart, so the whole range gradually paled towards Mont Blanc, whose ampler bosom still shone a in deep red blush and even appeared to us to retain a reddish tint to the very last,—just as one does not want to

---

[1] Johann Wolfgang von Goethe, "Briefe aus der Schweiz. Zweite Abteilung," in *Campagne in Frankreich, Belagerung von Mainz, Reiseschriften*, ed. Klaus-Detlef Müller, vol. 16, *Sämtliche Werke, Briefe, Tagebücher und Gespräche* (Frankfurt/Main: Deutscher Klassiker Verlag, 1994), 35–6.

[2] Goethe, "Briefe aus der Schweiz. Zweite Abteilung," 38.

acknowledge the death of a beloved right away, just as one does not want to cut short the very moment when the pulse ceases to beat.]³

Goethe's final description is at night, upon arriving in Chamonix on November 4th around nine o'clock:

> Es wurde dunkler, wir kamen dem Tale Chamouni näher und endlich darein. Nur die großen Massen waren uns sichtbar. Die Sterne gingen nach einander auf und wir bemerkten über den Gipfeln der Berge, rechts vor uns, ein Licht, das wir nicht erklären konnten. Hell, ohne Glanz wie die Milchstraße, doch dichter, fast wie die Plejaden, nur größer, unterhielt es lang unsre Aufmerksamkeit, bis es endlich, da wir unsern Standpunkt änderten, wie eine Pyramide, von einem innern, geheimnisvollen Lichte durchzogen, das dem Schein eines Johanniswurms am besten verglichen werden kann, über den Gipfeln aller Berge hervorragte und uns gewiss machte, daß es der Gipfel des Montblanc war. Es war die Schönheit dieses Anblicks ganz außerordentlich; denn, da er mit den Sternen, die um ihn herumstunden, zwar nicht in gleich raschem Licht, doch in einer breitern zusammenhängendern Masse leuchtete, so schien er den Augen zu einer höhern Sphäre zu gehören und man hatte Müh', in Gedanken seine Wurzeln wieder an die Erde zu befestigen.

> [It got darker, we approached the Valley of Chamouni and at last, we entered it. Nothing but the large masses were discernible. The stars came out one by one and we noticed above the peaks of the summits, to the right of us, a light which we could not explain. Clear, but without brilliancy like the milky way, yet closer, almost like that of the Pleiades, only bigger—it riveted our attention, until at last, as our position changed, it towered like a pyramid illuminated by a secret light within, which could best be compared to the gleam of a glowworm, high above the peaks of all the surrounding mountains and convinced us that it must be the peak of Mont Blanc. The beauty of this view was extraordinary. For while, together with the stars that clustered round it, it glimmered—not, indeed, with the same twinkling light, but in a broader and more continuous mass—it seemed to our eyes to belong to a higher sphere, and one had difficulty in thought to fix its roots again in the earth.]⁴

---

3   Goethe, "Briefe aus der Schweiz. Zweite Abteilung," 43.
4   Goethe, "Briefe aus der Schweiz. Zweite Abteilung," 48.

Goethe's four separate views of Mont Blanc can hardly be combined into one composite sketch of the mountain since they differ so greatly in mood and matter. Consequently, his renditions of Mont Blanc question the idea of description as an accumulative endeavor of representation. By Goethe's own account, Mont Blanc, the Alps' highest mountain, is at the same time organic—"ein gewaltiger Körper," "ein Johanniswurm"— yet inorganic, it is celestial—"wie die Plejaden," "zu einer höheren Sphäre zu gehören"—yet firmly grounded. The human senses falter before its grandness—"daß ein menschlich Auge nicht dazu hinreicht"— and the heretofore manageable task of seeing and describing suddenly becomes impossible for a poet, let alone for two: "Meine Beschreibung fängt an unordentlich und ängstlich zu werden, auch brauchte es eigentlich immer zwei Menschen, einen der's sähe und einen der's beschriebe." [My description begins to be irregular and forced: in fact, one wants two persons here,—one to see, and the other to describe.][5] Elsewhere in Switzerland, Goethe can neither draw nor write: "Meinem Gefährten beliebte es hier auszuruhen; er munterte mich auf, die bedeutenden Ansichten zu zeichnen. Die Umrisse mochten mir gelingen, aber es trat nichts hervor, nicht zurück; für dergleichen Gegenstände hatte ich keine Sprache." [My companion wanted to rest here; he encouraged me to draw the significant views. I was able to draw their outlines, but nothing stood out, nothing receded; I had no language for such things.][6] Writing in the presence of the mountain ultimately becomes an unpleasant, even painful task for Goethe, and he would much rather refer his reader to the works of others:

> Es ist immer eine Resolution, als wie wenn man in's kalte Wasser soll, ehe ich die Feder nehmen mag, zu schreiben; Hier hätt' ich nun gerade Lust, Sie auf die Beschreibung der Savoyschen Eisgebirge, die Bourit, ein passionierter Kletterer, herausgegeben hat, zu verweisen.

> [To take up one's pen and write, almost requires as great an effort as to go into a cold river. At this point I would rather refer you to the description of the icy Savoyard mountains published by Bourit, a passionate climber.][7]

---

[5] Goethe, "Briefe aus der Schweiz. Zweite Abteilung," 48.
[6] Johann Wolfgang von Goethe, *Aus meinem Leben. Dichtung und Wahrheit* in *Werke, Kommentare und Register: Hamburger Ausgabe in 14 Bänden*, ed. Erich Trunz, vol. 10 (München: C. H. Beck, 1999), 146.
[7] Goethe, "Briefe aus der Schweiz. Zweite Abteilung," 48–9.

By Goethe's own admission, experience and description emerge as inadequate when facing a mountain. Included in his failed accounts of Mont Blanc is not only his inability to faithfully transfer into text or image what he perceives but also a confrontation with an environment that resists representation and fits neither into ideas of description, narration, and composition, nor into those of scale, space, and selfhood. With this, the following book argues, the mountains as imposing, obdurate masses powerfully challenge older understandings of narration, description, and representation and force writers to grapple with how to write the mountains anew. Critical scholarship on mountains, for all its richness, has often focused on the social, political, ethnographic, cartographic, or scientific encounters with vertiginous heights. In *Romantic Rocks, Aesthetic Geology*, Noah Heringman argues that British literary culture was fundamentally shaped by many of the same forces that created geology as a science in the period 1770–1820.[8] Jason Grove's *Geological Unconscious* most recently traces geological knowledge in a series of readings of romantic, realist, and modernist German language works and shows the entanglement of the human and the mineral in periods well before the geological turn of contemporary cultural and literary studies.[9] In *Stone*, Jeffrey Jerome Cohen outlines an ecological enmeshment of man and minerals and argues that a stone's hardness and longevity is also an invitation to make sense of the world in other than human terms.[10] Caroline Schaumann's *Peak Pursuit* argues that mountaineering as sport and leisurely activity developed out of early scientific forays into the mountains, and shows how late eighteenth and early nineteenth-century scientists became increasingly fascinated by the idea of climbing for the sake of conquest.[11] In *The Mountain*, geographers Bernard Debarbieux and Gilles Rudaz trace the origins of the very concept of a mountain, showing how it is not a mere geographic feature but ultimately an idea, one that has evolved over time, influenced by changes in political climates and cultural attitudes.[12] Other publications, though wide-ranging in their traditional, literary approach, engage mountains as much more general, static entities, where the mountainous

---

[8] Noah Heringman, *Romantic Rocks, Aesthetic Geology* (Ithaca, NY: Cornell University Press, 2004).
[9] Jason Groves, *The Geological Unconscious: German Literature and the Mineral Imaginary* (New York: Fordham University Press, 2020).
[10] Jeffrey Jerome Cohen, *Stone: An Ecology of the Inhuman* (Minneapolis: University of Minnesota Press, 2015).
[11] Caroline Schaumann, *Peak Pursuits: The Emergence of Mountaineering in the Nineteenth Century* (New Haven, CT: Yale University Press, 2020).
[12] Bernard Darbieux and Gilles Rudaz, *The Mountain: A Political History from the Enlightenment to the Present* (Chicago: University of Chicago Press, 2015).

terrain creates a sense of place and provides a narrative backdrop for social or cultural negotiations.[13]

Writing the Mountains offers a different, albeit complementary approach. Here, mountains appear as disturbing spaces where principles of aesthetic representation are challenged, genres are deconstructed, and new ideas of narration are developed. The following book explores in a theoretically informed way the mountains' resistance to representation and the poetological complexities that arise when narratives attempt to adequately capture the rocky terrain. Each author in *Writing the Mountains* writes their own mountain and in so doing dispenses with the problematic of fidelity to a single idea of what a mountain is. Yet even when mountains are defined more narrowly, their meanings multiply. In these pages, it may mean a territory that is forbidden and inaccessible, a landscape that reveals itself as a repository of a brutal past, a summit that reaches deep underground, or a realm of perspectival extremes. Ultimately, this breakdown in representation is more than a mere rhetorical convention. At the point of Goethe's writing, the mountains have been vexing travelers for decades, if not centuries. Mountains were seen as hostile terrain, resistant to man's efforts to tame them. For a long time, writers, with the two oft-mentioned exceptions of the adventures of the sixteenth-century Swiss humanists Benedikt Marti and Konrad Gessner, questioned the value of expeditions such as Petrarca's 1336 ascension of Mont Ventoux.[14] And although he

---

[13] In chronological order, these volumes are *"Über allen Gipfeln . . .": Bergmotive in der deutschsprachigen Literatur des 18. bis 21. Jahrhunderts*, eds. Edward Bialek and Jan Pacholski (Dresden: Neisse Verlag, 2008); *Das Erschreiben der Berge: Die Alpen in der deutschsprachigen Literatur*, ed. Johann Georg Lughofer (Innsbruck: Innsbruck University Press, 2014); Martina Kopf, *Alpinismus—Andinismus: Gebirgslandschaften in europäischer und lateinamerikanischer Literatur* (Stuttgart: J. B. Metzler, 2016); Kathrin Geist, *Berg-Sehn-Sucht: Der Alpenraum in der deutschsprachigen Literatur* (Paderborn: Wilhelm Fink, 2018). I would be remiss, of course, not to note the two foundational volumes of U.S. American mountain studies, *Heights of Reflection: Mountains in the German Imagination from the Middle Ages to the Twenty-First Century*, eds. Sean Ireton and Caroline Schaumann (Rochester, NY: Camden House, 2012), and *Mountains and the German Mind: Translations from Gessner to Messner, 1541–2009*, eds. Sean Ireton and Caroline Schaumann (Rochester, NY: Camden House, 2020).

[14] Konrad Gessner, often referred to as the Swiss Pliny, vowed to climb at least one mountain per year—but only for scientific purposes. See Dan Hooley, "Gessner's Mountain Sublime," in *Mountain Dialogues from Antiquity to Modernity*, eds. Dawn Hollis and Jason König (London: Bloomsbury Academic, 2021), 21–36. Benedikt Marti's "Lob der Berge" and Konrad Gessner's "Brief über die Bewunderung der Berge, geschrieben vom Arzt Konrad Geßner und Jakob Vogel" and "Beschreibung des Frakmont, oder Pilatus mit dem gewöhnlichen Namen, bei Luzern in der Schweiz. 20. August 1555," are collected in *Die Entdeckung der Alpen. Eine Sammlung schweizerischer und deutscher Alpenliteratur*

used the mountains to elaborate his theories, Kant himself points out in *Kritik der Urteilskraft* that the good and sensible Savoyard mountain farmer deemed all lovers of icy mountains fools: "So nannte der gute, übrigens verständige savoyische Bauer (wie Hr. v. Saussure erzählt) alle Liebhaber der Eisgebirge ohne Bedenken Narren." [Thus the good and otherwise sensible Savoyard peasant (as Herr de Saussure relates) had no hesitation in calling all devotees of the icy mountains fools.][15] Kant, who famously never left Königsberg and thus never laid eyes on the Alps, received all of his examples of terrifying mountainscapes and overhanging rocks mediated through literature, and well into the eighteenth century, travel accounts and books about the Alps were filled with stories of toil and suffering.[16] The mountains not only presented travelers with the dangers of rock falls, deep crevasses, and avalanches, but the rocky wilderness was also home to fiery dragons. So many dragons, in fact, that the Swiss physician and naturalist Johann Jakob Scheuchzer was able to record multiple sightings, descriptions, and illustrations of dragons in his four-volume *Itinera per Helvetiae Alpinas Regiones Facta Annis 1702–1711*. Goethe, on his first journey through Switzerland in 1775, still proffers that the presence of dragons high up in the mountains is not inconceivable: "Hier kostet es der Einbildungskraft nicht viel, sich Drachennester in den Klüften zu

---

  bis zum Jahr 1800, ed. Richard Weiss (Frauenfeld: Huber, 1934), 1–5, 6–12, 13–14. See also Joachim Ritter, "Landschaft: Zur Funktion des Ästhetischen in der modernen Gesellschaft," *Subjektivität. Sechs Aufsätze* (Frankfurt/Main: Suhrkamp, 1974), 141–63, 141–3. Recent scholarship by Dawn L. Hollis, among others, powerfully contests the modern, exceptionalist transition from *terra incognita* to *locus amoenus*, from "mountain gloom" to "mountain glory," to borrow from Marjorie Hope Nicolson's homonymous book title, by showing that a positive reception of and engagement with mountains can be traced back as far as Greek and Roman antiquity. See Dawn L. Hollis, "Mountain Gloom and Mountain Glory: The Genealogy of an Idea," *ISLE: Interdisciplinary Studies in Literature and Environment* 26, no. 4 (Autumn 2019): 1038–61; Dawn L. Hollis and Jason Köng (eds.), *Mountain Dialogues from Antiquity to Modernity* (New York: Bloomsbury Academic, 2021); Marjorie Hope Nicolson, *Mountain Gloom and Mountain Glory: The Development of the Aesthetics of the Infinite* (New York: W. W. Norton, 1959).

15 Immanuel Kant, *Kritik der Urteilskraft. Werkausgabe*, volume 10, ed. Wilhelm Weischedel (Frankfurt/Main: Suhrkamp, 1974), B111–12; A110–11. Immanuel Kant, *Critique of the Power of Judgement*, trans. Paul Guyer (Cambridge: Cambridge University Press, 2000), 148. Kant here refers to the writings of Horace-Bénédict de Saussure, the third man to reach the summit of Mont Blanc in 1787. Horace-Bénédict de Saussure, *Voyages dans les Alpes: précédés d'un essai sur l'histoire naturelle des environs de Genève* (Paris: Samuel Fauche, 1779).

16 For an illuminating reading of Kant's literary sources, see Gernot Böhme, "Pyramiden und Berge," *Kants "Kritik der Urteilskraft" in neuer Sicht* (Frankfurt/Main: Suhrkamp, 1999), 83–107.

denken." [Up here, it is not difficult for the imagination to see dragons' nests in the clefts.][17] Until the late 1700s the mountains were a space of fear and horror, and a region devoid of any aesthetic merit. When in 1671 the English theologian Thomas Burnet set out on his Grand Tour—the traditional educational journey by Englishmen of the upper class—he was acquainted with the mountains from books, maps, and atlases only. Viewing the Alps from a distance and hence familiar with their structured representations, "Burnet could still believe in proportion and symmetry."[18] But once deep in the mountains and after his first ascent, he was awestruck by what he thought to be "wild, vast, and indigested Heaps of Stones and Earth":

> But suppose a Man was carried asleep out of a plain Country amongst the Alps, and left there upon the Top of one of the highest Mountains, when he wak'd and look'd about him, he wou'd think himself in an inchanted Country, or carried into another World; every Thing wou'd appear to him so different to what he had ever seen or imagin'd before. To see on every Hand of him a Multitude of vast Bodies thrown together in Confusion, as those Mountains are; Rocks standing naked round about him; and the hollow Valleys gaping under him; and at his Feet, it may be, a Heap of Frozen Snow in the midst of summer. He would hear the Thunder come from below, and see the black Clouds hanging beneath him; upon such a Prospect it would not be easy to him to persuade himself that he was still upon the same Earth; but if he did, he would be convinc'd, at least, that there are some Regions of it strangely rude, and ruin-like, and very different from what he had ever thought before.[19]

The idea that the mountains could be a source of pleasure appears first in the travel writing of the Englishmen Henry More, Joseph Addison, John Dennis, and Anthony Shaftsbury. Setting out on their Grand Tour, their ventures also took them across the Swiss Alps to Italy, where they describe their experiences as those of "delightful Horrour," or "terrible Joy." When Dennis writes to his friend to give him a first account of the mountains, he is met with resistance:

---

[17] Goethe, *Aus meinem Leben. Dichtung und Wahrheit*, 147.
[18] Nicolson, *Mountain Gloom*, 209.
[19] Thomas Burnet, *The Sacred Theory of the Earth: Containing an Account of the Original of the Earth, and of all the General Changes which it hath already undergone, or is to undergo, till the Consummation of all Things* (London: J. Hooke, 1726), 173, 191–2.

> 'Tis an easy thing to describe Rome or Naples to you, because you have seen something yourself that holds at least some resemblance with them; but impossible to set a mountain before your Eyes, that is inaccessible almost to the sight, and wearies the very Eye to climb it.

Dennis most likely failed in bringing the mountains before his friend's eye, yet he may have succeeded in conveying the sensations of finding oneself amidst the rocky structures for the first time:

> We entered into Savoy in the Morning, and past over Mount Aiguebellette. The ascent was the more easie, because it wound about the Mountain. But as soon as we had conquer'd one half of it, the unusual heighth in which we found our selves, the impending Rock that hung over us, the dreadful Depth of the Precipice, and the Torrent that roar'd at the bottom, gave us such a view as was altogether new and amazing. [. . .] In the very same place Nature was seen Severe and Wanton. In the mean time we walk'd upon the very brink, in a literal sense, of Destruction; one Stumble, and both Life and Carcass had been at once destroy'd. The sense of all this produc'd different motions in me, viz., a delightful Horrour, a terrible Joy, and at the same time, that I was infinitely pleas'd, I trembled.[20]

Addison, remarking on his own travels of 1699, wrote describing an analogous impression:

> At the one side of the walks you have a near prospect of the Alps, which are broken into so many steeps and precipices, that they fill the mind with an agreeable kind of horror, and form one of the most irregular misshapen scenes in the world.[21]

Though less prolific and verbose, descriptions by prominent German travelers are not too dissimilar from the English. Take, for example,

---

[20] John Dennis, *Miscellanies in Verse and Prose* (London: James Knapton, 1693).
[21] Joseph Addison, *Remarks on Several Parts of Italy, etc. in the years 1701, 1702, 1703* (London: J. Tonson, 1717), 300. In her analysis of the works of Dennis, Addison, Shaftsbury, and Moore, Marjorie Hope Nicolson shows how the notion of the sublime shifted from a technical term of rhetoric to a category applicable to phenomena in nature. Nicolson, *Mountain*. See also Ruth and Dieter Groh's two-volume study *Weltbild und Naturaneignung. Zur Kulturgeschichte der Natur* (Frankfurt/Main: Suhrkamp, 1991) and *Die Außenwelt der Innenwelt. Zur Kulturgeschichte der Natur 2* (Frankfurt/Main: Suhrkamp, 1996).

what can be called the Urtext of Alpine enthusiasm, Albrecht von Haller's 1732 *In den Alpen*. In the scopically and epistemologically most dominant position—on top of the mountain—the lyrical I must close their eyes because what lies before it is overwhelming:

> So wird, was die Natur am prächtigsten gebildet,
> Mit immer neuer Lust von einem Berg erblickt;
> Durch den zerfahrnen Dunst von einer dünnen Wolke,
> Eröffnet sich zugleich der Schauplatz einer Welt,
> Ein weiter Aufenthalt von mehr als einem Volke
> Zeigt alles auf einmal, was sein Bezirk enthält;
> *Ein sanfter Schwindel schließt die allzuschwachen Augen,*
> *Die den zu breiten Kreis nicht durchzustrahlen taugen.*

> [Thus is, what nature most magnificently formed,
> Seen from a mountain with renewed delight;
> Through the scattered haze from a thin cloud,
> At the same time, the scene of a world opens up
> A long stay of more than one people
> Shows everything its district contains at once;
> *A gentle dizziness closes the all too weak eyes,*
> *Who are not good enough to shine through the circle that is too wide.*][22]

The wanderer of Friedrich Schiller's 1795 *Der Spaziergang* suffers a similar faintness on a mountaintop and can only brace themselves with a literal banister alongside a mountain trail—"*ein geländerter Steig*":

> Unabsehbar ergießt sich vor meinen Blicken die Ferne,
> Und ein blaues Gebirg endigt im Dufte die Welt.
> Tief an des Berges Fuß, der gählings unter mir abstürzt,
> Wallet des grünlichten Stroms fließender Spiegel vorbei.
> Endlos unter mir seh' ich den Aether, über mir endlos,
> *Blicke mit Schwindeln hinauf, blicke mit Schaudern hinab,*
> *Aber zwischen der ewigen Höh' und der ewigen Tiefe*
> *Trägt ein geländerter Steig sicher den Wandrer dahin.*

> [Boundlessly seems the distance before my gaze to be stretching,
> And a blue mountain range terminates sweetly the world.
> Deep at the foot of the mountain, that under me falls away steeply,
> Wanders the greenish-hued stream, looking like glass as it flows.

---

[22] Albrecht von Haller, *Die Alpen*, ed. Harold T. Betteridge (Berlin: Akademie Verlag, 1959), 20; emphasis mine.

> Endlessly under me I see the ether, and endlessly over me,
> *Giddily I look up, shudderingly I look down,*
> *But between the infinite height and the infinite depth*
> *a well-guarded path safely guides the wanderer.*][23]

Peter H. Hansen recently identified this apotheotic "summit position" as fundamental to the development of modernity and mountaineering, two "mutually constitutive" phenomena, as he further contends, yet, as Haller and Schiller reveal, the inception of modernity and mountaineering appear to rest on epistemologically and ontologically unstable footing.[24] In other literary examples, as we will see, Schiller and Haller's dizziness turns to outright madness, as is the case in Georg Büchner's "Lenz," where the eponymous protagonist tries time and again in vain to order and structure the mountainous landscape that lies before him. Others face comparable difficulties. The classists Johann Joachim Winkelmann, while crossing the Alps from Innsbruck to Venice in 1755, is rumored to have drawn the curtains of his coach because the view of the mountains frightened him too much.[25] And about four decades after Winkelmann, in 1793, Jean Paul suffers a similar though slightly less nauseating experience in the mountains. Jean Paul's homonymous "Vorredner" writes the preface to his *Die unsichtbare Loge* as he is being carried in a sedan-chair to the summit of the Schneeberg, the highest mountain of the Fichtelgebirge. That is, the poet does not "climb" the entire mountain in the sedan-chair. He is first transported by coach to the Ochsenkopf, the second highest mountain of the Fichtelgebirge, where he is then transferred into the sedan-chair, with his eyes closed so as not to take in his surroundings:

> —Endlich hab' ich nun den Ochsenkopf.—Diese Zeile ist kein Vers, sondern nur ein Zeichen, daß ich droben war und da viel that: meine Sänfte wurde abgeschnallt und ich mit geschlossenen Augen hineingeschafft, weil ich erst auf dem Schneeberg, der Kuppel des Fichtelgebirges, mich umsehen will.
>
> [I've finally reached the Ochsenkopf.—This line isn't a verse but just a sign that I was up there and did a lot there: my sedan-chair

---

[23] Friedrich Schiller, "Der Spaziergang," in *Sämtliche Werke in 5 Bänden*, ed. Albert Meier, vol. 1 (München: Carl Hanser Verlag, 2011), 228–34, 229; emphasis mine.
[24] Peter. H. Hansen, *The Summits of Modern Man: Mountaineering after the Enlightenment* (Cambridge, MA: Harvard University Press, 2013), 2–3, 11, 16–17.
[25] See Jacek Wozniakowski, *Die Wildnis. Zur Deutungsgeschichte des Berges in der europäischen Neuzeit* (Frankfurt/Main: Suhrkamp, 1974), 317, and Albrecht Koschorke, *Die Geschichte des Horizonts* (Frankfurt/Main: Suhrkamp, 1990), 121.

was unbuckled, and I was put into it with my eyes closed, because I did not want to look around until the Schneeberg, the dome of the Fichtelgebirge.]²⁶

While in the coach, Jean Paul occupies himself with writing so as not to look outside and take in the landscape piece by piece, triangulated by scientific units of measurement, but to wait until he reaches the summit and behold everything at once:

Ich muß nun diese Vorrede schreiben, damit ich unter dem Fahren nicht aus der Schreibtafel und Kutsche hinaussehe, ich meine, damit ich die grenzenlose Aussicht oben nicht wie einen Frühling nach Kubikruten, die Ströme nach Ellen, die Wälder nach Klaftern, die Berge nach Schiffpfunden, von meinen Pferden zugebröckelt bekomme, sondern damit ich den großen Zirkus und Paradeplatz der Natur mit allen seinen Strömen und Bergen auf einmal in die aufgeschlossene Seele nehme.

[I must now write this preface, so that I don't look away from the writing tablet and out of the carriage while driving, I mean, so that my horses don't give me the limitless view above in crumbs like a spring by cubic rods, the streams by cubits, the forests by fathoms, the mountains by ship pounds, but so that my open-minded soul can absorb the great circus and parade ground of nature with all its streams and mountains all at once.]²⁷

Once at the summit, however, Jean Paul remains in the sedan-chair for an hour—with the curtains drawn. Instead of exiting and taking in the view as planned, he merely imagines the beauty of the mountains that could greet him: "Ich schrieb jetzt eine Stunde nicht; ich bin nun auf dem Schneeberg, aber noch in der Sänfte. Erhabne Paradiese liegen um mich ungesehen." ["I didn't write for an hour; I am on the Schneeberg now, but still in the sedan-chair. Unseen sublime paradises surround me."]²⁸ Ten years later, Goethe still displays the old contempt for seeing nature when he contemplates his "pointless travels" to Switzerland and through the Alps. And at the end of the *Wanderjahre*, in "Makariens Archiv," we find the following aphorism, where he writes disparagingly:

---

²⁶ Jean Paul, *Die unsichtbare Loge*, in *Jean Pauls Sämtliche Werke. Historisch-kritische Ausgabe herausgegeben von der Preußischen Akademie der Wissenschaften*, ed. Eduard Berend (Weimar: Herman Böhlaus Nachfolger, 1927), 18.
²⁷ Jean Paul, *Die unsichtbare Loge*, 14.
²⁸ Jean Paul, *Die unsichtbare Loge*, 21.

"Und diese Zickzackkämme, die widerwärtigen Felswände, die ungestalten Granitpyramiden, welche die schönsten Weltbreiten mit den Schrecknissen des Nordpols bedecken, wie sollte sich ein wohlwollender Mann daran gefallen und ein Menschfreund sie preisen!" [And these jagged ridges, the repugnant cliffs, the monstrous pyramids of granite, which cover the most beautiful areas of the world with the horrors of the North pole; how could any benevolent man enjoy them, and any philanthropist praise them!][29] Despite Goethe's multiple attempts at describing the highest peak of the Alps, the summit of Mont Blanc remained a pictorial blind spot until almost one century after its first ascent. In 1869, Charles Soulier was the first to present an unfocused, low-contrast photo, exposed on the mountain's summit. In its first publication, the grainy image was subtitled with the question, "What is it that reveals itself to our gaze?"[30] The undecipherable nature of the photograph was not surprising. Critics, from Chateaubriand on, were convinced that images were an entirely inappropriate medium to represent mountains. In 1841, the French painter Étienne Delécluse, for example, apodictically declared:

> L'homme est anéanti, il disparaît, il n'existe plus. Or l'expérience prouve que là où l'homme n'est plus le centre, là où il ne sert plus de mètre au moyen duquel on apprécie la grandeur relative (physique et morlae) des choses, il n'y a pas d'art possible. [. . .] Les Alpes ne sont pas pittoresques, elles tuent l'home.
>
> [Man is annihilated, he disappears, he no longer exists. Now, experience proves that where man is no longer the center, where he is no longer a yardstick by means of which one appreciates the relative size (physical and moral) of things, there is no art possible. [. . .] The Alps are not picturesque, they kill man.][31]

---

[29] Johann Wolfgang von Goethe, "Aus Makariens Archiv," *Wilhelm Meisters Wanderjahre* in *Werke, Kommentare, und Register, Hamburger Ausgabe in 14 Bänden*, ed. Erich Trunz, vol. 8 (München: C. H. Beck, 1999), 476. For an account of German mountain travels during the Goethe era, cf. Petra Raymond, *Von der Landschaft im Kopf zur Landschaft aus Sprache: Die Romantisierung der Alpen und die Literarisierung des Gebirges in der Erzählprosa der Goethezeit* (Tübingen: Max Niemeyer, 1993).

[30] See Wozniakowski, *Die Wildnis*, and Phillipp Felsch, "Mountains of Sublimity, Mountains of Fatigue: Towards a History of Speechlessness in the Alps," *Science in Context* 22, no. 3 (2009): 341–64, 352.

[31] Etienne Delecleuse to Wolfgang-Adam Töppfer, 1841, cited in *Mont-Blanc: Conquête de l'imaginaire*, eds. Paul Guichonnet et al. (Chambéry: La Fontaine de Siloé, 2002), 363.

Even from this cursory glimpse at some travel writing, we can see the change in the perception of the mountains. The mountains, heretofore avoided, begin to garner attention. What previously has been called terrible and frightening is now elevated to be sublime. For the mountains to "become" sublime, both the perception of the mountains and the notion of the sublime had to change. But the transformation of these concepts happens in tandem, in a kind of reciprocal relationship whereby the changing view of nature frees the sublime from a strictly rhetorical context, bringing it into the realm of nature. And simultaneously, the adaptation of the sublime in response to nature allows nature, once alien and terrifying, to generate aesthetic, pleasurable experiences. Additionally, these brief excerpts also show that the mountains confounded trusted strategies of comparison and analogy. Experiencing the mountains prompted not only questions about what is encountered but also about how that encounter can be represented. The act of writing the mountain is challenged by a terrain that resists representation and undermines an anthropocentric contingency between subject, object, and text. Subsequently, the mountains force authors to devise new narrative attempts to overcome these epistemological difficulties and to capture the vexing heights more adequately. This book's focus, then, is upon what might be called a poetics of the mountains: the strategies devised by authors to write the mountains. But *Writing the Mountains* also emphasizes the myriad ways the mountainous environment undermines this very endeavor at every turn.

MOUNTAINS AT REST? KANT AND THE SUBLIME

While the poets and artists struggled in the face of the mountains, it seemed for a short period as if at least the philosophers had managed to bring the rocky terrain to rest. In 1757, Edmund Burke published *A philosophical enquiry into the origin of our ideas of the sublime and the beautiful*, and by 1790, Immanuel Kant's analytic of the sublime had become the most widely known philosophical reference for those wishing to describe the experience of the mountains. Though Kant famously disliked the mountains, his name remains forever yoked to any aesthetic contemplation of the Alps. And even if we would like to avoid Kant, as some scholars have, we still ought to recognize the theoretical and aesthetic scaffolding his concept of the sublime provided over the last two centuries. Kant's notion of the sublime was exemplified by the panoramic view of and from the mountains: a limitless, massive, formless, and sometimes illegible vision of nature—from a safe distance—unfolding in front of the human gaze.[32] Though the mountains dwarf and overpower the observer, Kant remarks on their ability to empower the subject. Displeasure—terror evoked by the vastness of the mountains—is transformed into pleasure by the sense of understanding that the subject has vis-à-vis the sublime. The subject confronts the mountains, which are ungraspable and overwhelming. But then, using reason to make sense of these sensations, the subject renders them legible—he comprehends, masters, and even takes pleasure from the indomitable view. The power of nature seems to wane as man's rational capacity makes him superior to nature: in this reading, even the nature that overpowers man becomes an instrument of his intellect.

While earlier work on the sublime emphasized the emotional impact of sublime objects found in nature, Kant repositions the sublime as a sensation of the human mind—orders of experience and thought related to the outside world but manifest only as cognitive processes. Something is beautiful, Kant contends, when one experiences pleasure in the presence of an object that can hence be called beautiful. It is therefore a universal quality recognized through judgment, and communicable to others. The sublime, however, is experienced when the horror of expansive nature is transformed through a subject's sovereignty. It is therefore a universal quality achieved through reason. What was radically new in Kant's distinction is that the "true" sublime is a function of the mind, something internal to the thinking subject:

> Man sieht hieraus auch, daß die wahre Erhabenheit nur im Gemüte des Urteilenden, nicht in dem Naturobjekte, dessen Beurteilung diese Stimmung desselben veranlaßt, müsse gesucht werden. Wer sollte auch ungestalte Gebirgsmassen, in wilder Unordnung über einander getürmt, mit ihren Eispyramiden, oder die düstere tobende See, u.s.w. erhaben nennen? Aber das Gemüt fühlt sich in seiner eigenen Beurteilung gehoben, wenn es sich in der Betrachtung derselben, ohne Rücksicht auf ihre Form, der Einbildungskraft [...] überläßt [...].

---

[32] In an interesting reference to Burke's notion of the beautiful and the sublime, Herder, in *Kalligone*, chooses to read the beautiful and the sublime not as opposites, but as the stem and branches of the same tree. While much could be made of his tree metaphor, his shift in metaphor is more telling as he speaks of the highest order of the sublime. Instead of the tree's tip, he describes a mountain's summit: "[...] sein Gipfel ist das erhabenste Schöne." Johann Gottfried Herder, "Kalligone: Vom Angenehmen und Schönen," *Schriften zur Literatur und Philosophie 1792–1800*, ed. Hans Dietrich Irmscher, *Werke*, vol. 8 (Frankfurt/Main: Deutscher Klassiker Verlag, 1998), 641–964, 873. On the panoramic view, see Koschorke, *Geschichte des Horizonts*, 138–72.

[It is also evident from this that true sublimity must be sought only in the mind of the one who judges, not in the object in nature, the judging of which occasions this disposition in it. And who would want to call sublime shapeless mountain masses towering above one another in wild disorder with their pyramids of ice, or the dark and raging sea, etc.? But the mind feels itself elevated in its own judging if, in the consideration of such things, without regard to their form, abandoning itself to the imagination [...].][33]

The sensation of the sublime arrives with a shudder, a feel of danger that is terrifying—"das schreckhaft Erhabene" [the terrifyingly sublime].[34] For Kant, the sublime is an experience of major affective conflict in that the subject finds himself made insignificant by the sheer size of the natural world around him:

Kühne überhängende gleichsam drohende Felsen, am Himmel sich auftürmende Donnerwolken, mit Blitzen und Krachen einherziehende, Vulkane in ihrer ganzen zerstörenden Gewalt [...] machen unser Vermögen zu widerstehen, in Vergleichung mit ihrer Macht zur unbedeutenden Kleinigkeit.

[Bold, overhanging, as it were threatening cliffs, thunder clouds towering up into the heavens, bringing with them flashes of lightning and crashes of thunder, volcanoes with their all-destroying violence [...] make our capacity to resist into an insignificant trifle in comparison with their power.][35]

In light of nature's immensity, man discovers his own limitations and shortcomings and becomes aware of his physical powerlessness:

Denn so wie wir zwar an der Unermeßlichkeit der Natur, und der Unzulänglichkeit unseres Vermögens einen der ästhetischen Größeneinschätzung ihres Gebiets proportionierten Maßstab zu nehmen, unsere eigene Einschränkung [...] fanden: so gibt auch die Unwiderstehlichkeit ihrer Macht uns [...] unsere *physische* Ohnmacht zu erkennen [...].

---

[33] Kant, *Kritik der Urteilskraft*, §26, B 95–6; A 94–5. Kant, *Critique of the Power of Judgement*, 139.
[34] Immanuel Kant "Beobachtungen über das Gefühl des Schönen und Erhabenen," *Vorkritische Schriften bis 1768*, Band 2, *Werkausgabe*, ed. Wilhelm Weischedel, vol. 2 (Frankfurt/Main: Suhrkamp, 1977), A5, 827.
[35] Kant, *Kritik der Urteilskraft*, §28, B 104–5; A 103–4. Kant, *Critique of the Power of Judgement*, 144.

[For just as we found our own limitation in the immeasurability of nature and the insufficiency of our capacity to adopt a standard proportionate to the aesthetic estimation of the magnitude of its domain, [. . .] the irresistibility of its power certainly makes us [. . .] recognize our own physical powerlessness [. . .].][36]

But the sublime nature also awakens a sense of self-preservation—"eine Selbsterhaltung von ganz anderer Art," which empowers man to become a sublime subject. He comprehends what he sees and therefore recognizes his superiority to the vast nature that terrified him, his "Überlegenheit über die Natur selbst in ihrer Unermeßlichkeit."[37] This transition, from terror to domination, is what constitutes the sublime for Kant, as it mediates between imagination—"Einbildungskraft"—and reason—"Vernunft." Though this mediation seems at times precarious, as the rational subject remains aware of nature's size and force, the experience of the sublime is ultimately one in which the subject prevails over his environment. The mountains are unfathomable but stable forms that allow the rational observer to contemplate greatness, to refine his feelings—ultimately to turn back from the natural world toward what Kant calls "die Schönheit und Würde der menschlichen Natur, und eine Fassung und Stärke des Gemüts" [the beauty and dignity of *human nature*, the firmness and determination of the mind].[38]

In short, Kant's sublime is a process through which man transforms the mountains' greatness into his own. The ability to subdue terror through reason is experienced as a kind of triumph, so that the subject no longer feels threatened but empowered:

> Also ist das Gefühl des Erhabenen in der Natur Achtung für unsere eigene Bestimmung, die wir einem Objekte der Natur durch eine gewisse Subreption (Verwechslung der Achtung für das Objekt statt der für die Idee der Menschheit in unsrem Subjekte) beweisen, welches uns die Überlegenheit der Vernunftbestimmung unserer Erkenntnisvermögen über das größte Vermögen der Sinnlichkeit gleichsam anschaulich macht.
>
> [Thus, the feeling of the sublime in nature is respect for our own vocation, which we show to an object in nature through a certain subreption (substitution of a respect for the object instead for the

---

[36] Kant, *Kritik der Urteilskraft*, §28, B 104–5; A 103–4. Kant, *Critique of the Power of Judgement*, 145.
[37] Kant, *Kritik der Urteilskraft*, §28, B 105; A 103.
[38] Kant, "Beobachtungen," A 28–9; 839.

idea of humanity in our subject), which as it were makes intuitable the superiority of the rational vocation of our cognitive faculty over the greatest faculty of sensibility.][39]

Kant explains that what man perceives as the grandeur of nature is a product of confusion—subreption: it is man's greatness that allows him to see the greatness of nature. What he perceives in greatness is in fact a projection of his own qualities. By recognizing this confusion, the sublime emerges as a category of judgment wherein the mind is refined and the mountains made sublime. The sublime, in a double movement, allows man to become aware of his limitations and to transcend that which grants him this awareness. Sean Franzel addresses how the notion of the sublime moves from the natural world to the human subject when he says of Kant's influence: "[T]he discourse of the sublime gripped the imagination around 1800 in part because it enabled new ways of narrating human experience; that is, of situating experience in spatial and temporal frames of reference."[40] It is these "new ways of narrating"—spatial and temporal frames and forms—that shift when writers return to and revise Kant's treatment of the mountains.

In a wide range of canonical German works, mountains allow the rational observer to contemplate greatness, to refine his thoughts and feelings. But already during Kant's time, German authors were complicating, if not abandoning, Kant's notion of the sublime as the dominant principle to guide representations of the mountains. As early as the Romantic period, the classical stylistics of unity, proportion, and coherence are disrupted by the aesthetics of disharmony and fragmentation. The sublime gives way—or perhaps gives rise to mountains that serve as mutable spaces of transformation. Since the concept of the sublime in fact contains within it an implicit instability, the claim that German writers reject the sublime in favor of irrational or more malleable forms is an overstatement, and authors seize upon the mountains' transformative qualities already present in Kant's work. By focusing on mountains not as transcendent heights but rather as mercurial, labyrinthine forms, writers engage a familiar image of mountains in unfamiliar ways.

---

[39] Kant, *Kritik der Urteilskraft*, B 97, A 96. Kant, *Critique of the Power of Judgement*, 141.

[40] Sean Franzel, "Time and Narrative in the Mountain Sublime around 1800," in *Heights of Reflection: Mountains in the German Imagination from the Middle Ages to the Twenty-First Century*, eds. Sean Ireton and Caroline Schaumann (Rochester, NY: Camden House, 2012), 98–115, 98. Cf. also Claudia J. Brodsky, *The Imposition of Form: Studies in Narrative Representation and Knowledge* (Princeton, NJ: Princeton University Press, 1987), 21–87.

When the mountains appear as dynamic sites of material change and perspectival confusion, they frequently engender new forms of representation. Writers confront and transgress existing formal conventions; they seek out new modes that can adequately capture the strange, often illegible terrain that cannot easily be deemed sublime. It bears mentioning that this is not simply thematic criticism. The mountains are not just symbols; rather, they are explicitly present in the texts as setting and scenery. They are also written objects, functions of style as it changes in German-language prose since the early 1800s. As the once immovable mountains become shifting entities, boundaries between the animate and the inanimate dissolve, the observer and the observed seem to blur together and writers adapt new ways of writing.

The new poetic forms that arise in response to a shifting conception of the mountains are many and diverse. One frequent adaptation occurs in the realm of genre, as authors abandon poetry for prose, drama for narrative, or original stories for hybrid tales that blend fiction with documentary. It is as if the expansive, now dynamic terrain of the mountains exceeds the confines of an author's usual mode of address, causing them to turn to new genres that might better capture the enigmatic matter that was once just a site for remote contemplation. Writers turn to different forms in order to craft passages that could evoke the overwhelming, capricious landscape that both shapes and reflects a protagonist's mental state. Another effect on form that changing ideas of the mountains produces in German-language literature draws explicitly upon historical material. Some authors weave historical, scientific, and other cultural documents into their texts set in the mountains. This type of hybridity results in work that destabilizes the boundaries between "fact" and "fiction." It is not only that the mountains, once viewed as dynamic, liminal spaces, demand intertextual or postmodern forms. It is also the case that the mountains themselves, foundational to Austrian, Swiss, and German culture and thought, are figures through which questions of history and memory are addressed. Since the mountains are literary historical forms insofar as each representation of a mountain recalls the many peaks that have occurred in the long history of German-language literature, the explicit use and revision of earlier sources seems fitting. Hartmut Böhme sees mountains as foundational to human thought: "montane Metaphern strukturieren die Topographie des Geistes." [Mountainous metaphors structure the topography of thought.] They are clusters of meaning— "Bedeutungscluster"—and metaphorically as well as symbolically charged structures that comprise an inexhaustible texture. Böhme identifies three main clusters: mountains are cosmic markers, constituting the *axis mundi*, which separates the heavens from the earth;

secondly, they are remote domiciles and meeting places for Gods and men alike; lastly, mountains are sites of revelation or communication.⁴¹ The mountains become a site through which a literary genealogy can be established, revised, or even demolished.
As the writers navigate the twists and turns of mountains no longer held at a distance, their language also often undergoes contortions. Language folds upon itself as a nameless protagonist wanders through the mountainside, or snaking, tempestuous words transform the Austrian Alps into abject mountains of flesh. As the language of authors strives to document the mountains as a transformative zone, it is itself transformed. Language often seeks to overwhelm, to confuse, to mislead or waylay. In this sense, German-language authors move away from a treatment of the mountains aligned with the sublime and disband with the Kantian rational subject by composing texts in which prose can immerse the reader in a chaotic or dynamic experience of the terrain. Language itself reflects the dissolution of rigid boundaries and clear distinctions—characters go unnamed, phrases repeat, words carry double meanings, time seems to stand still, infinitely repeat itself, or rush ahead, and words are stripped of conventional meanings and assigned new ones.

GEORG SIMMEL AND THE RESISTANCE OF MOUNTAINS

But why do the Alps resist representation? Surprisingly, it was the sociologist, philosopher, and urban theorist Georg Simmel who most systematically investigated the Alps' resistance to representation. On January 19, 1911, the morning edition of the Berlin newspaper *Der Tag* ran an article by Simmel with the peculiar title "Zur Ästhetik der Alpen" [On the Aesthetics of the Alps]. Since Simmel spent almost every summer in the Swiss mountains, seeking calm away from the city to write or paint, it makes sense that the Alps appear more than once in his writing. In 1895, Simmel wrote "Alpenreisen" [Alpine Journeys] in which he contemplates the technological conquest of distance that transforms the mountains into an accessible escape for city dwellers.⁴²

---

[41] Hartmut Böhme, "Berg," *Wörterbuch der philosophischen Metaphern*, ed. Ralf Konsermann (Darmstadt: Wissenschaftliche Buchgesellschaft, 2007), 46–61, 46, 49, 52.
[42] Georg Simmel, "Alpenreisen," *Aufsätze und Abhandlungen 1894–1900, Gesamtausgabe in 24 Bänden*, eds. Heinz-Jürgen Dahme and David P. Frisby, vol. 5 (Frankfurt/Main: Suhrkamp, 1992), 91–5.

But in his piece from 1911, Simmel turned away from a strictly sociological treatment of the mountains to a consideration of their aesthetic power. In it, Simmel attempts to make sense of the appearance and effect of the rock formations that surrounded him during his summer retreats. Based on his knowledge of European art as well as aesthetic philosophy, he wonders why the art world lacks an aesthetically adequate depiction of the Alps. For Simmel, even the most successful mountain painters of his time, Giovanni Segantini and Ferdinand Hodler, failed to capture the mountains in all their might.

For Simmel, the aesthetic appeal of the Alps lies in what he calls the "Quantitätsmoment" [factor of quantity] or "Massenmoment" [factor of mass]—the mountains' sheer size and mass.[43] But this quantity, this mass, is also what impedes an accurate depiction of the mountains on canvas: "Die Alpen aber scheinen dies ihren Bildern zu versagen: keines erreicht den Eindruck der überwältigenden Masse der Alpen [. . .]." [Yet the Alps seem to deny this to their representations: none of them attains the impression of the overwhelming mass of the Alps [. . .].][44] Portraying the overpowering magnitude of the mountains, Simmel reasons, confounds artists, and they must therefore resort to a kind of subterfuge in order to avoid confronting the masses of the Alps head-on.[45] In "Zur Ästhetik der Alpen," Simmel elucidates this

---

[43] Cf. Georg Simmel, "Zur Ästhetik der Alpen," *Aufsätze und Abhandlungen 1909–1918, Band 1, Gesamtausgabe in 24 Bänden*, vol. 12, eds. Rüdiger Kramme and Angelika Rammstedt (Frankfurt/Main: Suhrkamp, 2001), 163; and Georg Simmel, "Die ästhetische Quantität," *Aufsätze und Abhandlungen 1901–1908, Band 1, Gesamtausgabe in 24 Bänden*, eds. Rüdiger Kramme et al., vol. 7 (Frankfurt/Main: Suhrkamp, 1995), 190–200, 191.

[44] Simmel, "Ästhetik der Alpen," 163. Elsewhere he writes, "Daß es eigentlich keine künstlerisch ganz befriedigende Alpenlandschaft gibt, schiebe ich auf das Quantitätsmoment." [That there is no artistically satisfactory representation of the Alpine landscape I blame on the factor of mass.] Simmel, "Die ästhetische Quantität," 191.

[45] "[. . .] und die größten Alpenmaler, Segantini und Hodler, suchen sich dieser Aufgabe durch raffinierte Stilisierung, Akzentverschiebung, Farbeneffekte mehr zu entziehen, als zu lösen." [[. . .] and the greatest painters of the Alps, Segantini and Hodler, try rather to avoid than to resolve this task through ingenious stylization, shift of accents, and color effects.], Simmel, "Ästhetik der Alpen," 163. Elsewhere Simmel writes that Segantini, in his opinion the greatest painter of mountains, " hat die Berge in den Hintergrund gerückt oder stilisierte Formen gewählt oder durch Beleuchtung und Luft von der Forderung eines nur durch die Quantität erzielbaren Eindruckes ganz abgelenkt." [moved the mountains to the background or chose composed forms or detracted entirely from the demand of an impression achievable purely through quantity.], Simmel, "Die ästhetische Quantität," 191–2.

resistance to artistic representation, a problem he had begun addressing earlier in his career.[46] Simmel opens his article by pointing out that, contrary to common belief, it is not only formal aspects that govern aesthetic experience but also the factors of size and scale. The mere enjoyment of "pure form" as such—the relationship of lines, planes, and colors—is impossible, and pleasure from these forms arises only when tied to a notion of quantity or size. Simmel claims that form and scale must work together to generate an aesthetic experience. In fact, form's "aesthetic value" depends on its relation to scale:

> Die Quantität hat einen gewissen Spielraum, aber sie bewegt sich zwischen einer oft ganz unzweideutigen Größe, bei der die Form, als solche ganz ungeändert bleibend, ihren ästhetischen Wert verliert, und einer Kleinheit, mit der der gleiche Verlust eintritt.

> [This quantity has a certain latitude, but it ranges between an often unambiguous largeness, in which the form, remaining as such wholly unchanged, loses its aesthetic value, and a smallness, with which the same loss sets in.][47]

In this passage, form is an immutable entity, which can grow or shrink in size but not in proportion or constitution. When form faces objects with radically expanded or reduced proportions, it loses its aesthetic value and, subsequently, its effect. This peculiar relationship between form and size and the precarity of form in the face of smallness and bigness becomes especially visible when artists try to capture or translate nature into an artwork, resulting in what Simmel calls a "Stufenleiter der Formen" [hierarchy of forms]. This hierarchy of forms ranges from those that can maintain their aesthetic value despite fluctuations in size or quantity to those whose aesthetic value is bound to one singular quantum. At one pole of this spectrum is man, and at the other, diametrically opposed, are the mountains: "An jenem einen Pole steht die menschliche Gestalt. [. . .] Am anderen Pol der Reihe stehen die Alpen." [At the first pole stands the human form. [. . .] At the other pole of the spectrum are the Alps.][48]

---

[46] Simmel wrote about the Alps' aesthetic resistance as early as 1892 in his *Einleitung in die Moralwissenschaft: eine Kritik der ethischen Grundbegriffe, Band 1, Gesamtausgabe in 24 Bänden,* ed. Klaus Christian Köhnke, vol. 3 (Frankfurt/Main: Suhrkamp, 1989), 216. In 1903, he writes about their defiance in "Über ästhetische Quantitäten" and "Die ästhetische Quantität." Cf. Simmel, *Aufsätze und Abhandlungen 1901–1908,* 184–9, 190–200.
[47] Simmel, "Ästhetik der Alpen," 162.
[48] Simmel, "Ästhetik der Alpen," 162.

Simmel attributes this opposition of man and mountain to a difference in empathy and experience. Artists can represent the human form—in the following passage Simmel speaks of *Gestalt*—across a wide spectrum of sizes because the artist has intimate, innate knowledge of the human shape:

> Wo wir nämlich den Sinn einer Gestalt von innen her durch Miterleben ihres Lebens ergreifen, da wird der Künstler verhältnismäßig leicht um die Verschiebung, die Akzente, die Abschwächung wissen, deren es bedarf, um bei veränderten Massen die rechte Bedeutung und Einheit der Form ungeändert wirken zu lassen [...].
>
> [For when we grasp the sense of a form from within by witnessing its life, the artist will know relatively easily the shifts, accents, and attenuations necessary to let the form's essential sense and unity take effect unaltered by a change in size [...].][49]

Because man knows no other creature or object as well as himself, and because he can relate himself to his environment and to changes in scale and size, he can create a full range of artifacts—from the miniature to the colossal—that bear a relation to the human form.[50] But with mountains, the artist's frame of reference falters, and form's intrinsic aesthetic value—its "ästhetischer Eigenwert"—vanishes with even the slightest change to quantum.[51] Simmel advocates neither a true-to-life realism nor a mimetic naturalism, and he does not ask for exact copies of man in art. Yet he argues for an unalienable essence of the object that cannot be distorted in an artistic representation. Capturing this essence in art, however, is what the Alps deny.

The latitude in changes to quantum available to the human form does not extend to the mountains. Both form and quantum are necessary

---

[49] Simmel, "Ästhetik der Alpen," 162.
[50] "Denn das Leben ist die unaufhörliche Relativität der Gegensätze, die Bestimmung des einen durch das andere und des anderen durch das eine, die flutende Bewegtheit, in der jedes Sein nur als ein Bedingtsein bestehen kann." [For life is the unceasing relativity of opposites, the determination of the one through the other and the other through the one, the surging restlessness in which all being can exist only as something conditioned.] Simmel, "Ästhetik der Alpen," 168.
[51] "Die Formen haben hier also offenbar nicht den ästhetischen Eigenwert, der die Änderung des Quantums überlebt, sondern er bleibt an dessen natürliches Maß gebunden." [Forms here, then, obviously do not have the intrinsic aesthetic value that survive the change in their quantum; instead, value remains bound to its natural scale.] Simmel, "Ästhetik der Alpen," 163.

to create an aesthetic effect. In the case of the Alps, however, quantity is most crucial to determining that aesthetic effect. The meaning of quantum itself appears to shift at this point in Simmel's essay. While earlier, quantum was a measure of size and scale—of "Maßstab"—it now seems to refer to a dynamic mass—"Massenmoment."[52] What Simmel here identifies as "Massenmoment" emerges as the primary characteristic of the mountains. The mountains' resistance to representation becomes less a problem of scale and size, a question of perhaps finding the appropriate canvas, but a problem of finding cohesion and unity in disparate forms:

> Die besondere Bedeutung des Massenmoments ruht auf der Eigenart der alpinen Gestaltung. Diese hat im Allgemeinen etwas Unruhiges, Zufälliges, jeder eigentlichen Formeinheit Entbehrendes – weshalb denn von vielen Malern, die auch die Natur als solche nur auf ihre Formqualität hin sehen, die Alpen schwer erträglich sind.

> [The special significance of the size factor rests in the peculiarity of Alpine formation, which in general has something restless and accidental about it, something lacking any real formal unity; and this is why for many painters, who look also at nature only for its formal aspects, the Alps are hard to bear.][53]

Usually, artists appeal to form—to harmonic or homologous shapes and lines—in order to tame restless nature into something palatable—to "Genießbarkeit."[54] But Simmel could not find the possibility of such aesthetic transformation in the Alps. The mountains lack a sense of cohesion or a formal "Gesamtlinie."[55] In fact, this lack of cohesion causes a great deal of irritation. Initially, the mountains' jagged peaks,

---

[52] Simmel, "Ästhetik der Alpen," 162, 163.
[53] Simmel, "Ästhetik der Alpen," 163.
[54] Simmel, "Ästhetik der Alpen," 163.
[55] "Wo aber die Formen so zufällig und durch keinen Sinn der Gesamtlinie verbunden nebeneinanderstehen wie in den Alpen, würde die einzelne peinlich isoliert sein und keinen Fußpunkt innerhalb des Ganzen haben, wenn nicht die Masse des Stoffes fühlbar wäre, deren Undifferenzierbarkeit sich einheitlich unter den Spitzen hinstreckt, und deren für sich sinnlose Individualisiertheit einen einheitlichen Körper gibt." [But where forms stand next to one another randomly and not connected by any sense of a unifying line as they do in the Alps, the individual form would be awkwardly isolated and devoid of any foothold within the whole, were it not for the palpable mass of the matter, whose undifferentiatedness stretches out uniformly among the peaks and gives their pointless individuality a unified body.] Simmel, "Ästhetik der Alpen," 163.

26   Writing the Mountains

deep valleys, and sharp ridges simply stand side by side without coherence. It is the mountains' mass that allows individual peaks to coalesce into a whole:

> Das Formlose [the mountain's quantum of mass; JK] muß hier im Eindruck ein sonst unverhältnismäßiges Übergewicht haben, damit das Chaos der gegeneinander gleichgültigen Gipfelprofile sozusagen ein Schwergewicht und einen Zusammenhalt finde.
>
> [Here, the formless materiality must have an otherwise disproportionate predominance in its impression for the chaos of the equally indifferent summit profiles to find, as it were, gravity and cohesion.]⁵⁶

At first, the heaviness of the mountains, their solidity and mass, unifies the "chaos" of many distinct peaks. It would seem then, that while the human form was flexible insofar as it could be aesthetically related to a wide array of other objects, both big and small, the mountains remain inert in their heaviness. But Simmel goes on to suggest that the mountains nonetheless possess a material dynamism that also thwarts attempts at representation. For Simmel, the mountains show an intricate interplay of form and formlessness, of agitating tension and calming balance. The form of the mountains is seen in sharp lines and pointed summits; but the material that "fills" these shapes is paradoxically formless and causes the Alps' artistically frustrating conjunction of placidity and tumult:

> Die zerflatternde Unruhe der Formen und die lastende Materialität in ihrem bloßen, formlosen Quantum erzeugen in ihrer Spannung und ihrer Balance den Eindruck, in dem sich Erregtheit und Frieden einzigartig zu durchdringen scheinen.
>
> [The fluttering restlessness of the forms and the burdensome materiality in their merely formless quantity engender in their tension and balance that impression in which agitation and quietude seem to penetrate each other inimitably.]⁵⁷

Here, Simmel attempts to describe the tension inherent to the mountains. Their forms "flutter," creating a sense of upward movement and lightness, while the heaviness of the mountains' matter exerts a

---

[56] Simmel, "Ästhetik der Alpen," 163–4.
[57] Simmel, "Ästhetik der Alpen," 163–4.

grounding, downward pull. The interplay of weightless form and formless mass causes the overwhelming aesthetic effect of the mountains, yet is also the reason that they resist artistic representation. Simmel goes on to explain that the mountains' formless mass contrasts with the upward movement of the peaks. As the mountains increase in altitude and their rocky flanks turn into snow- and ice-covered summits, the downward pull of the telluric wanes and a transcendental ascendance begins:

> Anderseits aber sind die übergroß aufsteigenden Felsen, die durchsichtigen und schimmernden Eishänge, der Schnee der Gipfel, der keine Beziehung mehr zu den Niederungen der Erde hat – all dies sind Symbole des Transzendenten [. . .].
>
> [On the other hand, however, are the enormously ascending cliffs, the transparent and glistening icy slopes, the snow of the peaks that no longer has a connection to the lowlands of the Earth—all these are symbols of the transcendental [. . .].][58]

In this liminal zone, where mountain rocks give way to snowy surfaces, Simmel sees another dynamic at work. The quantum mass of the material and the form of the peaks struggled earlier to come into equilibrium, but Simmel now identifies vectors pulling in opposite directions.[59] The glistening peaks draw an onlooker's gaze infinitely upward—yet only when the snow-covered heights have nothing but open sky above them. Unencumbered peaks in clear skies point upward, away from the telluric, toward the unearthly and transcendental, and to a new order: "Erst wenn nichts als Himmel über ihnen ist, weisen sie grenzenlos und ununterbrochen in das Überirdische hinauf und können einer anderen Ordnung als der Erde angehören." [Only when nothing but the heavens are above them do they boundlessly and ceaselessly point upward to the extraterrestrial and can belong to an order other than that of the Earth.][60] In turn, a cloudy sky would once again press

---

[58] Simmel, "Ästhetik der Alpen," 164.
[59] "Das Hochgebirge mit der Unerlöstheit und der dumpfen Wucht seiner bloßen materiellen Masse und dem gleichzeitigen überirdisch Aufstrebenden, über alle Lebensbewegtheit hinaus Verklärten seiner Schneeregion bringt beides in uns zu *einem* Klang." [The high mountain range, with the unredeemed state and blunt force of its bare material mass, and the concurrent celestial ascendency of the glorified radiance of its snowy regions above and beyond all vitality, unite both into one resounding harmony within us.] Simmel, "Ästhetik der Alpen," 165.
[60] Simmel, "Ästhetik der Alpen," 164.

the summits towards the ground and perhaps back into form.⁶¹ Much could be said about Simmel's mysterious metaphysics of mountains. What is of particular interest here is his connection of formlessness to the transcendental. "Gestalt"—form, which so often is the main focus of aesthetic theory—takes on an almost negative connotation in the following passage:

> Darum ist das Transzendente formlos: Gestalt ist Schranke, und so kann das Absolute, das schrankenlose nicht gestaltet sein. Es gibt also ein Formloses unter aller Gestaltung und eines über aller Gestaltung.
>
> [For this reason, the transcendental is formless: form is limitation, and thus the absolute, the unlimited, cannot be formed. There is hence one formlessness below all formation and another above all formation.]⁶²

Simmel claims that two types of formlessness can exist within one single mountain. Heavy, formless matter gives coherence to an otherwise chaotic assembly of peaks and valleys. This formless matter is contained within the shapes of the mountain itself and occurs in the area below the mountain's icy cap—"unter aller Gestaltung" [below all formation]. Another type of formlessness is seen above the rocks—"über aller Gestaltung" [above all formation]—in an area where matter and form are no longer distinguishable and blur together as they gesture toward transcendence.

In their pull toward the absolute, the icecaps, according to Simmel, belong to a different temporal order. In fact, the firn fields are the "absolutely ahistorical," removed from all time.⁶³ Situated in historical time are those sections of the mountains that are made of rock: grooves, erosion, and abrasion caused by glaciers and the brute force of lithic material working against each other are visible on the rock as temporal markers. Geomorphological forces pushed the mountains upward and

---

61 "Darum verschwindet der ästhetische Eindruck [...] sobald der Himmel über den Schneebergen dicht bezogen ist; den nun werden sie [the summits, the mountains; JK] von den Wolken zur Erde herabgedrückt, sie sind eingefangen und mit aller anderen Erde zusammengeschlossen." [Therefore, the aesthetic impression disappears [...] as soon as the skies above the snowy mountains cloud over; for now they are pressed down toward Earth by the clouds, they are captured and united with all of Earth.] Simmel, "Ästhetik der Alpen," 164.
62 Simmel, "Ästhetik der Alpen," 167.
63 "Das Firnrevier ist sozusagen die absolut 'unhistorische' Landschaft; [...]." [The realm of the firn is the absolutely "ahistorical" landscape, so to speak; [...].] Simmel, "Ästhetik der Alpen," 166.

brought them to their vertiginous heights, while erosive energies countervailed and wore down surrounding rock. Today, Simmel states, these antagonizing, historical forces are no longer so vividly at work, but can still be detected, and reconstructed by the observer who examines the stony mountains. Moreover, the observer can sense these forces still at work:

> Und noch einmal steigert sich diese Wirkung von der Felslandschaft aufwärts zu der reinen Firnlandschaft. An den Felsen spüren wir noch irgendwie die entgegengesetzt gerichteten Kräfte: die aufbauenden, die das Ganze gehoben haben, und die zernagenden, wegspülenden, abwärtsrollenden; in der momentanen Gestalt ist dieses Gegeneinander und Ineinander der Kräfte gleichsam zum Stehen gekommen, und es lebt wie mit einer instinktiv begreifenden, seelischen Rekonstruktion im Betrachter wieder auf.

> [And once more this effect intensifies from the rockscapes upward to the pure firnscape. On the rocks we still somehow perceive the antagonistic forces: the constructive forces that have lifted the whole upward, and those that gnaw away, wash away, roll downward; in its momentary shape this mutual opposition and penetration of forces has practically come to a standstill, and it comes to life again within the viewer like an instinctively comprehending spiritual reconstruction.][64]

What is it that Simmel thinks the mountain makes us feel but that artists fail to capture? It is not so much the appearance that eludes representation, but rather the temporal blurring and the combination of opposing forces—the sense that the mountains give an onlooker of both height and depth, of static rocks that somehow feel dynamic. For Simmel, it is the conflict and interplay of forces that defines the mountains, and that makes them so difficult to render in an artwork that must preserve a single, static image or moment. It is this interplay of forces and the refusal of the mountains to "stand still" that Simmel believes troubles artists; in *Writing the Mountains*, it is what generates new literary strategies for representation and new forms.

Simmel himself draws upon and reshapes existing work on the mountains, pressing known thought into new shapes. It is likely clear by now that Simmel's treatment of the mountains depends upon Kant's notions of the beautiful and the sublime. Although Simmel does not

---

[64] Simmel, "Ästhetik der Alpen," 167.

explicitly mention Kantian concepts, his repeated use of both "erhaben" and "schön" indicates that Kant's thought informs his own. Kant attributes beauty to form and the sublime to formlessness. Beauty in nature arises from the shape of an object, its form, whereas an experience of the sublime can result from formless objects that overwhelm and overpower:

> Allein sind es auch namhafte Unterschiede zwischen beiden in die Augen fallend. Das Schöne der Natur betrifft die Form des Gegenstandes, die in der Begrenzung besteht; das Erhabene ist dagegen auch an einem formlosen Gegenstande zu finden, sofern Unbegrenztheit an ihm, oder durch dessen Veranlassung, vorgestellt und doch Totalität derselben hinzugedacht wird [. . .]. Also ist das Wohlgefallen dort mit der Vorstellung der Qualität, hier aber der Quantität verbunden.
>
> [But notable differences between the two also strike the eye. The beautiful in nature concerns the form of the object, which consists in limitation; the sublime, by contrast, is to be found in a formless object insofar as limitlessness is represented in it, or at its instance, and yet it is also thought as a totality [. . .]. Thus the satisfaction is connected in the first case with the representation of quality, but in this case with quantity.][65]

As we have seen, Simmel takes up these concerns with quantity and form, but leaves his mountains suspended *between* the Kantian beautiful and sublime. Both formed and formless, Simmel's mountains cannot be squarely situated within Kant's frame. Rather, Simmel emphasizes that the mountains can be both beautiful and sublime, moving away from a clear distinction of the two: individual peaks that form an entire mountain range, masses that pull the viewer's gaze both upward and down, static masses that seem nonetheless to shift and change. The Kantian sublime describes the way that man transforms the fear inspired by the mountains into a rational perception of his surroundings. But Simmel insists that this transformation is not so quickly achieved and instead lingers with a generative ambiguity. Setting out from a Kantian notion of the sublime, Simmel takes his readers elsewhere, to a more ambivalent realm in which the mountains are as vexing as they are inspiring. If readers expect a text on the Alps to lead them to the familiar framework of the sublime, they are instead taken through unexpected twists and turns in which the mountains are productive of new ideas and forms while also exposing

---

[65] Kant, *Kritik der Urteilskraft*, B 75–6; A 74–5. Kant, *Critique of the Power of Judgement*, 128.

the limits of thought and of representation. Simmel's piece therefore resonates with the literature that is the subject of this book. For Simmel, the transformative properties of the mountains leave the onlooker and the artist to reckon with the coexistence of opposing, untamable forces.

SHIFTING FORMS

If, as Simmel suggests, form is intimately related to scale, then it makes sense that literary form should change as German-language writers interrogate the mountains from new perspectives. Once mountains are no longer the object of an observer who stands on a distant precipice to view inanimate masses, they can assume many different guises. The subject who enters the mountains, for instance, discovers not their transcendence but their obdurate materiality. They may also discover their own affiliation with stone or, conversely, the very vibrant, living nature of the mountain they previously conceived of as inanimate.[66] The contradictory forces that Simmel saw at play in the Alps, barely contained by the mountains themselves and thwarting the artists who sought to represent them, seem to ripple through the works that are the subject of this book. Scaling vertiginous heights, but seldom in a straight line, the authors discussed in *Writing the Mountains* undertake mountainous journeys that generate new narratives, perspectives, and new forms. Each chapter of this book examines narratives that are generated by mountains while also examining the ways in which the mountains are generated by means of narrative. Engaging literary theory, philosophy, and aesthetic theory, *Writing the Mountains* re-reads well-known texts, which turn out to be surprisingly relevant to mountain studies.

My analysis in the next chapter, "Figures from Mines—E.T.A. Hoffmann's 'Die Bergwerke zu Falun'," looks not only to mountainous heights, but also to their depths. This chapter traces a literary and historical genealogy of the curious factual story of a miner's petrified body, which was unearthed in Falun in 1720. Focusing on Hoffmann's treatment of this oft-retold story, I consider how the miner's body becomes a site of metamorphosis. The dramatically and repeatedly

---

[66] For an interesting reading of the relationship of the living and the lithic, see Hartmut Böhme, "Das Steinerne: Anmerkungen zur Theorie des Erhabenen aus dem Blick des 'Menschenfremdesten'," in *Das Erhabene. Zwischen Grenzerfahrung und Größenwahn*, ed. Christine Pries (Weinheim: VCH Acta Humaniora, 1989), 119–41. Böhme defines the fundamental characteristic of rock as that which is most foreign to human life. See also Noah Heringman's chapter "Geological Otherness; or, Rude Rocks and the Aesthetics of Formlessness," in his *Romantic Rocks, Aesthetic Geology* (Ithaca, NY: Cornell University Press, 2004), 54–93.

changing body is a useful point of departure for this book, as it illuminates the impact on human forms and relations that a changing conception of the mountains can have. As the miner's body moves through a variety of states—animate, inanimate, organic, inorganic, and something in between—it also moves as an object through a variety of texts. Hoffmann explicitly addresses the problems that the body poses for representation, as its recalcitrance comes as a direct response to the mountainous terrain in which it appears. Because, for Hoffmann, the body has the synchronic ability to exist in multiple states and textual registers at the same time, it exceeds the scope of linear narratives. Therefore, in addition to foregrounding the mercurial nature of the miner's materiality, I also attend to Hoffmann's narrative and poetic devices that reflect this dynamism. This chapter argues that the story's dissolution of the boundaries between life and death, between mountain and man, prompts a reflection on the boundaries of literary form.

Chapter three, "Lost in the Mountains—Perspective and Displacement in Georg Büchner's 'Lenz'," examines how Büchner uses the mountains as a setting to upend perspectival and narrative conventions. Moving between two perspectival extremes—expansive vistas of overwhelming, mountainous landscape and delineated views through windows and frames, the story addresses the challenge that mountains pose to representation. It argues that the oscillation between these perspectives, and the disorientation that it causes, establishes the protagonist's madness. But the story's focus on frames and ways of seeing the mountains does more than just reflect Lenz's psychological state. In this chapter, I demonstrate that Büchner's treatment of the mountains in fact creates a poetics in which rational perspectives are subverted. Madness, I suggest, is a form of *Verrückung*: of displacement, which is both spatial and formal in the story. The liminal, hostile terrain of the Vosges Mountains provides an appropriate setting for Büchner's anomalous ways of seeing; the transgression of frames that occurs in the story also explicitly challenges the role that mountains play in affirming a rational subject in Kant's thought.

Turning from Büchner's maddening mountains to Celan's serpentine landscape, the fourth chapter, "Folded Mountains—Paul Celan's 'Gespräch im Gebirg'," moves into the twentieth century. This chapter argues that the atrocities of the Holocaust and the crimes committed to European Jewry in the name of German culture render the literary landscape of mountains unusable to Celan.[67] Instead of continuing the

---

[67] For a comprehensive introduction to the deep relationship between the Alps and European Jewry, see *Hast du meine Alpen gesehen? Eine jüdische Beziehungsgeschichte*, eds. Hanno Loewy and Gerhard Milchrom (Hohenhems: Bucher Verlag, 2009).

traditional classicist or romantic topos of mountains as sublime or beautiful, as the place where the individual encounters nature or the subject comes into stable being, the mountains in "Gespräch im Gebirg" drive the story's strange and innovative poetics. From his experience in the mountains to his encounters with Leibniz's ideas of simple and composite substances, Celan appears to have been immersed in the images that his "Gespräch" deploys as part of a new poetic program. The fold, as represented by the geomorphological structure of the mountains and the symbolic structure of Leibniz's monad, serves as a model for Celan's text. Bringing together historical and biographical work with a reading of Celan's prose, this chapter illustrates how it is the mountains' folded structure that shapes the form and content of the "Gespräch." The fold, I argue, is a figure that allows Celan to write an impossible conversation into existence: the fold represents a multiplicity, a layering that can conceal at the same time as it uncovers, a singular object or perspective that is also double, a structural entity in which opposing forms can inhere.

"Liquid Mountains—Elfriede Jelinek's *Die Kinder der Toten*," my fifth chapter, considers another text in which the mountains, rather than initiating the sublime, are mutating and uncomfortably shifting sites that prompt reflections on historical memory and narrative possibility. In Jelinek's novel, the Alps serve as the repository of Austria's gruesome past, the denial of its all-too willing participation in the atrocities of the Third Reich. In this chapter, I show that the mountains are fundamental to Jelinek's treatment of this history—they are the terrain where history is confronted in the present and retold in new forms. Jelinek adapts her associative mode of writing to depict material eruption and collapse, as mountain ranges liquefy, and the earth yields up masses of flesh and bones. The novel makes the wounds of the past visible but refuses to confine them to the past or make them wholly legible or knowable. Material chaos and linguistic strangeness work together in this postmodern novel where mountains lead us to the height of uncertainty. In my analysis, the text's language represents and responds to the convulsions of the landscape that render the mountains a site of horror and of violence.

Though undeniably grim, this is a fitting place for this book to end, since Jelinek engages the history encoded by the mountains to move into dramatically new territory. Her novel demonstrates the enduring, generative role that the mountains have in German-language literature, as contemporary authors continue to revisit and revise the mountainous forms that have been central to German thought for so long. In a concise coda, I look at a more recent crop of Austrian and Swiss novels that take the mountains as their subject or setting. In Christoph Ransmayr's *Der fliegende Berg* (2006), Christian Kracht's *Ich werde hier sein im Sonnenschein und im Schatten* (2008), and Thomas Glavinic's *Das größere Wunder* (2013), the mountains offer heights and depths that characters long to reach—summits that motivate journeys and determine plots, remote valleys that promise retreat and threaten seclusion. But the authors make the mountains unconquerable, placing them beyond both reach and perspective. Readers are prompted to track vanishing peaks, question the outcome of an expedition, or enter the mountains as a counterfactual space in which real and alternate history collide. While Jelinek uses her postmodern prose and wordplay to depict the mountain as a material record of a violent history that is both immediate and elusive, the authors whose work I examine in the coda make the mountains themselves both remote and intensely social, resistant to territorial nomos and the site of ideological struggle and booked desire. The mountains in these books change hands, escape memory, and even vanish. They seem therefore suited to the current moment in which readers understand that history cannot be dismissed but also confront a world that seems increasingly immaterial and transient. In short, these contemporary novels demonstrate a central claim of *Writing the Mountains*—mountains, far from stable, static masses, are shifting entities. Recent fiction shows how literary genres and forms are likewise shifting, ready to be adapted to tell new stories about mountains in the twenty-first century. If, as Georg Simmel claimed, the problem of representing mountains remains vexing to contemporary artists, *Writing the Mountains* reveals that this problem is more than simply an impasse. Instead, in the terminology of Jane Bennett, mountains reveal themselves to be "vibrant" and demand that their story be told.[68] In sum, the mountains—transforming and transformative—prove to be fertile ground for writers whose poetic innovations break literary terrain and leave it shifting, thrillingly, beneath their readers' feet.

---

[68] Jane Bennett, *Vibrant Matter: A Political Ecology of Things* (Durham, NC: Duke University Press, 2010).

II Figures from Mines—E. T. A. Hoffmann's "Die Bergwerke zu Falun"

1720—SUMMER

In July and September of 1720, two Copenhagen newspapers, the *Nye Tidender om lærde Sager* and the *Extrait des Nouvelles*, reported a curious mining incident: in December of the previous year, deep inside an iron ore mine in Falun, Sweden, miners had discovered what, once brought to light, appeared to be a sculpture.[1] At a depth of 300 cubits inside the rock, between two unconnected mining shafts, workers found the body of a young man while cutting a crosshead linking the levels. The body was discovered in a previously undeveloped area of the mine, submerged in a water-filled cavern. Upon bringing it to the surface, his livery revealed the youth to have been a miner. He had sustained injuries to both legs, his right arm, and the back of his head. A liquid had soaked his corpse, and his flesh and skin were horn-like in texture.[2] Injuries aside, the miner's body, his face, and even his clothes were uncompromised. In fact, while underground, he was a pliant corpse, but upon being brought above ground, he immediately became hard and mineral-like.

At first, nobody could identify the remains; no one was currently posted missing, and the chronicles of the mine were considered complete. After some investigation, Magnus Johanssen stepped forward and testified before the mining council that he believed he recognized the deceased as Mathias Israelsson, also known as "Fet Mats"—"Big Mathias." Johanssen remembered that a miner had indeed gone missing in the fall of 1670, after descending into the mine alone, and was thought to have succumbed in a rockslide. Mayor Erik Michelsen and the ropemaker Erik Petersen corroborated Johanssen's statement. It was concluded that in 1670, Israelsson had gone into the mine by himself, perished in an underground explosion, and was buried. Further analysis showed that for fifty years, the dead man lay in a lake of blue vitriol known as cuperic sulfate, his body saturated by the crystalline solution, which preserved him.[3] The official identification should have solved the

---

1 *Nye Tidender om lærde Sager* (29), 20 July 1720, and "Extrait des Nouvelles" du Mois de Septembre 1720, 206–8, cited in Georg Friedmann, "Die Bearbeitung der Geschichte von dem Bergmann von Fahlun," diss. Königliche Friedrich-Wilhelms-Universität Berlin, 1887 (Berlin: Druckerei der Berliner Börsenzeitung, 1887), 9–11.
2 Adam Leyel, "Narratio accurata de cadavere humano in fodina cuprimontana ante duos annos reperto," *Acta litteraria Sveciae publicita* 1 (1722): 250–4, 252.
3 Vitriols, crystalline salt compounds of sulfur and metals like iron or copper, form dense, hair-like fibrous aggregates with varying degrees of hydration, ranging from hard crystals to complete dissolution. For a detailed analysis of the scientific findings, cf. Christiane Küchler Williams, "Was konserviert den Bergmann zu Falun—Kupfer- oder Eisenvitriol? Eine chemische Fußnote zu den Variationen des 'Bergwerks zu Falun'," *Athenäum* 10 (2000): 191–7.

mystery of the young man and earned him an entry in the annals of the mine, but one further witness came to the scene: an old woman who claimed to have finally found her long-lost love. She had been engaged to Mathias over fifty years ago, when the young man was sixteen, and now demanded that the body be returned to her.

These are the historic facts behind this story of a young miner, whose disappearance and reappearance prompted numerous writers and scholars to make it the topic of their work.[4] A male figure, discovered in an interstice, is brought to light. He mutates from man to statue, since he changes in compound structure from organic to inorganic and hardens upon surfacing. He becomes a disruption to the social and narrative cohesion of the mining community, as neither oral nor written accounts of the man exist. The sudden appearance of a mysterious body poses a problem in representation: what surfaces is an organic yet inorganic entity, and moreover, it is a presence marking an absence that should not exist. There is an inherent asynchrony, even diachrony, to Fet Mats: first, he inserts himself into a different time when he reappears fifty years later; then, the people at Falun must discuss him in order to make sense of him. Ultimately, Mats' materiality is a resistant materiality, as his body reluctantly engenders various literary forms. His body can be read as an instrument that causes an asynchronic interruption of a homogenous temporal continuum.[5] The appearance of Mat's body causes a rupture in space and time: from cave to surface, it switches into a different spatial realm, and from before to now, it changes orders of time. In the wake of this transition, Mat's body goes from pliant to rigid, but his surfacing also forces those in whose midst he suddenly appears

---

[4] Cf. Rolf Selbmann, "Unverhofft kommt oft. Eine Leiche und die Folgen für die Literaturwissenschaft," *Euphorion* 94 (2000): 173–204.

[5] Hebel emphasizes the interruption of a chronological historical time by the miner in his "Unverhofftes Wiedersehen." Here, the miner surfaces in 1809, and Hebel lists major world-historical events from the earthquake of Lisbon to the Napoleonic Wars that occurred while the miner was below ground. Most importantly, however, he synchronizes the temporal orders of historic-political events with quotidian tasks: "Unterdessen wurde die Stadt Lissabon in Portugal zerstört [...] Napoleon eroberte Preußen, und die Engländer bombardierten Koppenhagen, und die Ackerleute säeten und schnitten. Der Müller mahlte, und die Schmiede hämmerten, und die Bergleute gruben nach den Metalladern in ihrer unterirdischen Werkstatt." [In the meantime the city of Lisbon in Portugal was destroyed by an earthquake [...]. Napoleon defeated Prussia, the English bombarded Copenhagen, and the farmers sowed and reaped. The millers ground the corn, the blacksmiths wielded their hammers, and the miners dug for seams of metal in their workplace under the ground.] Johann Peter Hebel, "Unverhofftes Wiedersehen," *Die Kalendergeschichten. Sämtliche Erzählungen aus dem Rheinländischen Hausfreund*, eds. Hannelore Schlaffer and Harald Zils (München: Hanser, 1999), 328–32, 331.

to react, and thus to change themselves. To cope with this interruption, processes of transformation are necessary, and the body sets these transformations in motion.[6] As the body itself shifts ontological registers, so too do observers and readers of the scene who must make sense of the body's transformations.

Initially, the young man was the subject of scientific inquiries, most prominently in the 1722 study by the mining assessor Adam Leyel. Around 1800, the factual accounts surrounding the miner slowly gave way to fictional accounts, and the well-known naturalist and physician Gotthilf Heinrich Schubert was instrumental to the story's dissemination. His popular and widely read lectures held at the universities of Dresden and Erlangen, published as *Ansichten von der Nachtseite der Naturwissenschaft* in 1808, included a version of the miner's fate, fictionally amended by the love story of the reunited fiancées.[7] The republication of Schubert's romantic emendation in the same year in the literary magazine *Phöbus*, and in the following year 1809 in *Jason* with no other title than "Dichter Aufgabe"—a task for poets—admonished authors to take up this story and bring Schubert's already very imaginative narrative frame to further heights.[8] The petrified body subsequently inspired many aesthetic forms. Since *Jason*'s call, no fewer than thirty German-speaking artists and authors have retold the story of the miner in poems, novellas, librettos, and plays, among them most famously Johann Peter Hebel, Achim von Arnim, Clemens von Brentano, E. T. A. Hoffmann, Hugo von Hoffmannsthal, Richard Wagner, and

---

[6] Peter Schnyder identifies a metonymical shift in time and of temporal layers as central to romanticism's mining stories. Peter Schnyder, "Die Wiederkehr des Anderen: Ein Gang durch die Zeichenbergwerke zu Falun," *Figur, Figura, Figuration: E. T. A: Hoffmann*, eds. Daniel Müller Niebla et al. (Würzburg: Königshausen & Neumann, 2011), 31–43, 33.

[7] Schubert was widely read by many writers around 1800. Of greater importance, however, is the forefather of modern geology, Abraham Gottlob Werner, who was in personal contact with numerous authors, most notably Novalis, his student at the Bergakademie in Freiberg. Cf. Michaela Haberkorn, *Naturhistoriker und Zeitenseher. Geologie und Poesie um 1800. Der Kreis um A.G. Werner (Goethe, A.v.Humboldt, Novalis, Steffens, G.H. Schubert)* (Frankfurt/Main: Peter Lang, 2004). Theodore Ziolkowski showed that there was hardly a writer of that period not interested in the science of mining. Theodore Ziolkowski, "The Mine: Image of the Soul," *German Romanticism and its Institutions* (Princeton, NJ: Princeton University Press, 1989), 18–63. Jason Groves makes a compelling argument for the relationship of extraction and fiction in his chapter, "Of Other Petrofictions. Reimagining the Mine in German Romanticism," in *The Geological Unconscious*, 17–35.

[8] Gotthilf Heinrich Schubert, "Fragmente aus einer Vorlesung," *Phöbus* 4/5 (1808): 67–8. "Dichter-Aufgabe," *Jason. Eine Zeitschrift. Herausgegeben vom Verfasser des goldenen Kalbes*, vol. 1, January–April (Gotha: n.p., 1809), 394–6.

Georg Trakl.[9] Among its many adaptations, it is E. T. A. Hoffmann's 1819 "Die Bergwerke zu Falun" that most extensively inquires into the life of the miner before his death and thus allows us to speculate on the origins of the enigmatic body. Hoffmann tells the tale of a young sailor, Elis Fröbom, who becomes a miner and perishes in the mines.

In 1819, E. T. A. Hoffmann published "Die Bergwerke zu Falun" as a story in the four-volume collection of his *Serapions-Brüder* cycle, a project in narrative experimentation, published between 1818 and 1821. Taking its cue from Hebel—"ein sehr bekanntes und schon bearbeitetes Thema"—Schubert's *Nachtseiten*, as well as Johann Ludwig Hausmann's *Reise durch Skandinavien in den Jahren 1806 und 1807*, Hoffmann's tale draws upon a rich textual genealogy of sources, which documents the period's fascination with the curious find. The story appropriates and transforms elements of different epistemological and generic orders in light of a poetics of suspense.[10] Hoffmann's tale engages the mountains as a space of asynchronicity, where concepts of time, social space, and narrative order collide in the disruptive emergence of a miner's displaced body. A mine in a mountain-range—Hoffmann's choice of setting is neither arbitrary nor without precedence. The realm deep inside the mountain has been interpreted as charged with immense cultural and mythical importance, to be a space of initiation, and as a realm that leads to the inner self as well as to a cosmological heart and center. The mine's depths and dangers, hidden from human view, became the subject of intense fascination to a romanticist culture engaged in seeking out those realms not yet fully tamed or rendered transparent by Enlightenment rationality.[11] In this mine, the epistemological and taxonomic mutability of the miner's body complicates notions of stable form, and asks whether stability may be paradoxically strongest at the very point of form's dissolution.

---

[9] The most recent German-language adaptation is most likely Franz Fühmann's unfinished "Bergwerk Projekt." Franz Fühmann, *Im Berg. Texte aus dem Nachlass*, ed. Ingrid Prignitz (Rostock: Hinstorff, 1991). For a collection of Falun adaptations, see *Das Bergwerk von Falun: Varianten eines literarischen Stoffes*, ed. Thomas Eicher (Münster: Lit Verlag, 1996).

[10] Theodor, the narrator of the story, mentions that versions of the tale of Falun exist by other authors. When discussing the story, Ottmar explicitly mentions Schubert's *Nachtseiten*, and Hoffmann refers to Hausmann in a footnote. E. T. A. Hoffmann, "Die Bergwerke zu Falun," *Die Serapions-Brüder, Sämtliche Werke*, ed. Wulf Segebrecht, vol. 4 (Frankfurt/Main: Deutscher Klassiker Verlag, 2001), 208–41, 208, 220, 240.

[11] Cf. Regina Hartmann, "Technischer Fortschritt als menschheitlicher Progress? Reiseberichte über das Bergwerk von Falun zwischen Aufklärungshoffnung und Aufklärungsskepsis," *Zeitschrift für deutsche Philologie* 122 (2003): 184–99, 194–7.

The miner's body becomes a point of intersection for multiple processes of metamorphosis: it undergoes material transformations from animate to inanimate and from organic to inorganic, troubling principles of taxonomy in disconcerting ways. It also moves as object and protagonist through textual and poetic transformations, from factual to fictional accounts, from newspaper articles to scientific analysis, and from the historiographic to the literary. In the latter, Hoffmann, at the end of a long textual genealogy, problematizes the body's representation by addressing the process of fictionalization and the contingencies of narrative production, and consequently by asking for the appropriate form or medium to capture the miner's body. Hoffmann focuses on the body of the miner as a source of asynchrony and poetic impulse: its emergence from a grave in the mountain's depths causes a rupture in the closely knit fabric and order of contemporary knowledge production. The body resurfaces as an unruly relic from a different time, and it unsettles social order by resisting taxonomic and scientific explanations. The body of the miner engenders a new narrative that allows Hoffmann to explore the alternative potential of the literary imagination and to search for a form dynamic enough to capture the elusive miner.

Hoffmann's "Die Bergwerke zu Falun," set in the mountains and the mines, offers a poetics of suspended transformation and unresolved thresholds. By this I mean that Hoffmann's form works to move back and forth between forms and topics of study, often asking the reader to inhabit the space between multiple possibilities and conditions. "Die Bergwerke zu Falun" outlines the connection between considerations of poetic transformation—from *Stoff*, Aristotelian myth, historic source material, to literary narrative—and material transformation—from organic to inorganic, between different aggregate states of fluid, firm, and crystalline, from inanimate object to living being and back. The different orders depicted in the story comprise a taxonomy, a romantic order of knowledge that Hoffmann interrogates. "Die Bergwerke zu Falun" invokes this controversy by fictionalizing a factual, historical incident that in its own time already destabilized the taxonomic categories and binaries.

Historic events leave their traces in documents, changing from one aggregate state into another; textual sources transform from fact to fiction, from scientific description to historiography and literary narrative. Material objects are sometimes obdurate, resisting change and at other times malleable, moving from one state into another. Hoffmann's story is thus a story of metamorphosis; it deals with the transition from one space, from one realm of order to another. But it also questions the plausibility of such transitions, suggesting that transition is not always complete, logical, or legible. In particular, incomplete transformations in Hoffmann's text leave objects and readers suspended between temporal markers—poised in between origins and endings, the matter undergoing change often inhabits a strange, nearly timeless state. Tracking the transformations of the miner's body and the text in which the story is told exposes the relationship between physical matter and literary form. Ultimately, the miner's body that emerges from the mountains proves both resistant to change and generative of it; so too is literary form, which Hoffmann molds in order to narrate the dual, and sometimes in-between, state of his source material—the body of the miner found in the mines of Falun.

SOURCE MATERIAL

The most detailed and "scientific" account of the occurrence, written "in the style of the erudite," is given by the mining assessor Adam Leyel, who scrutinized the corpse and its story shortly after its appearance. "Narratio accurata de cadavere humano in fodina cuprimontana ante duos annos reperto," published in the first volume of *Acta litteraria Sveciae publicita* of 1722, is the extensive report of Leyel's examination.[12] After a thorough investigation—he washed the body, studied it, and gathered reports from the inhabitants of Falun—Leyel determines, "it is clear that this is in no way a petrified cadaver, or one changed into stone, but one that was only hardened by a supply of bubbling vitriolum."[13] Unmentioned by Leyel is the ensuing argument over the corpse, which ended with the former fiancée selling it for medical research and to be displayed in the Falun mining museum, first in a barrel, then on an iron chair, and finally in a glass vitrine.[14] Over the

---

[12] "[. . .] facti historiam sequentem in modum cum eruditis communicavero [. . .]." Leyel, "Narratio accurata de cadavere humano," 252.

[13] "[. . .] notitia haudquamquam petrificatum cadaver hoc, aut in lapidem mutatum, sed aquæ tantum victriolo scatentis beneficio induratum esse liquet." Leyel, "Narratio accurata de cadavere humano," 254.

[14] The *Extrait des Nouvelles* reports the following on the barter over the body: "[. . .] une chose aussi singulière, quoy que moins savante, est la dispute qu'il y a eue pur ce corps, l'école de Medicine le demandoit pour faire des observations, les ouvriers le pretendoient come un bien qui leur aoartenoit, on ne savoit à qui l'ajuger, lors qu'une fille ou feme [sic], à qui le deffunt, elle reclamé ce corps, sur le quel elle a soutenu ques a promesse de Mariage luy avoit donné des droits, que la mort mesme ne povoit par detruie, le corps lui a eté adjugé, et ayant offert de le remettre à ceux qui lui en donneroient le plus, la faculté de Medicine lui en a donnè [sic] cinq cens écus." [. . . something as peculiar, although less learned, is the dispute over this body. The school of medicine asked to analyze it and the miners claimed it as a good that belonged to them. Nobody knew to whom to

years, the body of the miner began to decay after all, and became rather unsightly.¹⁵ What remained of Mathias Israelsson was finally laid to rest on December 21, 1749, nearly eighty years after his disappearance and thirty years after his reappearance. Leyel, however, concluded his report with a striking remark:

> What is there that more strongly refutes the nature and character of vitriolum than the force of that kind of petrification? Indeed, since vitriolum never changes anything to rock, but bursts through everything with the true animated motion of the slightest vapor, binds everything together, and protects it from decay and decomposition.¹⁶

To what "force of that kind of petrification," capable of unhinging the inevitable process of breakdown and of establishing a moment of suspension between strength and suppleness, might Leyel refer? And why would it "strongly refute" the character of vitriols, a lapidescent substance, capable "of turning Bodies into a stony Nature"?¹⁷ In these

---

adjudge it, when a girl or woman, to whom the deceased body was given. She laid claim to the body, to which, she insisted, a promise of marriage had given her the right; a right, which even death could not destroy. The body was adjudged to her and she offered to give it to whomever would pay her the most: the faculty of medicine gave her five hundred crowns.] *Extrait des Nouvelles*, 206–8. Regarding the storage and exposition of the cadaver, see C. Wiman, "Über neue und einige alte Leichenwachsfunde," *Bulletin of the Geogical Institution of the University of Upsala* 28 (1941): 141–55, 149.

15 On July 2, 1737, Réginald Outhier makes the following entry in his travel log: "Le Mardi, nous fumes voir un Home que l'om difoit être pétrifié; il avoit été étouffé sous des cartiers de Rocher, qui s'étoient écroules dans le fond de la Mine. Au bout de 40 ou 50 ans, en fouillant on trouva son corps; ils étoit fi peu défiguré, qu'une Femme le reconnut; il y avoit seize ans qu'on le conservoit dans un fauteuil de fer par curiosité. Nous ne vîmes qu'un corps tout noir, fort desseché et fort éfiguré, qui exhaloit une odeur cadavereuse." [On Tuesday, we saw a man who must have been petrified; he had been suffocated under rock shells, when the bottom of the mine collapsed. After 40 or 50 years, a search discovered his body; it was so little disfigured that a woman recognized him; for sixteen years he had been preserved on an iron chair out of curiosity. We saw nothing but a black body, entirely desiccated and very disfigured, which exuded a cadaverous odor.] Réginald Outhier, *Journal d'un voyage au nord, en 1736 & 1737* (Amsterdam: H. G. Löhner, 1776), 282.

16 "Quid quod victrioli naturae & ingenio magis nil, quam ejusmodi petrificandi vis repugnant: quipped quod nil unquam in saxum convertat; tenuissimi vero vaporis vegetto motu omnia perrumpat, stringat, ac putredine interituque tueatur." Leyel, "Narratio accurata de cadavere humano," 254.

17 "lapidescent, adj. and n.," *OED* online, June 2022, http://www.oed.com/view/Entry/105720?redirectedFrom=lapidescent.

lines, Leyel attributes to vitriolic salts a great deal of dynamic energy: they are said to be "scantentis"—bubbling or effervescent, from the Latin *scantere*. And the process of saturation is not a slow infusion but an "animated motion of [...] vapor[s]" "bursting through everything." Judging by his comments, Leyel appears unsatisfied with the outcome of his examinations, and his discontent evokes an air of resistance in his text, as the hardened body continues to push against his analysis.

Leyel offers neither answer nor alternative, but in his treatise, we encounter the difficulties in translating or transcribing the external reality of the body into legible text. Leyel's language seems to exceed the norms of the scientific genre in which he writes. As he attempts to describe the energies of virtriol, which "bursts through everything with the true animated motion of the slightest vapor," his language becomes increasingly poetic. We are alerted here to the power that physical transformations seem to exert on language and might therefore usefully turn to the most significant text in which transformation is figured in prose. The precedent of such difficult transformations across binary limits, as fluid and complete, as each may seem, can be found in Ovid, whose *Metamorphoses* is foundational to any consideration of changes to the external world alongside changes in linguistic form on the page.[18] They are the textual template for the junction of the ontological problem of material transformation across taxonomic boundaries on the one hand, and the creative act and *poietic* principle on the other, yoking poetic transgression to the problem of material transformation. The most relevant, perhaps, of Ovid's transformation is the myth of Galatea's creation and animation by Pygmalion; a marble statue that comes to life. Yet Galatea "was born in a text" and her "animation is entrusted, in this case, to the power of words, and of words alone."[19] Just as words on the page conjure up the illusion of the real, they can also make it disappear, cause it to vanish behind the opacity of words. The materiality of the body turned to stone seems to resist full inclusion into the abstract poetics of the text. Time and again, this body disrupts the structure of the text. Its peculiar hardness, its radical materiality, is the immediate antagonist to the textual sign designated to replace it.

---

[18] Philip Hardie, *Ovid's Poetics of Illusion* (Cambridge: Cambridge University Press, 2002), 227.

[19] Victor I. Stoichita, *The Pygmalion Effect: From Ovid to Hitchcock*, trans. Alison Anderson (Chicago: University of Chicago Press, 2008), 6. For "pygmalionic reminiscences," cf. Edgar Pankow, "Medienwechsel: Zur Konstellation von Literatur und Malerei in einigen Arbeiten E. T. A. Hoffmanns," *E.T.A. Hoffmann Jahrbuch* 10 (2002): 42–57.

For the textual sign to come to the fore, the body must withdraw, or better, step down.[20]

Because of the noticeable hesitation in Leyel's account, one could even suggest that Leyel wants to preserve the miner, but to do so in a state of animation. In a more general introduction of vitriolic acids, he does indeed claim that human bodies, "nevertheless by their own brackishness, and their attractive force, so conspicuously condense and harden, that they leave their natural softness for the hardness of stone."[21] The transformation described by Leyel is a metamorphosis in matter and a change in the state of aggregation. He seems fascinated by the forces of petrification and vitriols, a binary opposition, which, by his account, renders difficult a clear taxonomy. By identifying an inorganic principle—the bursting energies of vitriols—that is animate but not alive, Leyel discloses the tension inherent in metamorphosis. These tensions arise when changes must take place across different epistemic, taxonomic, and ontic states, or more simply, from organic to inorganic, from soft to hard, and from fact to fiction.

Whether the youth was ever of stone, even for the briefest moment, cannot be proven—the sources are divided on this point. An inanimate, hardened body transfixed by an effervescing energy confronts us, and we can safely claim that the body found in the mine, pliable yet hard, organic yet mineral, was in a truly vitreous state. It was amorphous, as the mineralogical definition of vitreous has it: a solid state characterized by the peculiarity that its atoms are not arranged in any regular order. The vitriolated miner was not without *morphé*, form or shape; rather, he was amorphous, without a clear distinct form, able to move between states from solid, to gel, to liquid.

AN AESTHETIC EXISTENCE

The conflicted, "factual" accounts of the event at Falun surrounding the curious appearance of the miner already suggest the following points: a

---

[20] The problem posed by the miner's body is a question of presentation and representation. Though often used interchangeably, there is crucial difference between the German terms "Darstellung" and "Repräsentation," which are often translated synonymously as "representation" into English. Their difference could be grasped in "presentation" and "representation." Inherent in representation is a gap, as its semiosis refers to something that is absent, what it itself is not. "Darstellung," presentation, in return, contains an affirmative kernel: something presents itself.

[21] "[...] salitudine tamen sua, & contringendie vi, obvia quævis ita condensant & induranrtm ut nativa posita mollitie in lapidem duritatem deflectant." Leyel, "Narratio accurata de cadavere humano," 251.

metamorphosis took place when the dead miner was brought from the dark mines to the surface and touched by daylight. The frothing energies of the vitriolic salts hardened his supple body and rendered it like stone. The miner was transformed for some time into a statue and thus entered into an aesthetic as well as semiotic existence. As Leonard Barkan suggests, stone statues since Ovid carry, "even when they are not the product of metamorphic myths, [...] signs of essential life within."²² And indeed, by emphasizing the dynamic qualities of the vitriols, Leyel refuses to bring the case of the miner to a close. Even petrified, and thus lifeless and inorganic, inherent to the miner's body is a physical ambivalence that renders him dynamic and aesthetically potent. Containing life and death, the miner from Falun thus represents the vibrancy of art as well as the figurative death it imposes on its subjects.

The miner qua statue is *pro-duced*, brought forth, from the mines. *Bergwerk* literally translates as "mountain work" and has a productive, poetic valence. In a *poietic* act, through human τέχνη, *techné*, something is brought, as if in a process of enlightenment, "from concealment into the full light."²³ At Falun, it was the statuary body of the miner. Reminiscent of a mute witness from a distant past—after all, the miner was buried for fifty years—the corpse is now unearthed like an archeological find. But as we will see, something is amiss in this occasion of illumination and production, as neither formal, nor narrative, nor conceptual stability can be established. Seen through Agamben's Heidegger interpretation of poiesis and truth, ἀλήθεια, when the body comes from concealment to un-concealment, Fet Mats passes from nonbeing into being. In its simplest form, as a statue he was produced through human labor, through the *techné* of his fellow miners as skilled workers. Yet there is a second kind of production at work in this statue. Something brought forth by nature only, Aristotle distinguishes in his

---

²² "In all these cases the statue into which life has been frozen is not merely a conclusion to a story; it is an essence of that life; and, more important, it is to those of us who perceive the sculpture an unchanging sign of that essence. Indeed, Ovid often uses the word 'signum' for sculpture. At least from Ovid's time onwards, stone statues, even when they are not the product of metamorphic myths, will be signs of essential life within." Leonard Barkan, "Living Sculptures and the Winter's Tale," *English Literary History* 48 (1981): 639–67, 646. See also Leonard Barkan, *Unearthing the Past: Archaeology and Aesthetics in the Making of Renaissance Culture* (New Haven, CT: Yale University Press, 1999).

²³ Giorgio Agamben, "§8 Poiesis and Praxis," *The Man Without Content*, trans. Georgia Albert (Stanford, CA: Stanford University Press, 1999), 68–94, 68–9.

Physics, without *techné*, contains its own ἀρχή, arché, "its own principle and method of its entry into presence."²⁴

Let us remain with the miner as statue and attempt to capture it in more precise aesthetic terms and let us examine to what kind of art this relic belongs. Already Plato divides the arts of image-making into two categories: *eikastiké*, the art of the exact, proportional copy, and *phantastiké*, the art of the copy without resemblance.²⁵ Was the statue an *eikon*, a mimetic copy of a specific miner or of the idea of a miner in general, and hence based on likeness? Or was it a *phantasma*, an image without resemblance and hence a simulacrum? The simulacrum is often, and still in the dominant mimetic tradition, defined as a copy of a copy, or a copy without an original. Similar to a performative act, the simulacrum is that type of art whose object is also its aesthetic operation. Grounded only in the medium from which they arise, simulacra are thus by definition without profundity—ungrounded and without depth. The peculiarity of the young miner as statue is that it is non-mimetic. It is not a statue modeled according to someone's likeness; rather, model and statue, original and copy, are collapsed into one. The statue does not duplicate: the statue is the young miner, and the young miner is the statue. What is lacking at Falun, however, is both creator and artistic intention. In a hyper-authentic fashion, as simulacrum, the statue no longer simulates, that is, imitates, but creates its very own reality. Our statue as simulacrum implodes the difference between original and copy, body, and phantom. By occupying both categorical positions of the mimetic tradition, Fet Mats simultaneously negates them yet holds them in suspense. It therefore seems more originary than origin and copy ever could. There is a void where the origin should be. The void is physically present as the cave in which Fet Mats was discovered, but also as the textual void he produces by disrupting epistemic orders. On the one hand, this void becomes the catalyst for textual production; on the other, it is also a reminder of the perilous processes of transition. Reminiscent of Ovid's famous "Ars adeo latet arte sua"—"So does his art conceal his art"—the story of Fet Mats focuses on the precarious relationship of mimesis and fiction, toward a

---

²⁴ Giorgio Agamben, "§7 Privation is Like a Face," *The Man Without Content*, trans. Georgia Albert (Stanford, CA: Stanford University Press, 1999), 59–67, 60. Cf. Aristotle, "Physics," trans. R. P. Hardie and R. K. Gaye, *The Complete Works of Aristotle. The Revised Oxford Translation*, ed. Jonathan Barnes, vol. 1 (Princeton, NJ: Princeton University Press, 1995), 315–446, 219b.

²⁵ Plato, "Sophist," trans. F. M. Cornford, *Plato: The Collected Dialogues including the letters*, eds. Edith Hamilton and Huntington Cairns (Princeton, NJ: Princeton University Press, 1989), 957–1017, 236c.

staging of "naturalness" in the artificial play of "art."[26] In his repeated transformations throughout the many textual versions of his fate, the miner stands for the free play of mortification and animation.

Inherent to this free play of mortification and animation, and hence to the ambiguation of original and copy through the simulacra, is a dangerous disruptive force, which was trapped and lay dormant while the miner was still underground. In fact, the miner is trapped more than once: physically, rock prohibits him from returning to the surface; biochemically, vitriol prevents his body from decay; mythologically, he remains caught, whether below the surface or above, as in a *mise-en-abîme*. His story folds into story within story, creating the sense of an infinite depth. The emergence of the body from the mines initiates the many ambiguities outlined thus far. Hence the impulse to leave the body buried within the earth: "It is a question [. . .]," Gilles Deleuze says of the simulacrum, "of repressing simulacra, keeping them completely submerged, preventing them from climbing to the surface, and 'insinuating themselves' everywhere."[27] In a study of the simulacrum in Platonic thought, Deleuze provides a very useful figure for the case of Fet Mats. The metaphor of an image chained to the ground and thus hindered from surfacing seems especially apt here, given the circumstances of the miner trapped inside the rock. Deleuze repeatedly returns to the idea of grounding the simulacrum: "a foundational story," "the ground," "the proven ground," "well grounded." Fet Mats is thoroughly grounded in his miner's grave: "the simulacrum implies huge dimensions, depths, and distances that the observer cannot master."[28]

Returning to the notion of Kant's sublime, the unfathomable nature of the miner's body can be explicated further. We have already seen that overwhelming dimensions, depths, and distances, when not tamed through the sublime, unsettle the subject and thrust them into a state of uncertainty. This is precisely why the statue of the miner, the simulacrum, should have remained deep inside the mountain:

> In short, there is in the simulacrum a becoming mad, or a becoming unlimited [. . .] a becoming always other, a becoming subversive of the depths, able to evade the equal, the limit, the

---

[26] Ovid, *Metamorphoses*, trans. Frank Justus Miller, *The Loeb Classical Library*, vol. 42, ed. Jeffrey Henderson (Cambridge, MA: Harvard University Press, 2004), lib. X, 252.

[27] Gilles Deleuze, "The Simulacrum and Ancient Philosoph," *The Logic of Sense*, trans. Mark Lester, ed. Constantin V. Boundas (New York: Columbia University Press, 1990), 253–79, 257.

[28] Deleuze, "The Simulacrum and Ancient Philosoph," 258.

Same, the Similar: always more or less at once, but never equal. To impose a limit in this becoming, to order it according to the same, to render it similar—and, for that part which remains rebellious, to repress it as deeply as possible, to shut it up in a cavern at the bottom of the ocean [. . .]."[29]

As we shall see, Hoffmann's Elis longs to be in a cave on the bottom of the ocean in his deepest hour of despair: "Ach läg ich doch nur begraben in dem tiefsten Meeresgrunde!" [Oh, that I were lying deep, deep beneath the sea!][30] But his wish, though it foreshadows his death in the mine, does not come true. And neither can he remain at the bottom of the pit. Once he surfaces from his grave, the miner becomes a disruptive force, transgressing a great number of boundaries.

A TASK FOR POETS

In 1808, Fet Mats finds his way into the lecture hall, where the naturalist and physician Gotthilf Heinrich Schubert made him the topic of a lecture at the University of Dresden and later one at Erlangen.[31] Published collectively as *Ansichten von der Nachtseite der Naturwissenschaft*, the title of Schubert's collection refers to his counter-Enlightenment approach: he considers the interplay of bright and dark, of light and shade, and displays a fascination for that darkness which remained obscure. In a series of lectures on dreams, the harmony of man with nature, planetary orbits, animalistic magnetism, and clairvoyance, Schubert also takes up the case of the miner from Falun.

In lecture eight, "Die organische Welt," Schubert discusses the petrified miner as an example of an undecayed corpse and presents a two-part analysis of the episode. Part one consists of the factual details, part two of more emotional observations, rendered in an amplified, imaginative fashion. Schubert's account, however, is not as clear-cut as I have just presented it, since the two parts of his lecture envelope one another. An excerpt illustrates Schubert's intertwining of images and ideas:

> Auf gleiche Weise zerfiel auch jener merkwürdige Leichnam, von welchem Hülpher, Cronstedt und die schwedischen gelehrten

---

[29] Deleuze, "The Simulacrum and Ancient Philosoph," 259.
[30] Hoffmann, "Die Bergwerke," 211. For the English, I consulted E. T. A: Hoffmann, "The Mines of Falun," trans. L. J. Kent and E. C. Knight; E. T. A. Hoffmann, *Tales*, ed. Victor Lange (New York: Continuum, 1982), 163–87.
[31] Gotthilf Heinrich Schubert, *Ansichten von der Nachtseite der Naturwissenschaft* (Dresden: Arnoldsche Buchhandlung, 1808), 202–28, 217.

Tagebücher erzählen, in eine Art von Asche, nachdem man ihn, dem Anscheine nach in festen Stein verwandelt, unter einem Glasschrank vergeblich vor dem Zutritt der Luft gesichert hat. Man fand diesen ehemaligen Bergmann, in der schwedischen Eisengrube zu Falun, als zwischen zween Schachten ein Durchschlag versucht wurde. Der Leichnam, ganz mit Eisenvitriol durchdrungen, war Anfangs weich, wurde aber, so bald man ihn an die Luft gebracht, so hart als Stein. Funfzig Jahre hatte derselbe in einer Tiefe von 300 Ellen, in jenem Vitriolwasser gelegen, und niemand hätte die noch unveränderten Gesichtszüge des verunglückten Jünglings erkannt, niemand die Zeit, seit welcher er in dem Schacht gelegen, gewußt, da die Bergchronicken so wie Volkssagen bey der Menge der Unglücksfälle in Ungewißheit waren, hätte nicht das Andenken der ehemals geliebten Züge eine alte treue Liebe bewahrt.

[That peculiar corpse, of which is written in Hülpher, Cronstedt and the learned Swedish chronicles, disintegrated similarly into a kind of ash, after, presumed to be transformed into hard rock, it was sealed off unsuccessfully from fresh air in a glass cabinet. This former miner was found in the Swedish iron mine in Falun when a connecting tunnel was dug between two shafts. The body, entirely soaked with iron vitriol, was soft at first, but turned hard as stone as soon as it was exposed to the air. For fifty years it lay in the vitriol water at a depth of 300 cubits, and nobody would have recognized the young man's unchanged face, nobody would have known for how long he had been in the shaft, since the mining chronicles and folk tales offered little certainty considering the large number of accidents, had not an old true love remembered the once beloved features.][32]

Schubert's elaboration of the incident obviously unfolds in the context of an empirical inquiry: the miner is part of a discussion of Schubert's hypothesis that human bodies decay much faster than those of animals, which he illustrates through this example. Yet Schubert also asks why there are no findings of petrified humans. The first half begins in an objective, factual style, yet in part two, Schubert's text takes on a kind of plasticity when he touches upon the identity of the miner conserved in vitriolic water. In the course of the lecture, the features of the miner change from "jungendlich" and "unverändert" to "geliebt." Formally speaking, the scientific report gives way to an emotionally charged narrative. Schubert juxtaposes the imagery of youth, "noch jugendlicher Bräutigam,"

---

[32] Schubert, *Ansichten von der Nachtseite der Naturwissenschaft*, 215.

with old age, "altes Mütterchen," "Verwelken und Veralten des Leibes," depicting the progression from life to death. The report ends with an almost lyrically composed, nested opposition: on the one side is the youth, yet "starr und kalt," on the other the old bride filled with youthful, warm love. In a chiasmic combination, the lady and her young love possess complementary characteristics that bedizen one young and one old lover. However, each has the qualities normally assigned to the other.

> Denn als um dem kaum hervorgezogenen Leichnam, das Volk, die unbekannten jugendlichen Gesichtszüge betrachtend steht, da kömmt an Krücken und mit grauem Haar ein altes Mütterchen, mit Thränen über den geliebten Toden, der ihr verlobter Bräutigam gewesen, hinsinkend, die Stunde segnend, da ihr noch an den Pforten des Grabes ein solches Wiedersehen gegönnt war, und das Volk sah mit Verwunderung die Wiedervereinigung dieses seltnen Paares, davon das Eine, im Tode und in tiefer Gruft das jugendliche Aussehen, das Andere, bey dem Verwelken und Veralten des Leibes die jugendliche Liebe, treu und unverändert erhalten hatte, und wie bey der 50jährigen Silberhochzeit der noch jugendliche Bräutigam starr und kalt, die alte und graue Braut voll warmer Liebe gefunden wurden.

[For when a small crowd gathered around the recently recovered body, examining the unfamiliar features of the young man, a gray-haired old woman on crutches came forward, and in tears bent over the beloved departed, who was once her affianced bridegroom. She fell to the ground, blessing the very hour, which, at the threshold to her own grave, graced her with such an encounter. The crowd observed the reunion of the unusual pair with amazement. One had retained the youthful appearance in death, deep inside a tomb, whereas the other had preserved her youthful love, true and unwavering, in an aging body. As if it were their 50-year silver wedding anniversary, the youthful bridegroom was found stiff and cold, and the old and gray bride full of warm love.][33]

Taking a closer look at Schubert's language—the bodies described as wilting like plants, yet stiff and cold like inorganic minerals—we see several bold propositions. One concerns the transition from organic to inorganic matter, the other space and time. Time appears to have passed at different speeds in the two locations separated by the lithosphere. Above ground, time affects the external features of the physical body in

---

[33] Schubert, *Ansichten von der Nachtseite der Naturwissenschaft*, 216.

its customary fashion, yet an internal, emotional time appears to stand still, stalled at the height of the couple's youthful love. The inverse is true for the subterranean body: while its surface displays eternally young features, the core has grown cold and stiff. Schubert conjoins two moments in time that would never meet in a linear chronology. He also emphasizes the asynchrony of the miner's body, now in juxtaposition with that of his fiancée. Both represent an aberration from the presumed course of nature and an interruption of the chronology of an aging human body. Schubert observes the miner's state of youthful suspension, citing vitriol again as the instrument of deferral. But in a poetic digression from the factual accounts, Schubert begins his own narrative treatment of the event with its end.

While the facts of Schubert's account correspond to Leyel's, there is something peculiar about its opening. In the very first sentence of his text, Schubert reverses the petrification and turns the miner to ashes. The sources are divided with regard to the way, form, and exact state to which the corpse from Falun disintegrated during its years on display in the service of science. The descriptions by scientists and curious visitors range from praise for the body's miraculously pristine condition to observations of its black color and morbid stench. Schubert emphasizes a pulverulent condition. Dissolution into ashes may be an expected outcome, but Schubert foregrounds this particular condition before going on to depict the reunion of the lovers in the text's second part. He uses poetic license to accelerate the process of a slow and unsightly decay, thus revealing his own romantic interest in the subject matter. His interest in the love story prevents him from adhering to the factual accounts—though he does invoke them in his opening—and he glosses over the barter of the body and its decay. Between Schubert and Hoffmann, the miner's body disintegrates once at the beginning of an account and once at the end, reanimated several times in between. Like Schubert, Hoffmann also has the miner transform into ashes or dust:

> Die Bergleute traten hinan, sie wollten die arme Ulla aufrichten, aber sie hatte ihr Leben ausgehaucht auf dem Körper des erstarrten Bräutigams. Man bemerke, daß der Körper des Unglücklichen, der fälschlicher Weise für versteinert gehalten war, in Staub zu zerfallen begann.
>
> [The miners closed round. They would have raised poor Ulla, but she had breathed out her life upon her bridegroom's body. The spectators noticed now that it was beginning to crumble into dust. The appearance of petrifaction had been deceptive.][34]

---

[34] Hoffmann, "Die Bergwerke," 239.

E. T. A. Hoffmann's "Die Bergwerke zu Falun"   53

And there is yet another echo of Schubert in Hoffmann's ending. In itself, this is not very surprising, given Hoffmann's explicit reference to Schubert in his *Serapion's* cycle, as well as the widespread reception and inspirational history of the *Nachtseiten* lectures. But Hoffmann, instead of focusing on the facts of the story, picks up Schubert's fictionalization, amplifies it, and enacts a process of strong, literary metamorphoses. Hoffmann recounts the reunion of the former lovers in dramatic detail:

> Da geschah es, daß die Bergleute, als sie zwischen zwei Schachten einen Durchschlag versuchten, in einer Tiefe von dreihundert Ellen im Vitriolwasser den Leichnam eines jungen Bergmanns fanden, der versteinert schien, als sie ihn zu Tage förderten. [...] Es war anzusehen als läge der Jüngling in tiefem Schlaf, so frisch, so wohl erhalten waren die Züge seines Antlitzes, so ohne alle Spur der Verwesung seine zierliche Bergmannskleider, ja selbst die Blumen an der Brust. [...] Man stand im Begriff den Leichnam weiter fortzubringen, nach Falun, als aus der Ferne ein steinaltes eisgraues Mütterchen auf Krücken hinankeuchte. [...] Und damit kauerte sie neben dem Leichnam nieder und faßte die erstarrten Hände und drückte sie an ihre im Alter erkaltete Brust, in der noch, wie heiliges Naphtafeuer unter der Eisdecke, ein Herz voll heißer Liebe schlug.
>
> [[...] when it chanced that some miners who were making a connection-passage between two shafts, found, at a depth of three hundred yards, buried in vitriolated water, the body of a young miner, which seemed, when they brought it to the daylight, to be turned to stone. The young man looked as if he were lying in a deep sleep, so perfectly preserved were the features of his lace, so wholly without trace of decay his new suit of miner's clothes, and even the flowers in his breast. [...] The body was going to be taken to Falun, when out of the distance an old, old woman came creeping slowly and painfully up on crutches. [...] And she cowered down beside the body, took the stony hands and pressed them to her heart, chilled with age, but throbbing still with the fondest love, like some naphtha flame under the surface ice.][35]

Hoffmann adopts some of Schubert's language verbatim to present the basic elements of the story. The description of the mine and the discovery of the miner is lifted from Schubert, as is the old woman on her crutches, and the fact that nobody recognized the young man. Hoffmann

---

35   Hoffmann, "Die Bergwerke," 238–9.

continues by describing the body's pristine state and renders the miner in a dainty portrait as he limns his handsome face, his delicate clothes, and the still fresh boutonnière. Well rested and invigorated, we can imagine the young man might awaken at any moment from his slumber, in good health and ready to return to work in the mines. Ulla, the fiancée, is rendered as his exact inverse—an old, crippled woman. Ulla herself is transformed from organic to inorganic matter: old as stone and grey as ice, her hybrid state complements that of Elis. Neither the young miner nor the fiancée, now an aged woman, remain stable beings. The identity of the miner takes shape through the narration of someone who herself had to first abdicate her own identity. It is curious that Hoffmann, in the very moment of identification and formation, has the miner crumble to ashes. His physical stability seems replaced by semantic stability. Like Schubert's text, Hoffmann's ending plays with and reverses the roles assigned to the two figures. Hoffmann also concludes the portrait of the miner with a description of thriving flowers. It mirrors the vegetal language used by Schubert in his portrayal of Ulla, but it also points to that peculiar affinity between the realms of the plants and of minerals.

Hoffmann tells us that the body was falsely thought to be of stone. We can now speculate whether he does so because it falls to dust and hence cannot possess a rock's hardness, or because he simply follows Schubert's model. Both writers emphasize the miner's stony nature and subsequent pulverization. I am hesitant to dismiss this similarity too quickly. Schubert begins his account with the pulverization and Hoffmann places it at his story's end. In both cases, it accelerates the processes described in the narrative: a solid state dissolves once more. United at last, the two lovers could form a stable pair in death. But as Ulla expires, clutched to Elis's chest, he is paradoxically invigorated and transforms a final time. Ulla is transformed as well, but in the other direction: from living to dead, from flexible to rigid. Hoffmann undermines the notion that death could provide closure to the story of a life.

Turning to humus, dirt, and dust is not only a thematic connection on the diegetic level between Schubert and Hoffmann. Already during the inaugural meeting of the Serapiontic brothers, when they contemplate revivifying their friendship, Theodor refers to the mutability of life and illustrates his point by associating the process of aging with accumulating soil:

> Daß wir zwölf Jahre älter worden, daß sich wohl mit jedem Jahr immer mehr und mehr Erde an uns ansetzt, die uns hinabzieht aus der luftigen Region, bis wir am Ende *unter* die Erde kommen, das will ich gar nicht in Anschlag bringen.

[I say nothing of the circumstance that we are twelve years older; that, no doubt, every year lays more earth upon us, which weighs us down from aerial regions, till we go *under* the earth at last.][36]

What Theodor describes with the downward pull of soil are in fact those very stories of life that must be reanimated. The six friends decide to rekindle their bond by forming a literary club and meeting regularly to tell stories from different times and places, all of which have been told elsewhere. We already saw that Hoffmann incorporates word-for-word excerpts of Schubert's lectures. By including the novella of the miner in his *Serapion's* cycle, Hoffmann weaves it into a larger narrative fabric and a frame, which indicates the effort to enclose obtrusive material. It creates a border around possibly otherwise unconnected stories and attempts to better contain them. The mountainous landscape of the mine elicits attempts at this kind of literary enclosure or formal taming. One of the aspects of the Serapiontic principle is to adapt, that is transform, and therefore attempt to tame, already existing literary material. And it is Theodor's turn to recount the story of the miner:

> Es wird spät, und das Herz würde es mir abdrücken, wenn ich euch nicht noch heute eine Erzählung vorlesen sollte die ich gestern endigte. Mir gab der Geist ein, ein sehr bekanntes und schon bearbeitetes Thema von einem Bergmann zu Falun auszuführen der Breiteren, und ihr sollt entscheiden, ob ich wohl getan der Hingebung zu folgen oder nicht.
>
> [It is late; and I should be sorry not to read you, tonight, a tale which I finished yesterday. The spirit moved me to treat, rather more fully than has been done previously, a well-known *thema* concerning a miner at Falun; and you must decide whether I have done well to yield to the spirit's prompting, or not.][37]

Before Hoffmann, Achim von Arnim's ballad *Des ersten Bergmanns ewige Jugend* appeared in 1808, three years later Johann Peter Hebel published his "Unverhofftes Wiedersehen" as a calendar story for *Der rheinländische Hausfreund*, and of course there were Schubert, Leyel, and the newspaper articles. In both Schubert and Hoffmann, the corporeality of the miner's body achieves its significance only once the body itself is beyond recognition and has fallen to ashes. The material body of the miner and the materiality of the text cannot coexist in time. For the illegible

---

[36] Hoffmann, *Die Serapions-Brüder*, 15; emphasis original.
[37] Hoffmann, *Die Serapions-Brüder*, 208.

physical body to become a legible textual sign, the physical body must disappear through a metamorphosis into a text. It is this second disappearance of the body that paradoxically emphasizes the figural corporeality of the miner and demands his reformation and reanimation.

Hoffmann gives the miner a back-story. He introduces Elis Fröbom, a sailor, who followed his father's career path. Elis was destined to be a sailor from childhood and he experiences the ocean and the seas as invigorating and life-sustaining. In fact, he was unharmed by the same storm that took his father's life. Yet Fröbom does not share the joy of homecoming with his fellow sailors. He had lost his father and his mother, and he begins to realize a dark sense of meaning in his labor and life. "'Ach', begann er endlich, wie sich besinnend, 'ach, mit meiner Freude, mit meiner Lust ist es nun einmal gar nichts.'" ["Ah!" he said, as if collecting his thoughts, "it's no use talking about my enjoying myself. [. . .] there's no pleasure in it, for me."][38] Joy and delight, feelings Elis shared with his mother upon his usual returns to the port, when he showered her with ducats and told her of his voyages, give way to a sense of futility and disgust concerning his life at sea: "Auf die See mag ich nicht mehr, *das* Leben ekelt mich an." [I shan't go to sea any more; I'm sick of existence altogether.][39] Gradually, these sentiments overtake him, and Elis longs for death: "Ach läg' ich doch nur begraben in dem tiefsten Meeresgrunde!" [Oh, that I were lying deep, deep beneath the sea!][40]

Separated from all that is dear to him and at a moment of total loss, Elis meets Torbern. Tobern is an old miner who is in fact undead. He is a traveller from a different time, an asynchronous entity able to traverse ontological and categorical boundaries. He is convinced that Elis is at an age when his life is just about to begin instead of end, and points him toward a new way of life. He encourages Elis to forsake his life at sea, certain that Elis was never suited to be a sailor. Instead, Elis should follow the calling nature had destined for him: "Aber zum Seemann habt Ihr Eure Lebtage gar nicht im mindesten getaugt. [. . .] Folgt meinem Rat, Elis Fröbom! Geht nach Falun, werdet ein Bergmann." [[. . .] but you were never in all your born days in the least cut out for a sailor. [. . .] Take my advice, Elis Froebom; be a miner.][41]

Torbern advises Elis to undergo a transformation: to move from sea to land.[42] From the beginning of the tale, it is apparent that Elis's path

---

[38] Hoffmann, "Bergwerke," 211.
[39] Hoffmann, "Bergwerke," 213.
[40] Hoffmann, "Bergwerke," 211.
[41] Hoffmann, "Bergwerke," 214.
[42] For a detailed discussion of Elis's transition from sea to land, cf. Vera Bachmann, *Stille Wasser—Tiefe Texte? Zur Ästhetik der Oberfläche in der Literatur des 19. Jahrhunderts* (Bielefeld: Transcript, 2013), 145–68.

from sailor to miner is anything but accidental. Hoffmann places Elis at a juncture where he must contemplate the beginnings and endings of his life. Elis could surrender to his grim desires and end his worldly existence, or he could leave behind his life as a sailor and find new meaning in the life of a miner. Ellis chooses the life of the pitman, and what follows is the story of Fröbom's passage from sea to land. Although Elis does relocate from sea to land, his transition remains incomplete. In fact, as we will see, Elis remains caught in an eternally transitory state, in an intermediary realm between what he was before and what he could be; and finally, between life and death.

AN EMPTY CIPHER

Because neither chronicle nor lore knew of the miner, we can argue that he was socially dead and hidden in a space without meaning and time. Unlike Schubert, or his predecessor Hebel, Hoffmann emphasizes that the people of Falun had forgotten the story of Elis and Ulla:

> Längst war der wackre Masmeister Altermann Pehrson Dahlsjö gestorben, längst seine Tochter Ulla verschwunden, niemand in Falun wußte von beiden mehr etwas, da seit Fröboms unglückseligem Hochzeitstage wohl an die funfzig Jahre verflossen.
>
> [Long had stout Pehrson Dahlsjoe been dead, his daughter Ulla long lost sight of and forgotten. Nobody in Falun remembered them. More than fifty years had gone by since Froebom's luckless wedding-day [. . .].][43]

Ulla's father had passed away and Ulla herself disappeared, only to return every year on their intended anniversary as the "Johannismütterchen," unrecognized by anyone. Trapped in rock, between two passageways, unmarked by time, and changing his form in his movement from dark to light, from the depth of the mine to the surface, Fet Mats was always of more than one form, category, and order. He was perpetually in a liminal state. Hoffman's text offers a description of Mats in his early years that is intelligible, if marked by transition and instability. But upon discovery, Fet Mats presented the people of Falun with more than the problem of a corpse on their hands. He was a semiotic problem, a cipher that no one could decode. Although

---

[43] Hoffmann, "Bergwerke," 238.

the body moves from darkness to light and therefore from geology to geography, it remains illegible. Despite the body's emergence, its movement into the realm of the geo-*graphein*, the miner remains inscrutable. The miner as cipher is precisely at the semantic margins of the known and the unknown. In both Leyel and Schubert, the curious body is indecipherable to science. Hoffmann writes such a detailed prehistory of the miner in order to emphasize the power of literary imagination vis-à-vis scientific observation. Where Leyel's taxonomic efforts were frustrated and Schubert expanded a scientific account through poetic license, Hoffmann frees the case from the shackles of the factual. Although the opacity of the miner's body frustrates scientific efforts and defies taxonomic order, its cryptic nature becomes the creative catalyst for Hoffmann's literary endeavor.

INVERSIONS, TRANSFORMATIONS, TRANSITIONS

At first it seems that Hoffmann structures the fictional space of his story according to the same topography as Tieck would in his "Runenberg" of 1804 and Novalis in the posthumously published *Heinrich von Ofterdingen*. There is a clear division between the lowlands and the mountainous region, and each is ascribed a specific role.[44] Yet a similar distinction cannot be upheld in Hoffmann. Hoffmann's scenery can be divided roughly into four theaters: the open sea, the seaport Göthaborg, the mining village, and finally, the mine itself. Initially, the topographic demarcations are clear, but soon the boundaries begin to blur as the transition from ocean to mountains takes place. And this transition is a narrative transition. "Du weißt nichts von dem Bergbau, Elis Fröbom, laß dir davon erzählen." [You know nothing about mining, Elis. Let me tell you a little.][45] Elis has not yet set out for the mountains, but is still in Göthaborg when, for the first time, he has the mines "vor Augen."[46] Elis's first encounter with the mine is through a story. The revenant Torbern tells Elis of the mine, and he tells of it in such a way that Elis imagines that he is standing in it. Through his descriptions, the old miner introduces Elis to the realm deep within the mountain. Yet instead of merely telling Elis about the mining business, as initially

---

[44] Ludwig Tieck, "Runenberg," *Phantasus*, ed. Manfred Frank (Frankfurt/Main: Deutscher Klassiker Verlag, 1985), 184–209; Novalis, "Heinrich von Ofterdingen," *Werke, Tagebücher und Briefe Friedrich von Hardenbergs*, vol. 1, ed. Richard Samuel (München: Hanser Verlag, 1978), 237–383. Cf. Böhme, "Adoleszenskrisen," 136.
[45] Hoffmann, "Bergwerke," 215.
[46] Hoffmann, "Bergwerke," 215.

suggested, the revenant brings the mines to life, as if they were a magic garden: "Immer lebendiger und lebendiger wurde seine Rede [...]. Er durchwanderte die Schachten wie die Gänge eines Zaubergartens. Das Gestein lebte auf, die Fossile regten sich [...]." [More and more vivid grew his words [...]. He went, in his description, through the different shafts as if they had been the alleys of some enchanted garden. The jewels came to life, the fossils began to move [...].]⁴⁷ Concerning the liveliness of Torbern's speech, Hoffmann makes an interesting distinction. Through his speech, Torben takes Elis into the mines, and he walks through the shafts of the mine *as if* they were paths in a magical garden. But once inside the fictional mine, the rocks and fossils come to life in actuality. Elis's second visit to the mine is also not a physical visit. After his conversation with the old miner, Elis falls asleep and encounters this same enchanted space in his dreams, which possesses strange forces that put him into a state of delight and terror. Within the fantastical space of his dream, Elis feels wistfully drawn to rocks and metals that come to life and take on vegetal and human forms.

[...] aber in dem Augenblick regte sich alles um ihn her, und wie kräuselnde Wogen erhoben sich aus dem Boden wunderbare Blumen und Pflanzen von blinkendem Metall, die ihre Blüten und Blätter aus der tiefsten Tiefe emporrankten, und auf anmutige Weise ineinander verschlangen. Der Boden war so klar, das Elis die Wurzeln der Pflanzen deutlich erkennen konnte, aber bald immer tiefer mit dem Blick eindringend, erblickte er ganz unten— unzählige holde jungfräuliche Gestalten, die sich mit weißen glänzenden Armen umschlungen hielten, und aus ihren Herzen sproßten jene Wurzeln, jene Blumen und Pflanzen empor, und wenn die Jungfrauen lächelten, ging ein süßer Wohllaut durch das weite Gewölbe, und höher und freudiger schossen die wunderbaren Metallblüten empor. Ein unbeschreibliches Gefühl von Schmerz und Wollust ergriff den Jüngling, eine Welt von Liebe, Sehnsucht, brünstigem Verlangen ging auf in seinem Inneren.

[[...] but, at that moment, every thing around him began to move, and wonderful plants and flowers, of glittering metal, came shooting up out of the crystal mass he was standing on, and entwined their leaves and blossoms in the loveliest manner. The crystal floor was so transparent that Elis could distinctly see the roots of these plants. But soon, as his glance penetrated deeper

---

⁴⁷ Hoffmann, "Bergwerke," 215.

and deeper, he saw, far, far down in the depths, innumerable beautiful maidens, holding each other embraced with white, gleaming arms; and it was from their hearts that the roots, plants, and flowers were growing. And when these maidens smiled, a sweet sound rang all through the vault above, and the wonderful metal-flowers shot up higher, and waved their leaves and branches in joy. An indescribable sense of rapture came upon the lad; a world of love and passionate longing awoke in his heart.][48]

The order in which the transformation occurs is noteworthy. Inorganic, mineral forms take on animate human and vegetal shapes that appeal to the dreamy Elis. Conversely, when the primary form is organic or human, it appears awesome, overpowering, and repellant in its subsequent inorganic rigidity, brought about by the influence of fire and lightning. In his dream, Elis re-encounters the old miner as well as a mystical mountain queen, both of whom have undergone a transformation from organic to inorganic:

Elis gewahrte neben sich den alten Bergmann, aber so wie er ihn mehr und mehr anschaute wurde er zur Riesengestalt aus glühendem Erz gegossen. Elis wollte sich entsetzen, aber in dem Augenblick leuchtete es auf aus der Tiefe wie ein jäher Blitz und das ernste Antlitz einer mächtigen Frau wurde sichtbar. Elis fühlte, wie das Entzücken in seiner Brust immer steigend und steigend zur zermalmenden Angst wurde.

[But as Elis looked at him, he seemed to expand into gigantic size, and to be made of glowing metal. Elis was beginning to be terrified; but a brilliant light came darting, like a sudden lightning-flash, out of the depths of the abyss, and the earnest face of a grand, majestic woman appeared. Elis felt the rapture of his heart swelling and swelling into destroying pain.][49]

The synesthetic experience of dual, contradictory forces of pleasure and horror, delight and fear, continue to guide Elis when he compares his visions of the mining world with the reality of life near the pits in Falun. Fröbom witnesses destruction and misery and succumbs to torpor in light of what he encounters. The vegetal forces and qualities, which were the source of pleasure and allure for Elis in his dreams, have been destroyed by man's exploitations. As Elis stands before the hellish gates

---

[48] Hoffmann, "Bergwerke," 216–17.
[49] Hoffmann, "Bergwerke," 217.

to the mine, which Hoffmann describes in great detail, he witnesses miners emerging, presumably after having completed their day's work.

> Es geschah, daß eben einige Bergleute aus der Teufe emporstiegen, die in ihrer dunklen Grubentracht, mit ihren schwarz verbrannten Gesichtern, wohl anzusehen waren wie häßliche Unholde, die aus der Erde mühsam hervorgekrochen sich den Weg bahnen wollten bis auf die Oberfläche.
>
> [Two or three miners happened, just then, to be coming up from work in the mine, and in their dark mining clothes, with their black, grimy faces, they were much like ugly, diabolical creatures of some sort, slowly and painfully crawling, and forcing their way up to the surface.][50]

These are not the proud colliers described to Elis by the old miner, but Acherontic creatures digging their way to the surface. The earth's surface becomes a liminal barrier or an inverting mirror and the miners are transformed when they break it open and pass through it. In his description of the pit, Hoffmann not only vividly describes the destruction and exploitation with all is coloric and olfactoric concomitants in their various shades of black and brown to sulfuric yellow, but he also makes mention of the exact dimensions and construction of the pit: "Bekanntlich ist die große Tagesöffnung der Erzgrube zu Falun zwölfhundert Fuß lang, sechshundert Fuß breit und einhundert und achtzig Fuß tief." [It is well known that the great open pit of the iron ore mine in Falun is twelve hundred feet long, six hundred feet wide, and one hundred and eighty feet deep.][51] This data corresponds to the mines of Falun as described in the mineralogist Johann Friedrich Ludwig Hausmann's travelogue *Reise durch Skandinavien*. Hoffmann's prosaic rendering of the mine is interesting insofar as the mine of Falun was, according to Hausmann's report, a highly productive and technologically advanced enterprise. This can be gleaned not only from the travelogue, but also from a detailed map and cross-section of the mine in the appendix. In comparison to the gigantic subterranean sprawl of the mine, the visible part above ground seems miniscule. The sketch shows an older section of the mine that was apparently worked in open-cast style, while the younger section is a vast network of horizontal, subterranean tunnels accessible by vertical shafts. The buildings above ground are dwarfed in comparison to the

---

[50] Hoffmann, "Bergwerke," 221.
[51] Hoffmann, "Bergwerke," 220–1.

dimensions of the mine. Hoffmann presumably read Hausmann's sketch as an allegorical emblem of what is visible and what remains invisible. This proportional asymmetry is relevant not only to the infrastructure of the mine but, also to the relation of what is rationally explicable and what must remain irrationally vague and unknowable in nature and in the mind.[52]

In fact, the world of Fröbom seems disjointed from the outset. In her analysis of the romantic notion of "depth," Inka Mülder-Bach suggests that profundity is not achieved through a downward motion.[53] Rather, it is a movement that points in all directions, especially upwards. Already Martin Luther had associated both *abyssus* and *altitudo* with *Tiefe*—depth. Three hundred years later, Jean Paul claimd that depth is the inversion of *altitude*, and Novalis referred to geologists as "inverted astrologers."[54] We can witness this strange curvature also in Hoffmann: when the old miner first tells Elis about the wonders of the pit, he describes the bottom of the rock as a reflection of the heavens above, rendering the mine an inverted mountain.

> Wenn der blinde Maulwurf in blindem Instinkt die Erde durchwühlt, so möcht es wohl sein, daß in der tiefsten Teufe bei dem schwachen Schimmer des Grubenlichts des Menschen Auge hellsehender wird, ja daß es endlich sich mehr und mehr erkräftigend, in dem wunderbaren Gestein die Abspiegelung dessen zu erkennen vermag, was oben, über den Wolken verborgen.

> [[. . .] the mole tunnels the ground from blind instinct; but, it may be, in the deepest depths, by the pale glimmer of the mine candle, men's eyes get to see clearer, and at length, growing stronger and stronger, acquire the power of reading in the stones, the gems, and the minerals, the mirroring of secrets which are hidden above the clouds.][55]

---

[52] Cf. Johann Friedrich Ludwig Hausmann, *Reise durch Skandinavien in den Jahren 1806 und 1807* (Göttingen: Johann Friedrich Römer, 1818), Tab. IV, 434.
[53] Inka Mülder-Bach, "Tiefe: Zur Dimension der Romantik," *Räume der Romantik*, eds. Inka Mülder-Bach and Gerhard Neumann (Würzburg: Königshausen & Neumann, 2007), 83–102.
[54] Mülder-Bach, "Tiefe," 85–7. Cf. also Johann Gottfried Herder, "Kalligone: Vom Angenehmen und Schönen," *Schriften zur Literatur und Philosophie 1792–1800*, ed. Hans Dietrich Irmscher, *Werke*, vol. 8 (Frankfurt/Main: Deutscher Klassiker Verlag, 1998), 641–964, 892.
[55] Hoffmann, "Bergwerke," 215.

The mine is strangely lit in Torbern's description. In response to the mine's increasing darkness, both eyesight and reflection become stronger. And as the reflections increase in intensity, so does the inversion of the space. Later in his dream, Elis is sailing on a smooth sea during a dark and starry night.[56] In his dream, Elis finds himself back aboard the vessel, sailing on the smooth, glassy surface of the ocean, above which vaults the dark firmament—a concave, cavernous space. When he looks into the water, its surface becomes a crystal floor—"ein Kristallboden"—above which now cambers a roof of glistening stones— "ein Gewölbe von schwarz flimmernden Gestein." [[. . .] a vault of black rock above him [. . .].][57] To speak of an *ordo inversus*, however, would maintain the evenly-structured duality of above ground and below ground, of light and dark. Rather, Elis's world above and below ground is an environment of perpetual change without clear demarcations. Here, Elis is suspended between worlds and forms as if caught in a perpetual passage of a threshold.

Hoffmann's story of the miner from Falun is a narrative of thresholds that informs his poetics. Within the narrative itself, the protagonist attempts to undergo various transitions, which are none other than *rites de passage*. Elis returns from sea to land, death separates him from his mother, he decides to become a miner instead of continuing his life as a sailor, and his fiancée Ulla, as we will soon see, invites him to join the miners and to cross the threshold of the home as her husband. The *passage* can illicit desires for relief and renewal, for movement and motion, change, and self-discovery. It can also be a quest for stability, for connection, and for the inclusion within a new social order and environment. The *passage* is simultaneously a quest for detachment and containment. What appears paradoxical at first unites in one coherent movement, *supra limen*, in the crossing of the threshold, which, however, is denied to Elis.

---

[56] "Es war ihm, als schwämme er in einem schönen Schiff mit vollen Segeln auf dem spiegelblanken Meer und über ihm wölbte sich ein dunkler Wolkenhimmel. Doch wie er nun in die Wellen hinabschaute, erkannte er bald, daß das, was er für das Meer gehalten, eine feste durchsichtige Masse war, in deren Schimmer das ganz Schiff auf wunderbarste Weise zerfloß, so daß er auf dem Krystallboden stand, und über sich ein Gewölbe von schwarz flimmerndem Gestein erblickte. Gestein war das nämlich, was er erst für den Wolkenhimmel gehalten." [He thought he was sailing in a beautiful vessel on a sea calm and clear as a mirror, with a dark, cloudy sky vaulted overhead. But when he looked down into the sea he presently saw that what he had thought was water was a firm, transparent, sparkling substance, in the shimmer of which the ship, in a wonderful manner, melted away, so that he found himself standing upon this floor of crystal, with a vault of black rock above him, for that was rock which he had taken at first for clouds.] Hoffmann, "Bergwerke," 216.

[57] Hoffmann, "Bergwerke," 216.

Hoffmann stresses the force of this passage and its ambivalence in several ways. One of them is through dates, or more precisely, through one date. The reader will remember that the historic Fet Mats was returned to the earth on December 21, 1749, the day of the winter solstice and hence the shortest day of the year. In itself, this may be nothing but a nice coincidence, which could motivate elaborate speculation, if it were not for Hoffmann's fictional date of Elis and Ulla's wedding, the date of Fröbom's disappearance, and the day of reappearance: St. John's day, June 24, midsummer's eve.[58] A solstice marks a tipping point, resulting either in an increase or decrease of illumination after a moment of instability. Hoffmann's insistence on this date evokes the narrative movement between clarity and opacity; the way that Hoffmann's telling hinges on unstable figures and ambiguous events. Hoffmann further emphasizes the role of passages by constantly placing Elis right in their middle through instances of foreshadowing. The story of Elis points toward various future scenarios, of which only a few manifest. The anticipatory force of such predictions and the expectation of their fulfillment are introduced in a wise warning to Elis and to the reader by an old sailor. Many years ago, the sailor told Elis of a vision he had during a delirium, in which he saw the waves part before him and an evil grimace appear. The sailor interpreted the dream as an omen of his demise, and the sudden disappearance of the sailor elevates the premonition to an inescapable truth:

> Ein solches Gesicht, meinte der alte Seemann, bedeutet den baldigen Tod in den Wellen, und wirklich stürzte er auch bald darauf unversehens von dem Verdeck in das Meer und war rettunglos verschwunden.
>
> [The old sailor said that to see such a vision meant death, ere long, in the waves; and in fact he did very soon after fall overboard, no one knew exactly how, and was drowned without possibility of rescue.][59]

But these premonitions never come true for Elis. Though he follows in the footsteps of his father, he does not become his father, and the substitutive chain from mother to Ulla is never fully linked. Instead, Hoffmann stresses the contingency of these "inevitable" or "prophesied" events:

---

[58] Hoffmann, "Bergwerke," 236, 238.
[59] Hoffmann, "Bergwerke," 221, 212.

Und doch war es ihm wieder, als habe ihm der Alte eine neue unbekannte Welt erschlossen, in die er hineingehöre, und aller Zauber dieser Welt sei ihm schon zur frühsten Knabenzeit in seltsamen geheimnisvollen Ahnungen aufgegangen.

[And yet it seemed as though the old man were opening to him a new and unknown world, to which he really properly belonged, and that he had somehow felt all the magic of that world, in mystic forebodings, since his boyhood.][60]

By showing how the seemingly predestined events may *not* come to pass, Hoffmann unhinges notions of teleology and inevitability. Causal consistency is actually frustrated doubly in the above quoted passage. "Und doch war es ihm wieder," "er glaubte," "er meinte," and "ihm schien" are not only indirect but also conditional or hypothetical speech, creating a sense of "as-if-ness," which opens up a "dual set of coordinates" that dissolves all clear contours and renders events and things unstable.[61] A dual set of coordinates, an existence suspended above and below ground, an illegible cipher, a corpse that is a statue, who is a sailor as well as a miner: Hoffmann continually forces the reader to suspend the miner in contradictory states.

The peculiarity of Hoffmann's text lies in his lapidary poetic principle. *Lapidescence* and *lapidescent* is the "process of becoming stone; having a tendency to solidify into stone; said chiefly of 'petrifying' waters and the salts dissolved or suspended in them," a definition apt since Leyel's first description.[62] The etymology of *lapidary* refers to the brevity and conciseness of inscriptions on tombs or memorial stones. And Hoffmann treats the miner as if he is such an inscription. According to the *OED*, *lapidary*, as an adjective, is first and foremost "concerned with stones." But further also "Of an inscription, etc.: Engraved on stone, esp. monumental stones. Of style, etc.: Characteristic of or suitable for monumental inscriptions."[63] Elis's petrified body marks his own death; in this way Hoffmann suggests that the miner's body is both the corpse and the tomb, the object to be mourned and the matter that enables such mourning.

---

[60] Hoffmann, "Bergwerke," 215–16.
[61] Norbert Miller, "E. T. A. Hofffmann's doppelte Wirklichkeit. Zum Motiv der Schwellenüberschreitung in seinen Märchen," *Literaturwissenschaft und Geschichtsphilosophie. Festschrift für Wilhelm Emrich*, eds. Helmut Arntzen et al. (Berlin : De Gruyter, 1975), 357–72, 370.
[62] "lapidescent, adj. and n.," *OED* online, June 2023, http://www.oed.com/view/Entry/105720?redirectedFrom=lapidescent.
[63] "lapidary, adj. and n.," *OED* nnline, June 2023, http://www.oed.com/view/Entry/105713?redirectedFrom=lapidary.

Hoffmann takes the curious case of the miner to explore the transformative power of the literary imagination. The story is lapidary insofar as it is a tale about a curious death, but Hoffmann expands the horizon of literary imagination to make the episode a story of origins and metamorphosis, of collapse and *mise-en-abîmes*. He tells the story of the miner and imagines the winding path from the stages of his previous life until his disappearance on his wedding day. Where Leyel represented the transition from the factual to the scientific, and Schubert occupied the realm in between the scientific and the poetic, Hofmann draws upon the scientific in order to reveal the full power of literary form.

After Theodor finishes his story, the Serapion's brothers, as is their custom, discuss its merits. During his introductory remarks, Theodor already cautioned his listeners that his story, which he calls a picture or painting, would be of a much drearier nature than Cyprian's, whose reading preceded his. As he expected, his friends were rather laconic upon the story's conclusion. They criticize Theodor's story for its effect, suggesting how it could have been told differently. Lothar bemoans the strong local color and the heavy technical terminology of the tale. Ottmar claims that he much preferred Schubert's brief version to Theodor's colorful rendition with ghosts, visions, and carnivals. Only Cyprian concedes that he did not dislike Theodor's story as strongly as the others did. He speaks of the possibility to be split from oneself, or as he puts it, "als im ganzen Leben mit sich entzweit"—cut in two, or perhaps to be suspended between forms.[64] By providing three, even four critical reactions to his story, Hoffmann offers alternative versions. He emphasizes the inherent contingencies of fictional and factual metamorphoses. On a poetic level, Hoffmann ultimately renders processes of transition unstable, and he refrains from giving his story a robust sense of closure. Instead, he lingers with the possibility of material metamorphoses as guiding principle for the openness of the literary. While his coevals Tieck and Novalis treat the mountains as a

---

[64] "Wie oft stellen Dichter Menschen, welche auf irgend eine entsetzliche Weise untergehen, als im ganzen Leben entzweit [. . .]. Ich habe Menschen gekannt, die sich plötzlich im ganzen Wesen veränderten, die entweder in sich hien erstarrten oder wie von bösen Mächten rastlos, verfolgt in steter Unruhe umhergetrieben wurden und bald dieses, bald jenes entsetzliche Ereignis aus dem Leben fortriß." [Writers very often show us people who perish in some disastrous way as having been themselves separated from their very own lives [. . .] I have known people who have suddenly seemed to alter and change completely—who have appeared to be suddenly petrified (so to speak) within themselves, or driven hither and thither by hostile powers, in constant unrest, till some fearful catastrophe has torn them from life.] Hoffmann, *Die Serapions-Brüder*, 240.

space of initiation that can be entered, and most importantly, again also exited, Hoffmann decides to leave Elis Fröbom in the mines, stuck in a liminal phase.

The mountains in Hoffmann's story are neither a space of sublime contemplation nor exalted heights to be conquered; rather, they are masses that harbor secrets of transformation. The many stories of the miner of Falun a journey through an inverted peak; a visit to a mine out of which a most curious figure emerges. Hoffmann's text establishes what requires further exploration: that the mountains encode, congeal, and sometimes even disgorge matter that demands innovations in form. For Hoffmann, the miner's body itself becomes a landscape through which ideas of transformation—both physical and literary—are worked out. The miner from Falun, as he vacillates between living and dead, overdetermined and utterly inscrutable, flesh, stone, and dust, serves as inspiration and corollary for Hoffmann's literary innovations. The author likewise vacillates between generic conventions, formal registers, and different endings. This unceasing movement between states and forms seems, for Hoffmann, a source of literary pleasure. It allows for the incorporation of various source materials, the writing of dreams, and the stitching together of fantasy and science. As we ascend from the depths of Hoffmann's mines to the heights of Büchner's mountains, we will encounter even greater oscillation—the kind that leads not only to a multiplicity of bodily states or fictional ones, but to a type of madness as intimately linked to the mountains as Elis is to the mines.

III Lost in the Mountains—Perspective and Displacement in Georg Büchner's "Lenz"

ARRIVALS

On the fifth day of his "recuperative" stay in the Vosges Mountains, the eponymous protagonist of Georg Büchner's unfinished work from 1837, "Lenz," is told by his father's friend Kaufmann to return home to Strasbourg. Lenz, plagued by emotional and mental disturbances, replies in exasperation:

> Hier weg, weg! Nach Haus? Toll werden dort? Du weißt, ich kann es nirgends aushalten, als da herum, in der Gegend, wenn ich nicht manchmal auf einen Berg könnte und die Gegend sehen könnte; und dann wieder herunter in's Haus, durch den Garten gehen, und zum Fenster hineinsehen. Ich würde toll! Toll! Laßt mich doch in Ruhe!
>
> [[A]way from here, away! Go home? Go mad there? You know I can't stand it anywhere but here, in this area; if I sometimes couldn't go up a mountain and see the countryside and then back into the house, walk through the garden and look in through the window. I'd go mad! Mad! Leave me in peace!][1]

But whatever calm—"Ruhe"—Lenz might hope to find in the mountainside parish eludes him throughout the story, in large part because of the terrain in which it is set. Here, Lenz claims that the parish of Oberlin, set in the Steintal of the Vosges Mountains, affords him an environment for respite and restoration. He can climb the mountains and look out over the land or look from the garden through a window into the parish house. Lenz claims that the multiplicity of views offers him freedom that is lacking in Strasbourg—freedom without which he will go mad, "Toll!" But it is precisely the coexistence of the two perspectives Lenz names—the vast expanse seen from a mountain's summit and the delimited interior of a house framed by a window—that establish and sustain Lenz's madness. Büchner's story explores these two perspectives, oscillating between the two without ever establishing one scopic mode as superior or stabilizing. The movement between these two visual modes lends the story a formal quality that

---

[1] Georg Büchner, "Lenz," *Dichtungen, Sämtliche Werke, Briefe und Dokumente*, ed. Henri Poschmann, vol. 1 (Frankfurt/Main: Deutscher Klassiker Verlag, 1992), 223–50, 236. For the English, I consulted Georg Büchner, "Lenz," *Complete Works and Letters*, eds. Walter Hinderer and Henry J. Schmidt, trans. Henry J. Schmidt (New York: Continuum, 1968), 139–59 and Georg Büchner, *Leonce and Lena. Lenz. Woyzeck*, trans. Michael Hamburger (Chicago: University of Chicago Press, 1972), 35–62.

mirrors its protagonist's mental state: unsettled, irrational, unable to find calm or achieve mastery of the surroundings. In other words, the story's setting in an untamable mountainscape allows Büchner to craft and explore an aesthetic of madness. While other scholars have read "Lenz" as a psychopathography—an early depiction of mental illness—I want to instead call attention to Büchner's emphasis in the text on perspective.[2] Rather than considering a description of madness in "Lenz" as the story's ultimate aim or result, Büchner investigates the incompleteness and inadequacy of perspective in order to narrate a story that is *about*—both literally and formally—madness. A subtle, but nonetheless radical disavowal of the rational subject described in Kant's sublime, Büchner's "Lenz" engages the mountains to suggest that spatial displacement and discomfort is in fact a new and surprisingly modern form of madness.

Büchner's protagonist takes his name from the *Sturm und Drang* writer Jakob Michael Reinhold Lenz, who in 1777 visited the clergyman Oberlin in Waldersbach after suffering from a nervous breakdown. Despite the care he received at the Alsatian parish, the author Lenz's condition continued to deteriorate until the end of his life. This aspect of Lenz's biography not only lends Büchner's story a central plot element; it also is suggestive of Büchner's interest and literary intervention in discourses of madness circulating at the time of Lenz's life and later during the composition of the tale. During Reinhold Lenz's life, his mental illness would have likely been diagnosed as melancholia and mania. Oberlin says that the historical Lenz suffers from suicidal compulsions, "Entleibungssucht" and "Melancholie."[3] While contemporary medical discourse would likely diagnose Büchner's Lenz as schizophrenic, the author himself stresses different aspects of his character's psychic state. Although he drew extensively from Oberlin's notes about Reinhold Lenz's condition and occasionally even lifts entire passages from these documents, Büchner makes several

---

[2] Cf. Benedikt Decurvières, "Der Wahnsinn als Kraftfeld: Eine symptomatische Lektüre zu Georg Büchners Erzählung *Lenz*," *Weimarer Beiträge* 52 (2006): 203–26; Sabine Kubik, *Krankheit und Medizin im literarischen Werk Büchners* (Stuttgart: Metzler, 1994); Harald Schmidt, *Melancholie und Landschaft. Die psychotische und ästhetische Struktur der Naturschilderungen in Büchners "Lenz"* (Opladen: Westdeutscher Verlag, 1994); Harald Schmidt, "Melancholie und Landschaft: Zur problematischen Differentialdiagnostik in Georg Büchners 'Lenz'," *Zeitschrift für deutsche Philologie* 117 (1998): 516–42.

[3] Cf. Oberlin's diary on Lenz's stay in his parish. Johann Friedrich Oberlin, "Herr L . . . . . ., (synoptischer Text)," in Georg Büchner, *Lenz, Georg Büchner: Sämtliche Werke und Schriften* (Marburger Ausgabe), vol. 5, eds. Burghard Dedner and Hubert Gersch (Darmstadt: Wissenschaftliche Buchgesellschaft, 2001), 219–41, 238.

decisions that indicate his interest is not madness as an internal, subjective disruption, but as a condition that results from a troubled relationship to the external world.[4] For instance, Büchner chooses not to use the term "Melancholie," but makes the semantic shift to "Wahnsinn" in order to name Lenz's condition.[5]

The concept of *Wahnsinn*, as it was understood during Büchner's time, helps lead to a definition of Lenz's ailment that aligns with Büchner's formal program. In 1812, the physician Adolph Henke wrote of *Wahnsinn* when he lamented the hazy terminology used to describe madness:

> Der *Wahnsinn*, d.h. im allgemeinen die Störung des freien Selbstbewußtseyns, wodurch der Kranke außer Stand gesetzt wird, das Subjektive vom Objektiven, seine innere Empfindungen von äußern sinnlichen Eindrücken zu unterscheiden, wird von den Ärzten oft als gleichbedeutend mit *Verrückung oder Verrücktheit* betrachtet, und Schwermuth und Melancholie, partieller Wahnsinn (fixe Ideen) und Manie waren sodann als verschiedene Formen und Grade des Wahnsinns angesehen.

> [Physicians often equate *madness*, that is generally the disturbance of the "independent consciousness," which renders the patient unable to distinguish between subjectivity and objectivity and between internal feelings and external sensory perceptions, with *derangement or insanity* [Verrückung oder Verrücktheit; JK], and deep sadness and melancholia, partial madness (obsessions) and mania were seen as variations and degrees of madness.][6]

Although Henke complains about the loose interchangeability of terms, he productively suggests that madness is foremost an inability to distinguish between the subjective and the objective—a collapse between the internal and the external world. This definition, then, points to the form of madness that Büchner explores as an aesthetic property, the form that might be best captured by one of the many terms Henke lists: *Verrückung oder Verrückheit*. This term for madness has a

---

[4] For a detailed anaylsis of Lenz's position within the medical discourses from 1800 to the present, see Carolin Seling-Dietz, "Büchners *Lenz* als Rekonstruktion eines Falls 'religiöser Melnacholie'," *Georg-Büchner-Jahrbuch* 9 (1995–9), 2000: 188–236.

[5] Seling-Dietz, "Büchners *Lenz* als Rekonstruktion," 205.

[6] Adolph Henke, *Lehrbuch der gerichtlichen Medicin. Zum Behuf academischer Vorlesungen und zum Gebrauch für gerichtliche Ärzte und Rechtsgelehrte* (Berlin: Ferdinand Dümmler, 1832⁷), 182–3; second emphasis mine. Also cited in Seling-Dietz, "Büchners *Lenz* als Rekonstruktion," 205–6.

particular history that helps illuminate the shifts in perspective that Büchner deploys in his text to contemplate and evoke his protagonist's state of mind. Büchner came across the term *Verrücktheit* in the second volume of Friedrich Bird and Franz Amelung's 1836 *Beiträge zur Lehre von den Geisteswissenschaften* while researching for a model for *Woyzeck*'s caricature of contemporary psychiatry. Here, Büchner also found, in addition to the source for the "schöne fixe Idee, eine köstliche alientio mentis" [beautiful fixation, a delightful alientio mentis], with which the doctor sends Woyzeck to the madhouse, "verrückt" as "Verrückheit," "Allgemeine Verrücktheit," right next to "*Alientio mentalis*" and "*Alientio mentis sive vesania totalis.*"[7] Büchner chooses not to use *verrückt* to describe poor Woyzeck's state of mind. But he uses the term elsewhere, in the negative, and only once throughout the entirety of his oeuvre, in "Lenz," where the protagonist, unmoved, in a state of total calm and composure—*unverrückt*—stares at a cat:

> Einst saß er neben Oberlin, die Katze lag gegenüber auf einem Stuhl, plötzlich wurden seine Augen starr, er hielt sie unverrückt auf das Tier gerichtet, dann glitt er langsam den Stuhl herunter, die Katze ebenfalls, sie war wie bezaubert von seinem Blick [. . .].

> [Once he was sitting next to Oberlin, the cat was lying opposite him on a chair. Suddenly his eyes became fixed, he kept them riveted (unverrückt) upon the animal; then slowly he slipped off his chair, likewise the cat; it seemed spellbound by his gaze [. . .].][8]

In this passage, *verrückt* or *unverrückt* has more of a spatial than a mental connotation and is closer to its etymological roots. *Verrücktheit*, from Middle High German *verrucken*, means to move out of place, to shift, to remove something from its proper place. This notion of disorder or

---

[7] Georg Büchner, *Woyzeck. Sämtliche Werke und Briefe*, vol. 1, ed. Henri Poschmann (Frankfurt/Main: Deutscher Klassiker Verlag, 1992), 197. Friedrich Bird and Franz Amelung, *Beiträge zur Lehre von den Geisteswissenschaften* (Darmstadt and Leipzig: Carl Willhelm Keske, 1836), 167–8. Cf. Seling-Dietz, "Büchners *Lenz* als Rekonstruktion," 236. Cf. also the entry for "Verrückung" in *Grammatisch-kritisches Wörterbuch der Hochdeutschen Mundart*: "Der Zustand, da man verrückt, des Verstandes beraubt ist, ohne Plural." Johann Christoph Adelung, *Grammatisch-kritisches Wörterbuch der Hochdeutschen Mundart*, vol. 4 (Wien: Bauer, 1808), 1111.

[8] Büchner, "Lenz," 247. For an intriguing reading of Lenz's feline encounter, see Roland Borgards, "'Wie in Verzweiflung stürzten beide aufeinander los!' Büchner's Lenz is encountering a cat." in *Animal Encounters. Mensch-Tier-Kontakte in Kunst, Literatur, Kultur und Wissenschaft*, eds. Alexandra Böhm and Jessica Ullrich (Stuttgart: J. B. Metzler, 2019), 85–100.

displacement can be traced to a discussion of shifts and transpositions in music. In a work from 1771, *Allgemeine Theorie der schönen Künste*, Johann Georg Sulzer writes that "Verrückung" is the deliberate destruction of harmony and order in music that is achieved by removing one or more notes from their proper place in the harmonic sequence:

> Durch dieses Wort bezeichnen wir eine, nur eine kurze Zeit dauernde oder aus gewissen Absichten glücklich veranstaltete Zerstörung der Harmonie oder Ordnung, da ein oder mehr Töne aus ihrer Stelle entweder völlig oder zu früh weggerückt werden.

> [With this word we refer to a brief or for certain reasons auspicious destruction of harmony or order, in which one or several notes are either completely or prematurely shifted from their position.]

When used prudently by the composer, and always with the larger order of the musical piece in mind, such displacement can be cause for "much freedom and greatness in composition." But when used unwisely, when this excision does not occur in its "proper place," the "transgression of rules" fails to bring about beauty.[9]

Though writing from different fields and entirely different subject matters, both Sulzer and Henke touch on the transgression of what we might call aesthetic norms: Henke on the blurred boundaries between

---

[9] "Verrückung. (*Musik*) Durch dieses Wort bezeichnen wir eine, nur eine kurze Zeit dauernde oder aus gewissen Absichten glücklich veranstaltete Zerstörung der Harmonie oder Ordnung, da ein oder mehr Töne aus ihrer Stelle entweder völlig oder zu früh weggerückt werden. [...] Alle diese Verrückungen der Zeit, des Rhythmus und der Bewegung gehen über das Gewöhnliche hinaus und bringen, wenn sie sparsam und mit Überlegung angebracht werden, viel Freies und Großes in die Schreibart. [...] Große Meister bringen damit die größten Wirkungen hervor; Stümper legen damit ihre Unwissenheit und ihre Ungeschicklichkeit an den Tag. Bei jenen stehen sie allezeit am rechten Ort und die Übertretung der Regeln wird in ihren Werken oft zur größten Schönheit; bei diesen stehen sie niemals recht, sie zerstören die Ordnung und bringen Verwirrung und Unsinn hervor." [Shift. (*music*) With this word we refer to a brief or for certain reasons auspicious destruction of harmony or order, in which one or several notes are either completely or prematurely shifted from their position. [...] All of these shifts in timing, rhythm and movement go beyond the ordinary and bring, when applied sparingly and thoughtfully, much that is unrestrained and great into the composition. [...] Great masters use them to create the greatest effects; dilettantes reveal in them their ignorance and clumsiness. With the former, they always appear in the right place, and the exaggeration of the rules can bring about the greatest beauty; with the latter they are never right, they destroy the order and produce confusion and nonsense.] Johann Georg Sulzer, "Verrückung," *Allgemeine Theorie der schönen Künste* (1771), vol. 4 (Leipzig: Weidmanns Erben und Reich, 1787), 551–2.

subject and object and Sulzer on the intentional disruption of musical order. What is striking is that both see *Verrückung* as a form of displacement: a shift in sequence or position that disrupts perception. This form of madness manifests itself as disorientation in both cases, and therefore returns us to the constantly fluctuating perspectives that comprise Büchner's "Lenz." We might also read Büchner's relation to his source material—Oberlin's notes on Reinhold Lenz—as a practice of *Verrückung*, in which particular notes are used without attribution, while others are carefully removed.[10] In both cases, a notion of *Verrückung* as a kind of madness that results from and in spatial modulations is extremely productive for tracking Büchner's protagonist as he makes his way uncertainly though the Vosges mountains. As Lenz attempts to make sense of the vast mountains, oftentimes by seeking out constrained views, it is his tenuous relationship to space that becomes the main symptom of his madness.

Given the importance of spatial order to this image of madness, a brief return to Kant's work on the sublime is warranted. When Kant describes the overhanging rocks, thundering clouds, and boundless oceans that might make an onlooker aware of his own insignificance, he also stresses the strength of understanding and reason that can be increased by such encounters with the sublime. The reasoning subject, as we have seen previously, measures himself against the expanse of nature—aware of his meager stature but finding superiority in the power of thought. The vision of sublime scenes is all the more appealing for the chance it offers the viewer to refine his thoughts:

Aber ihr Anblick wird nur um desto anziehender, je furchtbarer er ist, wenn wir uns nur in Sicherheit befinden; und wir nennen

---

[10] Burghard Dedner writes extensively on the textual genesis of Büchner's "Lenz." Burghard Dedner, "Büchners 'Lenz.' Rekonstruktion der Textgenese," *Georg Büchner Jahrbuch* 8 (1990–4), 1995: 3–68. Cf. also his editorial report "Textgenese" in the *Marbacher Ausgabe*. Burghard Dedner, "Textgenese," in Georg Büchner, "Lenz," *Sämtliche Werke und Schriften. Historisch-kritische Ausgabe mit Quellendokumentationen und Kommentar*, eds. Burghard Dedner et al., vol. 5 (Darmstadt: Wissenschaftliche Buchgesellschaft, 2001), 127–65. Cf. also Henri Poschmann, "Textgrundlage und Textgestaltung," and "Entstehung," in Georg Büchner, *Dichtungen, Sämtliche Werke, Briefe und Dokumente*, ed. Henri Poschmann, vol. 1 (Frankfurt/Main: Deutscher Klassiker Verlag, 1992), 791–802. To prevent a conflation and over-identification of Büchner's fictional Lenz with the historical Lenz, Burghard Dedner also edited a volume compiling historical records documenting J. M. R. Lenz's madness. Without reference to Büchner's citational practices, its title is *Lenzens Verrückung*. Burghard Dedner et al. (eds.), "*Lenzens Verrückung*" *Chronik und Dokumente zu J. M. R. Lenz von Herbst 1777 bis Frühjahr 1778* (Tübingen: Max Niemeyer, 1999).

diese Gegenstände gern erhaben, weil sie die Seelenstärke über ihr gewöhnliches Mittelmaß erhöhen und ein Vermögen zu widerstehen von ganz anderer Art in uns entdecken lassen, welches uns Muth macht, uns mit der scheinbaren Allgewalt der Natur messen zu können.

[But the sight of them only becomes all the more attractive the more fearful it is, as long as we find ourselves in safety, and we gladly call these objects sublime because they elevate the strength of our soul above its usual level, and allow us to discover within ourselves a capacity for resistance of quite another kind, which gives us the courage to measure ourselves against the apparent all-powerfulness of nature.][11]

This triumph of the human mind over an overpowering landscape occurs, Kant maintains, only if the subject can view the scene from the appropriate position. The onlooker must be a certain distance from the object of the sublime: the high mountains or cascading waterfalls. From this distance, the subject perceives the expanse of the scene, as it occupies their entire field of vision. But they are also able to contemplate this expanse because they manage it optically; that is, they are far enough away from the object of their perception to appreciate or measure its grandeur.

Kant illustrates the importance of this distance with the example of a pyramid: when too far away, the viewer has no sense of the structure's composition, built as it is from many small units. When too close, the onlooker finds themself unable to apprehend the structure as a whole, so that the entirety (*die Zusammenfassung*) of the pyramid requires many viewings.[12] In a sense, Kant's concept of the sublime already contains the two scopic poles that Büchner takes up in "Lenz." Here, in the *Kritik der Urteilskraft*, we see that perception depends largely on the position of the viewer; hence the subject's ability to master and rationalize the sublime is a matter of space and location. Distance facilitates summary and holistic views, while nearness to an object of perception reveals the

---

[11] Kant, *Kritik der Urteilskraft*, §28, B 104–5; A 103.
[12] "Ist es aber das erstere, so bedarf das Auge einige Zeit, um die Auffassung von der Grundfläche bis zur Spitze zu vollenden; in dieser aber erlöschen immer zum Teil die ersteren, ehe die Einbildungskraft die letzteren aufgenommen hat, und die Zusammenfassung ist nie vollständig." [In the former case, however, the eye requires some time to complete its apprehension from the base level to the apex, but during this time the former always partly fades before the imagination has taken in the latter, and the comprehension is never complete.] Kant, *Kritik der Urteilskraft*, §26, B 88–9; A 87–8.

details that give a larger structure its power. In any case, Kant treats both positions as part of the reflective subject's interaction with their environment. For Büchner, as we shall see shortly, neither the "long view" nor a constrained image can grant his protagonist a feeling of calm or of mastery. In turn, Lenz wishes that he could measure out the world with but a few steps. Büchner devotes significant space to Lenz's movement and progress through the mountains. His halting motion might readily be seen as an attempt to measure, and therefore "conquer" the landscape he traverses.[13]

The story begins, however, with an enigmatic opening sentence that sets Lenz out on his journey through the mountains: "Den 20. ging Lenz durch's Gebirg." [On the 20th Lenz went through the mountains.][14] Despite its apparent specificity and clarity—on the 20th, Lenz walked through the mountains—the sentence quickly gives way to a multiplicity of meanings. The precision of the date fades once we consider that the

---

[13] Büchner. "Lenz," 225. In his discussion of motion, Kant writes that "Messung eines Raums (als Auffassung) ist zugleich Beschreibung desselben, mithin objektive Bewegung in der Einbildung und ein Progressus" [measurement of a space (as apprehension) is at the same time the description of it, thus an objective movement in the imagination and a progression], indicating that motion itself can be a measurement. Kant, *Kritik der Urteilskraft*, §27, B 99; A99.

[14] Büchner, "Lenz," 225. The opening phrase affirms the topos of mountains in German literature, but a widely circulated amended version makes the connection to the mountains even more palpable. A rather recalcitrant, false opening, penned by neither Büchner nor Oberlin, has been in circulation for many decades, and due to uncorrected editions, electronic libraries, and online databases, it is reluctant to disappear: "Den 20. Jänner ging Lenz durchs Gebirg." The most famous misuse of the faulty opening is probably by Paul Celan, who, in his *Meridian*, writes, "Ich hatte mich, das eine wie das andere Mal, von einem '20. Jänner', von meinem '20. Jänner', hergeschrieben." Paul Celan, "Der Meridian," *Prosa I: Zu Lebzeiten publizierte Prosa und Reden, Werke: Historisch-Kritische Ausgabe*, vol. 15.1, eds. Andreas Lohr and Heino Schmull (Frankfurt/Main: Suhrkamp, 2014), 33–51, 48. The missing apostrophe as well as the date stamp for January should not be of too great concern. Oberlin's records show that Lenz came to him on January 20, 1778: "Den 20. Januar [1778] kam er hieher." In the course of several transcriptions by August Stöber, suddenly the word "Jänner" appeared in Oberlin's text. Oberlin, "Herr L . . . . . .," 230. The change to "Jänner" first appeared during the serial publication of August Stöber's biographical essay "Der Dichter Lenz. Mittheilungen von August Stöber," which was published irregularly between October 19, 1831 and December 10, 1831 in Cotta's *Morgenblatt für gebildete Stände* (Stuttgart & Tübingen, Jg. 25, nos. 250–95). For a detailed editorial history of Oberlin's report and August Stoiber's transcriptions, cf. Hubert Gersch, *Der Text, der (produktive) Unverstand des Abschreibers und die Literaturgeschichte* (Tübingen: Max Niemeyer, 1998). Though not causing any factual alterations, "Jänner," a regional variation of *Januar*, January, and only used in Austria, Switzerland, Southern Tyrol, and the southeast of Germany—the Alpine region—moves Büchner's text closer to the mountains.

"20th" may refer to any month or any year. The specificity of the location likewise dissolves when the mountains, referred to here as if there could be only one set of mountains, remain unnamed. Büchner appears to have revised the line that opens the section in Oberlin's diary concerning Reinhold Lenz, which reads, "Den 20. Januar [1778] kam er hierher." [He came here on the 20th of January 20th [1778].][15] Oberlin provides an exact date, a clear sense of motion—hither, toward the parish in the Steintal. While Lenz *comes* in Oberlin's diary, he *goes* in Büchner's text, toward an unknown destination, through the mountains.

Even more relevant to the strangeness of Büchner's opening line and the way that it establishes the story immediately as a study in fluctuating perspectives is the sentence's orthographic anomaly. Büchner omits the last letter of *das Gebirge*, shortening the word by eliminating its final vowel—practicing the kind of *Verrückung* that we encountered in Sulzer's work on music. This change in spelling lends the mountains a striking singularity that stands in tension with the universality that the sentence might otherwise evoke. Although "das Gebirg" might conjure any number of actual or figurative mountains, the apocope *Gebirg* initiates Lenz's journey into a landscape made immediately unfamiliar by Büchner's linguistic craft. While both *Gebirg* and *Gebirge* appear in the text, Büchner uses them to indicate different relations to the mountains. The shortened *Gebirg*, with its sharp end-consonant, appears only in conjunction with Lenz and his actions. *Gebirge*, however, are the mountains of others' reports and tales: an old man, for instance, in a cabin located safely in a valley, tells of the voices he heard in the mountains and the sheets of lightening he saw there; Oberlin speaks of the people who live in the mountains, of young women who can feel the streams of water and veins of metal pulsing deep within the earth. In these stories, *Gebirge* are distant, nearly mythical peaks.[16] *Gebirg*, by contrast, seems threatening, immediate—not the distant mountains of fantastical tales, not those located in a distant field of perception, awaiting the imposition of Kantian thought, but the hard, immovable masses of stone that Lenz must traverse in his efforts to become healthy.

---

[15] Oberlin, "Herr L......," 230.
[16] "Das führte sie weiter, Oberlin sprach noch von den Leuten im Gebirge, von Mädchen, die das Wasser und Metall unter der Erde fühlten [...]." [That led them further, Oberlin also spoke about the people in the mountains, about girls who sensed water and metals under the earth [...].] "Es war finsterer Abend, als er an eine bewohnte Hütte kam, im Abhang nach dem Steintal. [...] Einige Zeit darauf kam ein Mann herein [...] Er erzählte, wie er eine Stimme in Gebirge gehört, und dann über den Tannen ein Wetterleuchten gesehen habe [...]." [It was dark when he came to an inhabited hut on a slope toward the Steintal. [...] A little later a man entered [...] He told of hearing a voice in the mountains and the seeing sheet lightning over the pines [...].] Büchner, "Lenz," 232, 238.

Following the opening line, the narrative offers a description of the landscape that Lenz traverses:

> Den 20. ging Lenz durch's Gebirg. Die Gipfel und hohen Bergflächen im Schnee, die Täler hinunter graues Gestein, grüne Flächen, Felsen und Tannen. Es war naßkalt, das Wasser rieselte die Felsen hinunter und sprang über den Weg. Die Äste der Tannen hingen schwer herab in die feuchte Luft. Am Himmel zogen graue Wolken, aber Alles so dicht, und dann dampfte der Nebel herauf und strich schwer und feucht durch das Gesträuch, so träg, so plump.

> [On the 20th Lenz went through the mountains. The peaks and high slopes in snow, gray rock down into the valleys, green fields, boulders, and pine trees. It was cold and damp, water trickled down the rocks and sprang over the path. Pine branches hung down heavily in the moist air. Gray clouds moved across the sky, but everything so dense, and then the fog steamed up, and trailed, oppressive and damp, through the bushes, so sluggish, so shapeless.][17]

In medias res, Büchner sends protagonist and reader through the disenchanting mountains without any exposition that might lend a sense of orientation. The landscape encroaches, heavy, damp, and stifling, as Büchner' truncated syntax shuffles along. The paratactical sequence of short, verbless phrases presents the mountainous landscape as a series of still-life images, a string of unconnected static tableaux that contains no action. There is no verb in the second sentence, so that the environment appears as a motionless space. Although the passage has an ekphrastic quality, it does not depict a scene that can be easily called picturesque or hospitable. The damp, wet air, heavy with grey clouds smeared across the sky, feels oppressive, halting Lenz's progress and enveloping him with a cloying embrace. Paradoxically, although the passage is painting-like, it submerges the viewer, depriving him of the distance required to contemplate the landscape it describes. Büchner plays with the formal elements of a rationally constructed image space to write a failed attempt at achieving a sensation of the sublime. The fact that Lenz is unable to compose a coherent image from the individual paratactical impressions is evidence that a sensation of the sublime, produced in part through the notion of a visual and rational totality, fails to set in. The mountains are quickly established as impassive

---

[17] Büchner, "Lenz," 234.

masses that loom at a distance and as invasive, impinging forms that threaten to overcome Lenz.

At first, Lenz is only dimly aware of the difficulty that the mountains pose, both to his journey and to his sense of perception. Büchner stresses the fact that Lenz fails to accurately perceive the mountains—that he sees the peaks simultaneously as too grand and too small. Quickly then, we face the impossibility of taming the mountains through a sensation of the sublime and the inadequacy of reducing the landscape to something manageably apportioned:

> Es war ihm alles so klein, so nahe, so naß, er hätte die Erde hinter den Ofen setzen mögen, er begriff nicht, daß er so viel Zeit brauchte, um einen Abhang hinunter zu klimmen, einen fernen Punkt zu erreichen; er meinte, er müsse Alles mit ein paar Schritten ausmessen können.

> [Everything seemed to him to be so small, so close, so wet, he would have liked to set the earth behind the stove, he could not understand why he needed so much time to climb down a steep slope, to reach a distant point; he felt he should be able to cover any distance in a few steps.[18]

Because everything is so "small" and "near," Lenz cannot estimate the distance he has left to travel or appreciate the true scale of the mountains, which cannot be measured in a few footsteps. He seems both naïve in his ignorance and overly proud in his desire to set the whole earth behind the stove to dry. In short, from the story's opening, Lenz's perspective is entirely unsteady. Focalizing his story through this oscillating gaze, Büchner deprives Lenz and his reader of the stability and distance that might work to tame nature.

As Lenz continues his journey, he responds to the overwhelming terrain not by fleeing and finding a vantage point from which he can safely view the scene, but by wishing for his own dissolution or submersion. In a remarkable passage, Büchner describes the competing urges that Lenz feels in response to the environment:

> Nur manchmal, wenn der Sturm das Gewölk in die Täler warf [. . .] und die Stimmen an den Felsen wach wurden, [. . .] und dann gewaltig heran brausten [. . .] und die Wolken wie wilde, wiehernde Rosse heransprengten [. . .] und alle Berggipfel scharf und fest, weit über das Land hin glänzten und blitzten, riß es ihm in der

---

[18] Büchner, "Lenz," 225.

Brust, er stand, keuchend, den Leib vorwärts gebogen, Augen und Mund weit offen, er meinte, er müsse den Sturm in sich ziehen, Alles in sich fassen, er dehnte sich aus und lag über der Erde, er wühlte sich in das All hinein, es war eine Lust, die ihm wehe tat; oder er stand still und legte das Haupt in's Moos und schloß die Augen halb, und dann zog es weit von ihm, die Erde wich unter ihm, sie wurde klein wie ein wandelnder Stern und tauchte sich in einen brausenden Strom, der seine klare Flut unter ihm zog.

[Only at times when the storm hurled the clouds into the valley [...] and voices awakened on the rocks [...] and the clouds galloped along like wild neighing horses [...] and all the mountain peaks, sharp and firm, gleamed and flashed far across the countryside: then pain tore through his chest, he stood, panting, his body bent forward, eyes and mouth wide open, he thought he must draw the storm into himself, contain all within him, he stretched out and lay over the earth, he burrowed into the cosmos, it was a pleasure that hurt him, or he stood still and rested his head on the moss and half-closed his eyes, and then it all moved far away from him, the earth receded below him, it grew small like a wandering star and plunged into a rushing stream flowing limpidly beneath him.][19]

The mountains here are an utterly wild space—with voices that awake within the rocks and clouds that rush like neighing horses toward an entirely overwhelmed Lenz. But even within this fantastical scene, the mountain peaks stand sharp and solid, "scharf und fest," immovable masses that might, in other conditions, be a thing of beauty or even comfort. But for Lenz, the surroundings penetrate his body and his thoughts. He is struck by the urge to take the storm into himself, "den Sturm in sich ziehen," and to expand and lay over the entire globe, "er dehnte sich aus und lag über der Erde." If there is an impulse to encompass or incorporate the landscape into his own body, Lenz also wants to surrender to the environment, to dig himself into the universe, "er wühlte sich in das All hinein," and surrender to the currents of the roiling stream, "tauchte sich in einen brausenden Strom." Here is madness as *Verrückung*—a torturous state of mind in which distances

---

[19] Büchner, "Lenz," 225–6. Lenz's experience in the mountains is congruent with how Christian Begemann describes the cosmological unsettledness following the Copernican restructuring of the astronomical world order and its influences on the perception of natural space. Christian Begemann, *Furcht und Angst im Prozeß der Aufklärung: Zu Literatur und Bewußtseinsgeschichte des 18. Jahrhunderts* (Frankfurt/Main: Athenäum Verlag, 1987), 118–19.

collapse, object and subject interpenetrate, and the distinction between fantasy and reality dissolves.[20]

WINDOWS TO THE WORLD

We might expect that Lenz's confusion would abate once he escapes from the tumultuous mountainside into the orderly village of Waldbach. However, even when Lenz is no longer overwhelmed by the landscape, his desire to vanish remains. When he arrives at the parish, Büchner shifts his focus from the threatening, vital elements of the natural world that cannot be tamed through perspective to the vacillations of language that make achieving a stable sense of self equally difficult for Lenz. The greeting he receives upon arrival furthers the erosion of firm boundaries that the journey through the mountains has initiated. When Oberlin sees Lenz, he misidentifies the visitor:

> Oberlin hieß ihn willkommen, er hielt ihn für einen Handwerker. "Sein Sie mir willkommen, obschon Sie mir unbekannt." – Ich bin ein Freund von ... und bringe Ihnen Grüße von ihm. "Der Name, wenn's beliebt" ... *Lenz*. "Ha, ha, ha, ist er nicht gedruckt? Habe ich nicht einige Dramen gelesen, die einem Herrn dieses Namens zugeschrieben werden?" Ja, aber belieben Sie mich nicht danach zu beurteilen.
>
> [Oberlin welcomed him, welcomed him for a laborer. Welcome, although I don't know you." I am a friend of ... and bring you greetings from him. "Your name, if you please?" Lenz. "Ha, ha, ha, hasn't it appeared in print? Haven't I read several dramas ascribed to a man of that name?" Yes, but I beg you not to judge me by them.][21]

First Oberlin mistakes Lenz for a craftsman, albeit one unknown to him. Lenz responds by saying that he brings the greetings of an unnamed

---

[20] Prior to this scene, Büchner describes Lenz's desire to disappear in different terms: "Müdigkeit spürte er keine, nur war es ihm manchmal unangenehm, daß er nicht auf dem Kopf gehn konnte." [He felt no fatigue, but at times he was irritated that he could not walk on his head.] Büchner, "Lenz," 225. Paul Celan famously interprets' Lenz's desire to walk on his head as a truly grim desire, one that leads to a kind of eternal abjection: "Wer auf dem Kopf geht, meine Damen und Herren,—wer auf dem Kopf geht, der hat den Himmel als Abgrund unter sich." [He who walks on his head, ladies and gentlemen—he who walks on his head, has the sky beneath himself as an abyss.] Celan, "Meridian," 42.

[21] Büchner, "Lenz," 227.

mutual friend. When Lenz at last tells Oberlin his name, Oberlin recognizes it, but not in association with the Lenz that stands before him. Rather, Oberlin has read plays by a writer named Lenz. Lenz's vague response—that he hopes not to be judged by this—leaves the reader to wonder if he has indeed written the plays or if he only hopes not to be evaluated on the basis of works that are not his own. Emerging from the wild space of nature, the orbit of culture here seems equally as strange and opaque. This is in part the result of Büchner's play here on the idea of craft and of writing. Is this Lenz a craftsman or a writer who has already written his own story? If not, and Oberlin is simply mistaken, then we might still wonder about the Lenz with which the protagonist is confused. Büchner implicitly alludes to the existence of another Lenz whose story might be the origin of the tale at hand, but not its exact analog. That Lenz's identity is so uncertain asks the reader to inhabit the uncertainty that has thus far plagued Lenz—to look at the text and its events with blurred vision.[22]

In an ongoing attempt to stabilize his oscillating vision and find a clear view of the world that surrounds him, Lenz turns from the limitless views of the mountainous terrain to the delimited scene glimpsed through a window. In the short space of the novella devoted to Lenz's stay with Oberlin, Büchner depicts seven scenes of windows. Contrasted to the wild, untamed mountains that Lenz has come through on his journey to Waldbach, the windows offer deliberately apportioned views. Lenz's repeated encounters with windows suggest that he is seeking a rational perspective through which the hostile, unknowable world can be domesticated and circumscribed by the imposition of a clear frame. These windows also explicitly evoke the medium of painting—the windows in "Lenz" are suggestive of canvases on which a particular space or moment is elected by the artistic gaze and preserved through technique. But instead of presenting these framed views as viable instances of a sustained, stable perspective, Büchner places them in a constant state of flux and fluidity. As Lenz continues to search for a way of seeing that would make the world more easily comprehensible, all he discovers are scenes that present the illusion of stability and control.

---

[22] It has been established that Oberlin's 1778 account of Reinhold Lenz's stay in his parish is the intertext underlying Büchner's "Lenz." Many other sources—down to the level of individual words—have been identified, yet they offer very little orientation and hermeneutic aid. In a nice pun on the German "Quelle" for textual source and aquatic spring, Helmut Müller-Sievers states that the identified intertextual sources rather admix—"verquellen"—with Büchner's own text then form a solid basis on which original source and adaptation could be distinguished. Helmut Müller-Sievers, *Desorientierung: Anatomie und Dichtung bei Georg Büchner* (Göttingen: Wallstein, 2003), 149–50. Cf. also Büchner, "Lenz" (Marburger Ausgabe); Michael Will, *"Autopsie" und "reproductive Phantasie": Quellenstudien zu Georg Büchners Erzählung "Lenz"*, 2 vols. (Würzburg: Königshausen und Neumann, 2000).

Windows, and the paintings they evoke, ultimately turn menacing as the relationships they posit between interior and exterior quickly dissolve. Before looking in some detail at the window scenes in "Lenz," I want to briefly touch upon the relationship between windows and paintings that becomes operative in Büchner's text. Because Büchner uses windows in "Lenz" to comment upon the illusion of unity, wholeness, and repose that artistic works seem to offer, it is useful here to quickly consider Leon Battista Alberti's notion of the *finestra aperta*. In his treatise *De pictura* of 1435, Alberti provides what is perhaps the most widely known definition of the early modern concept of a picture: "First I trace as large a quadrangle as I wish, with right angles, on the surface to be painted, in this place, it [the rectangular quadrangle] certainly functions for me as an open window through which the *historia* is observed [. . .]."[23] Alberti's description is generally regarded as the origin of the metaphorical comparison of the window and picture, which has significantly shaped modern thinking about images.[24] His concept of the picture as a clearly demarcated space that opens out onto a view of the world shapes art from the Baroque period through romanticism, where the window becomes emblematic of the split between subject and object.[25] In Büchner's text, windows indeed represent the notions at work in Alberti's theory: they are tools that the author uses to shift literary perspective, to depict Lenz's gaze as he struggles to locate himself inside or outside, to place himself as subject or object. While the textual windows of Büchner's story do serve as pictures that open out onto or into another world, they fail to evoke the kind of masterful hand that Alberti describes constructing the frame that will delineate the view of the world. Instead, the windows are pictoral illusions that serve as an untenable pole in Lenz's ongoing perspectival oscillations. The first window in the tale appears shortly after Lenz's arrival in Waldbach:

---

[23] Leon Batista Alberti, *De pictura* I, 19; Leon Battista Alberti, *On Painting: A New Translation and Critical Edition*, trans. Rocco Sinsigalli (Cambridge: Cambridge University Press, 2011), 39.

[24] For a thorough discussion of Alberti's ideas and how they depend upon the viewer standing at a certain distance from the window-picture, see Johannes Grave, "Reframing the *finestra aperta*: Venetian Variations on the Comparison of Picture and Window," *Zeitschrift für Kunstgeschichte* 72 (2009): 49–68.

[25] For a discussion of the relationship of windows, framing, and literature in relation to Alberti, consult Albrecht Koschorke, "Das Bild als Fenster," *Geschichte des Horizonts*, 70–5. Cf. also Richard Alewyn, "Ein Wort über Eichendorf," *Eichendorf heute: Stimmen der Forschung mit einer Bibliographie*, ed. Paul Stöcklein (Darmstadt: Wissenschaftliche Buchgesellschaft, 1966), 7–18. The notion of image and perspective in relation to the window is particularly insightful in E. T. A. Hoffmann's "Des Vetters Eckfenster." E. T. A. Hoffmann, "Des Vetters Eckfenster," *Späte Prosa. Briefe. Tagebücher und Aufzeichnungen. Juristische Schriften. Werke 1814–1822, Sämtliche Werke in sechs Bänden*, vol. 6, eds. Gerhard Allroggen et al. (Frankfurt/Main: Deutscher Kassiker Verlag, 2004), 468–97.

Er ging durch das Dorf, die Lichter schienen durch die Fenster, er sah hinein im Vorbeigehen, Kinder am Tische, alte Weiber, Mädchen, Alles ruhige, stille Gesichter, es war ihm, als müsse das Licht von ihnen ausstrahlen [. . .].

[He went through the village, lights shone through the windows, he looked in as he passed by, children at the table, old women, girls, all calm, quiet faces, it seemed to him as if the light must be radiating from them [. . .].]²⁶

---

26 Büchner, "Lenz," 226. Hillary P. Dannenberg sees windows in "Lenz" as "an intensifier of Lenz's perspective, not only in purely expressionistic visual terms, it will be seen, but also as a key indicator of Lenz's attitudes to two central themes of the *Novelle*: art and religion." Hillary P. Dannenberg, *The Changing Heavens: Major Recurrent Images in the Poetic Writings of Georg Büchner* (Rheinbach: H. P. Dannenberg Verlag, 1994). Gerda Bell, in the first extensive study of windows in Büchner's œuvre, reads windows as a dichotomous structure of inclusion and exclusion: "When the protagonists appear at a window they are either looking *out* from a room, i.e., they are 'shut in' and try to overcome their feeling of claustrophobia which is both physical and psychological; or they are looking *in* from outside. In this case they are 'locked out', they are outsiders of society. There is also the contrast between 'open' and 'shut' (windows and doors), between night and day (observed through the window) and between perception by eye and ear, again through the medium of the window." Gerda Bell, "Windows: A study of a Symbol in Georg Büchner's Work," *Germanic Review* 46 (1972): 95–108, 95–6. Walter Jens briefly considers windows in terms of experience and loss of self: "Gerade die Fenstersituation markiert bei Büchner immer jenen Moment, in dem der Mensch, sich selbst 'abhanden kommend,' der Andersartigkeit des Universums inne wird; wo sich aber auch greifbar Nahes mit Fernstem verschwistert, wo Austausch möglich ist, weil die Konturen nicht mehr solide erscheinen [. . .] In den Fensterszenen erfährt der saturnische Mensch am intensivsten jene ebenso ersehnte wie gefürchtete Chance der Verschwisterung mit dem All." [For Büchner, the window-scenes in particular mark that moment in which man loses himself and becomes aware of the otherness of the universe. Yet it is also the moment when what is tangibly close resembles what is far away, when exchange is possible because the contours no longer appear solid [. . .]. In the window scenes, the Saturnian person experiences most intensively that longed-for yet feared chance of becoming one with the universe.] Walter Jens, *Euripides. Büchner* (Pfullingen: Neske, 1964), 41. For windows in literature, cf. Cathrin Senn, *Framed Views and Dual Worlds: The Motif of the Window as a Narrative Device and Structural Metaphor in Prose Fiction* (Bern: Lang, 2001); Gotthart Frühsorge, "Fenster: Augenblicke der Aufklärung über Leben und Arbeit. Zur Funktionsgeschichte eines literarischen Motivs," *Euphorion* 77 (1983): 346–58; Jürgen Daiber, "Fenster-Metaphorik: Zum historischen Spannungsfeld von Text-Bild-Relationen," *Grenzen der Germanistik: Rephilologisierung oder Erweiterung?*, ed. Walter Erhart (Stuttgart: Metzler, 2004), 392–409.

As he walks through the village, Lenz sees an idyllic image that would at first seem a stark contrast to the imposing views he encountered in the mountains. Light shining from a window compels Lenz to look inside, where he glimpses the tranquil faces of women and children who sit at a table. The light seems to emanate from within the figures themselves, as if their calm, silent stature grants them a kind of iridescence. Once again Büchner uses parataxis to give this description the feel of a still-life: although verbs position Lenz and locate his perspective, the scene inside the window lacks action altogether. The scene inside the window, syntactically marked by verbal ellipses, presents a stillness that Lenz, even in looking upon it, cannot achieve, as he only remarks on the scene in passing.

This glimpse into a tranquil home initially suggests that windows frame and depict scenes of order and calm from which Lenz feels deeply alienated. But a similar scene becomes the topic of the pivotal, oft-discussed *Kunstgespräch*, in which Lenz discusses art and literature in a conversation with Kaufmann. The conversation comprises approximately one tenth of the text's total volume and has been repeatedly studied for its programmatic nature and its connection with the aesthetics of Büchner as well as with those of the historical Lenz.[27] Instead of examining the conversation as a model for Büchner's own formal principles, I want to consider the pronouncements that Lenz makes on art in close conjunction with the window scenes he encounters in Waldbach. The aesthetic declarations that Lenz makes in the conversation are directly connected with his own experiences—not abstract principles for high art, Lenz's statements reveal between perspective and madness the impossible desire to create and sustain a world as benevolent as the one he has seen through the glowing window in Waldbach.[28]

In the course of the *Kunstgespräch*, Lenz supports his arguments about artistic merit with reference to Dutch canvases, the works of the

---

[27] For a lengthy overview of many of the significant, scholarly investigations of the *Kunstgespräch*, see Peter K. Jansen, "The Stuctural Function of the *Kunstgespräch* in Büchner's *Lenz*," *Monatshefte* 67, no. 2 (1975): 145–56. See also Hans-Jürgen Schings, "Der mitleidigste Mensch ist der beste Mensch," *Poetik des Mitleids von Lessing bis Büchner* (München: Beck Verlag, 1980), 68–84; Jürgen Schwann, *Georg Büchners implizite Ästhetik: Rekonstruierung und Situierung im ästhetischen Diskurs* (Tübingen: Gunter Narr, 1997); Robert C. Holub, "The Paradoxes of Realism: An Examination of the Kunstgespräch in Büchner's Lenz," *Deutsche Vierteljahrsschrift für Literaturwissenschaft und Geistesgeschichte* 59 (1985): 102–24.

[28] Peter Jansen claims that past experiences of "indeterminate significance"— sightings of girls on narrow mountain paths, for instance—assume sudden value in the conversation when Lenz's creative memory seizes upon them to enhance his argument. Jansen, "Structural Function," 149.

Altdeutsche Schule, like Albrecht Dürer, Martin Schongauer, or Albrecht Altdorfer, as well as of Dutch and Italian masters.[29] Whether the paintings mentioned are real or fictitious is less relevant here than the fact that the second canvas depicts a scene evoking that which Lenz has just seen through the window in Waldbach:

> Die Frau hat nicht zur Kirche gekonnt, und sie verrichtet die Andacht zu Haus, das Fenster ist offen, sie sitzt darnach hingewandt, und es ist als schwebten zu dem Fenster über die weite ebne Landschaft die Glockentöne von dem Dorfe herein und verhallet der Sang der nahen Gemeinde aus der Kirche her, und die Frau liest den Text nach.
>
> [The woman was unable to go to church, and she performs her devotions at home, the window is open, she sits turned toward it, and it seems as if the sound of the bells from the village were floating over the wide, flat landscape into the window, and from the church the singing of the nearby congregation were drifting over to her, and the woman is following the hymnal.][30]

The painting shows a woman who has to say her prayers at home because she has been prevented from joining the congregation for the service. The woman in the painting seems to be listening to the "sound of the bell" wafting "into the window [...] from the village [...]." Though the mood of the painting—one of expectant tranquility—is like the mood of the scene around the table that Lenz has seen earlier, there is something destabilizing about the image. The woman in the painting is excluded from the community of parishioners—her tranquility comes in part from her isolation. Furthermore, Lenz's description emphasizes the window in the painting. The window gives the viewer access to the scene and carries the sounds of the church service to the woman who performs her devotions alone. Resembling Alberti's *finestra aperta*, the window in Waldbach and the painting Lenz describes attain their beauty by, to some degree, excluding Lenz. They also disclose their own

---

[29] *Christus und die Jünger von Emaus*, the painting mentioned by Lenz during the conversation, has been identifed as *Christus in Emmaus* by the Dutch master Carel von Savoy (1621–65).

[30] Büchner, "Lenz," 236. According to Hubert Gersch, the scene described by Lenz is not an actual painting but the description of the interior in the first scene of Ludwig Tieck's tragic fairy tale "Leben und Tod des kleinen Rotkäppchens. Eine Tragödie." Ludwig Tieck, "Leben und Tod des kleinen Rotkäppchens. Eine Tragödie," *Phantasus. Schriften in zwölf Bänden*, vol. 6, eds. Manfred Frank et al. (Frankfurt/Main: Deutscher Klassiker Verlag, 1985), 362–93, 363. Cf. "Anmerkungen," *Georg Büchner: Werke und Briefe (Müchner Ausgabe)*, eds. Karl Pörnbacher et al. (München: Hanser, 2007), 534–62, 547.

artifice—either in the distinctively crafted language that Büchner uses to describe the images or in the emphasis on perspective that places a viewer always at a remove, distanced by his awareness that what he sees is, in fact, a constructed scene. It's constructedness is underscored by the frame of the window, with its window cross as perspectival grid or *velum*, at the front as well as at the back of the painting. The painting, then, is not only an example to support Lenz's preference for art that shows the world in its most "real form"—"Der Dichter und Bildende ist mir der Liebste, der mir die Natur am Wirklichsten gibt [. . .]" [I most prefer the poet or painter who makes nature most real to me [. . .]]—but subtly reflects the ambivalence of the carefully delineated view.[31]

At the end of the *Kunstgespräch*, the narrator tells us that, "Er hatte sich ganz vergessen" [He had totally forgotten himself].[32] Scholars have for long debated whether this curious phrase may indicate that the conversation has been restorative for Lenz—that he has forgotten his existential plight by returning to artistic concerns.[33] But the phrase also points to Lenz's desires to disappear or to be obliterated that run like a current from the text's beginning to its end. Even in the course of the conversation with friends, Lenz is unable to find a position of stability as his agitated mood fluctuates between lightness and despair: "In der Art sprach er weiter [. . .] er war rot geworden über dem Reden, und bald lächelnd, bald ernst, schüttelte er die blonden Locken." [He continued in this manner [. . .] his face had flushed from speaking, and often smiling, often serious, he shook his blond curls.][34] It is as if looking through windows, looking onto scenes of repose and calm, cause Lenz to forget himself because they depict a state so opposite to his own. The conversation about art is thus not an exception to Lenz's madness but rather a consideration of how perspective, so central to all artwork and especially to Büchner's text, is fundamental to that madness. If the only perspective that can offer respite and stability proves to be constructed, artificial, and exclusionary, then Lenz must once again seek alternate views. He does just this shortly after Kaufmann's departure, when he decides to accompany Oberlin into the mountains.

---

[31] Büchner, "Lenz," 235.
[32] Büchner, "Lenz," 236.
[33] For a few early examples of this longs-tanding debate (given here in chronological order), see Albrecht Schöne, "Interpretationen zur dichterischen Gestaltung des Wahnsinns in der deutschen Literatur" (diss. Münster, 1952); Benno von Wiese, *Die deutsche Novelle von Goethe bis Kafka: Interpretationen*, 2 vols. (Düsseldorf: August Bagel Verlag, 1956–62); and Erna Kritisch Neuse, "Büchners *Lenz*. Zur Struktur der Novelle," *German Quarterly* 43 (1970): 199–209. Holub argues that the *Kunstgespräch* is in line with Lenz's madness; cf. Holub, "Paradoxes of Realism."
[34] Büchner, "Lenz," 236.

RETURN TO THE MOUNTAINS

Lenz follows Oberlin but turns back where the mountains meet the plains, "wo die Täler sich in die Ebne ausliefen"—and he retreats into the structured space of hills and valleys as if to avoid the expansive mountains before him:

> Er ging allein zurück. Er durchstrich das Gebirg in verschiedenen Richtungen, breite Flächen zogen sich in die Täler herab, wenig Wald, nichts als gewaltige Linien und weiter hinaus die weite rauchende Ebne [. . .].
>
> [He went back alone. He wandered through the mountains in various directions, broad slopes led down into the valleys, few woods, nothing but mighty lines, and farther out, the broad smoking plain [. . .].]³⁵

On the heels of the *Kunstgespräch*, the mountains here figure as massive lines and surfaces, planes that Lenz traverses as if marking them out in an act of composition. But even as they are transposed into perspectival, potentially artistic lines, the mountains remain overwhelming, even menacing. The geometric planes, so characteristic of Büchner's mountains that they appear no less than seven times in the text, seem to stretch infinitely, rarely offering a tree or a rock on which the scanning eye can rest.³⁶ The mountains once again become the space of *Verrückung*,

---

35 Büchner, "Lenz," 237.
36 The novella opens with "Die Gipfel und hohen Bergflächen im Schnee, die Täler hinunter graues Gestein, grüne Flächen, Felsen und Tannen." [Snow on the peaks and upper planes, down into the valley grey stone, green planes, rocks, and pine-trees.] Followed by "Schneeflächen," [snowey planes] and "so weit der Blick reichte, nichts als Gipfel, von denen sich breite Flächen hinabzogen [. . .]." [nothing so far as the eye could see but mountain peaks from which broad planes descended] "[B]reite Bergflächen, die aus großer Höhe sich in ein schmales, gewundnes Tal zusammenzogen, das in mannichfachen Richtungen sich hoch an den Bergen hinaufzog, [. . .] eine Aussicht nach Westen in das Land hinein und auf die Bergkette, die sich grad hinunter nach Süden und Norden zog, und deren Gipfel gewaltig, ernsthaft oder schweigend still, wie ein dämmernder Traum standen." [[B]road planes narrowing from on high to form a strait, winding valley that climbed and twisted far into the mountains, [. . .] westward a view of the countryside and of a chain of mountains that stretched straight down to north and south, and whose peaks stood massive, grave, and silent still.] And finally "breite Flächen zogen sich in die Täler herab, wenig Wald, nichts als gewaltige Linien [. . .]." [broad plains narrowed down into the valley, sparse woods, nothing but bold lines [. . .]] Büchner, "Lenz," 225, 226, 228, 237.

when Lenz loses all sense of orientation, and the skies and the earth melt into a single mass:

> Er wurde still, vielleicht fast träumend, es verschmolz ihm Alles in eine Linie, wie eine steigende und sinkende Welle, zwischen Himmel und Erde, es war ihm als läge er an einem unendlichen Meer, das leise auf- und abwogte.
>
> [He grew still, perhaps almost dreaming, everything seemed to melt into a single line like a rising and falling wave between heaven and earth, it seemed as though he were lying at an endless sea that gently rose and fell.][37]

The mountains eradicate the clear demarcations that Büchner evokes in his descriptions of windows. Here, lines that would otherwise delineate mountain from sky, observer from observed, blur into an infinite sea of uninterrupted, undulating horizontals that seduces Lenz with what seems like an all-consuming, even lethal calm. Underneath it all, to borrow from art historian Rosaling Krauss, might be the longing for the organizing grid. "Unlike perspective, the grid does not map the space of a room or a landscape [. . .]," Krauss writes. "It is a transfer in which nothing changes place. [. . .] something that freezes and locks the self into the space of its own reduplicated being."[38] In Sulzer's terms, perhaps, Krauss's grid promises a transposition without change.

Drifting aimlessly on this hazy sea of mountain and sky, Lenz happens upon a cabin. Here, once again, a window interrupts the foggy, fathomless terrain of rocky planes and the encroaching sky. Büchner establishes the view through the window in direct contrast to the environment that has yet again overcome Lenz, and the text asks readers explicitly to consider the two perspectives as the poles between which the protagonist vacillates. A look into the cabin's window evokes a darker version of the previous tableaux glimpsed through windows and discussed in the *Kunstgespräch*:

> Die Türe war verschlossen, er ging an's Fenster, durch das ein Lichtschimmer fiel. Eine Lampe erhellte fast nur einen Punkt, ihr Licht fiel auf das bleiche Gesicht eines Mädchens, das mit halb geöffneten Augen, leise die Lippen bewegend, dahinter ruhte. Weit weg im Dunkel saß ein altes Weib, das mit schnarrender Stimme aus einem Gesangbuch sang.

---

[37] Büchner, "Lenz," 237.
[38] Rosalind Krauss, "Grids," *October* 9 (1979): 50–64, 52, 59.

[The door was locked, he went to the window, through which a faint light came. A lamp illuminated little more than one spot, its light fell in the pale face of a girl resting behind it, eyes half open, softly moving her lips. Farther off an old woman sat in the dark, singing from a hymnal in a droning voice.]³⁹

The image again brings together familiar elements: a glimmer of light, a scene of piety, and the sounds of private devotion. The single lamp that illuminates the scene directs Lenz's gaze to a young girl, whose pallid face seems both inviting and immoveable. It is only because the door is locked, because Lenz's entry into the cabin is barred, that he witnesses this scene. While the mountainous expanse threatens to consume Lenz, the painting-like scenes of domesticity seen through windows exclude him. The comfortably constrained, orderly images seem to depend on the viewer remaining outside, at a distance not as great but just as significant as the viewer who contemplates the sublime.

But in this instance, Lenz succeeds in crossing the threshold and entering into the pictorial space framed by the window. The women open the cabin door to Lenz and give him shelter for the night. Once granted entry into the scene that he admired, however, Büchner does not integrate Lenz into the welcoming picture he has seen from the outside. Instead, the following morning, Büchner positions Lenz once again at the window, this time looking outward onto the landscape where he had previously stood:

> Er trat an's Fenster und öffnete es, die kalte Morgenluft schlug ihm entgegen. Das Haus lag am Ende eines schmalen Tales, das sich nach Osten öffnete, rote Strahlen schossen durch den grauen Morgenhimmel in das dämmernde Tal, das im weißen Rauch lag und funkelte am grauen Gestein und trafen in die Fenster der Hütten.

> [He went to the window and opened it, the cold morning air struck him. The house lay at the end of a narrow, deep valley open toward the east, red rays shot through the gray morning sky into the half-lit valley lying in white mist, and they sparkled on gray rocks and shone through the windows of the huts.]⁴⁰

Now inside the cabin, Lenz can contemplate the mountainous surroundings from a position of relative safety. Instead of an

---

³⁹ Büchner, "Lenz," 237.
⁴⁰ Büchner, "Lenz," 238–9.

undifferentiated, overwhelming panorama, the landscape now appears framed by the window, apportioned for Lenz's view. The outside world, its narrow valleys illuminated by the red rays of morning sunshine, is suggestive of a landscape painting. When Lenz opens the window and looks out at the valley, he is standing near the vanishing point of the image he saw the evening before, and now looks outward into the valley, past the picture plane to where he, the observer, stood the evening before. Perspectivally, the house, located at the end of a narrow valley, is the vanishing point, and the extension of the valley form the perspectival vectors. Lenz now stands inside the picture and can look out into the world. He sees it constructed according to the same perspectival principles, as the red rays of the sun, the valley and mountainside structure the picture. But the image Lenz sees out of the window seems also to penetrate the interior space of the cabin and the image points toward the dissolution of the boundary between inside and outside. The cold morning air rushes through the open window and hits Lenz in the face, reminding the reader that the force of the natural world remains untamed. The description of the valley, beautiful in one moment, seems sinister in the next—white smoke meeting grey stone in an indistinct twilight.

This reversal of perspective—first Lenz looks into the window and then he looks out—also erodes the reader's perspectival stability. No longer entirely clear how to differentiate between inside and outside, between a welcoming image and a hostile one, or between the environment and Lenz's interpretation of it, the reader, like Lenz, engages in a futile search for a single, stable vantage point. The multiple, malleable views enact formally what the text narrates. The constantly shifting perspectives cast the reader into the same "dämmernder Traum," the "dawning dream" through which Lenz has traveled earlier:

> Mit Oberlin zu Pferde durch das Tal; breite Bergflächen, die aus großer Höhe sich in ein schmales, gewundenes Tal zusammenzogen, das in mannichfachen Richtungen sich hoch an den Bergen hinaufzog, große Felsenmassen, die sich nach unten ausbreiteten, wenig Wald, aber alles im grauen ernsten Anflug, eine Aussicht nach Westen in das Land hinein und auf die Bergkette, die sich grad hinunter nach Süden und Norden zog, und deren Gipfel gewaltig, ernsthaft oder schweigend still, wie ein dämmernder Traum standen.

> [With Oberlin through the valley on horseback; broad mountain slopes contracting from a great height into a narrow, winding valley that led high up into the mountains in many directions, large masses of rock, spreading out toward the base, few woods,

but all in a gray, somber hue, a view toward the west into the country and to the mountain range running straight from south to north, immense, grave or silent peaks standing like a dusky dream.][41]

Here, the mountains are unframed—seen not through a window but from the perspective of Lenz as he moves across the valley on horseback. Büchner again emphasizes their overwhelming contours. The description moves along a vertical axis of high and low, peaks and plains, and the mountains are in part structured as planes and perspectival lines and diagonals, though without a clear vanishing point or central perspective. But this movement feels impossible to track, as the grey rocks spread both upward and downward and occupy every corner of the image that Büchner creates. Every view seems to yield only more rocky masses and the reader struggles to envision the path that Lenz and Oberlin will take across the valley as it is subsumed by the serious, silent peaks that loom over the scene. Once again Büchner rejects the organizing principles of the sublime and further scrambles the conventions of perspective that would render such a landscape legible. The mountains are, as they have been previously in the text, dynamic spaces of change and even terror. But they are simultaneously still, as static and placid in moments as the scenes that Lenz has glimpsed through windows. The final phrase of this passage encapsulates the tension that Büchner sustains through his protagonists' views of the landscape: the mountains stand like a dawning dream. The rocky masses are solid fortresses of land paradoxically emerging in an ephemeral moment that Lenz records at the same moment as it overwhelms him.

A LETHAL GAZE

If it is the perspectival shifts between expansive mountain views and domestic scenes perceived through windows that is the substance of Lenz's madness, his desire for stillness becomes intelligible as his search for relief. The cessation of movement between the perspectival poles that Büchner establishes would seem to deliver the protagonist from his suffering. While several critics have suggested that Lenz suffers, first and foremost, from boredom, the text's emphasis on the maddening movement between untenable viewpoints demonstrates instead that it is primarily a sense of spatial displacement caused by a mountainous

---

[41] Büchner, "Lenz," 228.

environment that plagues its protagonist.⁴² When Lenz comes upon a scene that he wishes to preserve, to petrify, to utterly still, it is therefore a desire born out of the relentless movement—physical, mental, and perspectival—that he has thus far endured.

In the *Kunstgespräch*, Lenz recalls a walk up into the mountains. On it, he comes upon a scene that he finds indescribably beautiful and therefore wishes to preserve forever:

> Wie ich gestern neben am Tal hinaufging, sah ich auf einem Steine zwei Mädchen sitzen, die eine band ihre Haare auf, die andre half ihr; und das goldne Haar hing herab, und ein ernstes bleiches Gesicht, und doch so jung, und die schwarze Tracht und die andre so sorgsam bemüht. Die schönsten, innigsten Bilder der altdeutschen Schule geben kaum eine Ahnung davon. Man möchte manchmal ein Medusenhaupt seyn, um so eine Gruppe in Stein verwandeln zu können, und den Leuten zurufen.
>
> [As I went by the valley yesterday, I saw two girls sitting on a rock, one was putting up her hair, the other was helping her; and the golden hair hung down, and a serious, pale face, and yet so young, and the black dress, and the other one working with such care. The most beautiful, most intimate paintings of the Old German School barely hint at it. At times one would like to be a Medusa's head in order to transform such a group into stone and summon everyone to see it.]⁴³

The girls, with their pale, serious faces, black dresses, and golden hair evoke and even exceed in beauty the paintings that Lenz has discussed earlier as well as the window scenes that he gazed upon. At first Lenz is, as I have mentioned, fascinated by the possibility of fixing this moment in time—to become the Medusa's head so as to freeze the girls' in a lifeless tableaux that could then be displayed for others. But this wish, as with so much in Büchner's text, is double-edged: preserving the beauty requires the death of its subjects and the transformation of the viewer into a monstrous being. I will say more about this monstrous being later, but first, let us consider the end of the passage, in which

---

⁴² For just two examples of scholars who consider Lenz's madness to be due to boredom, see Dennis F. Mahoney, "The Sufferings of Young Lenz: The Function of Parody in Büchner's *Lenz*," *Monatshefte* 76, no. 4 (1984): 396–408; and Dennis Tate, "'Ewige deutsche Misere?' GDR Authors and Büchner's *Lenz*," *Culture and Society in the GDR*, eds. Graham Bartram and Anthony Waine, GDR Monitor Special Series 2 (Dundee: GDR Monitor, 1983), 85–99.

⁴³ Büchner, "Lenz," 234–5.

Lenz himself realizes the danger in his desires for stillness. He concludes his description of the wondrous scene by noting how it changes but remains equally beautiful in its altered form:

> Sie standen auf, die schöne Gruppe war zerstört; aber wie sie so hinabstiegen, zwischen den Felsen, war es wieder ein anderes Bild. Die schönsten Bilder, die schwellendsten Töne, gruppieren sich, lösen sich auf. Nur eins bleibt, eine unendliche Schönheit, die aus einer Form in die andre tritt, ewig aufgeblättert, verändert, man kann sie aber freilich nicht immer festhalten und in Museen stellen und auf Noten ziehen und dann Alt und Jung herbeirufen, und die Buben und Alten darüber radotieren und sich entzücken lassen.

> [They stood up, the beautiful group was destroyed; but as they climbed down among the rocks they formed another picture. The most beautiful pictures, the richest sounds group together and dissolve. Only one thing remains, and endless beauty moving from one form to another, eternally unfolding, changing, one surely cannot always hold it fast and put it into museums and write it out in notes and then summon young and old and let boys and old men chatter about it and go into raptures.][44]

The girls stand up and the scene is wrecked. But quickly, as they descend among the rocks, they form another picture. Lenz relays that the most beautiful pictures are those that take shape and then dissolve, changing in form but retaining their beauty. In fact, what Lenz conveys is the sense that beauty itself exists in this very movement, which cannot be captured and displayed in museums, or fixed onto musical scores, those very musical scores that first made room for Sulzer's notion of *Verrückung* as the movement of a note from its proper place. It is movement above all else, the very oscillation that has plagued Lenz from the text's opening, that here becomes the true content of beauty. What Lenz observes here in the mountains echoes what he has described to Kaufmann in the *Kunstgespräch*:

> Ich verlange in allem Leben, Möglichkeit des Daseins, und dann ist's gut; wir haben dann nicht zu fragen, ob es schön, ob es häßlich ist, das Gefühl, daß Was geschaffen sei, Leben habe, stehe über diesen Beiden, und sei das einzige Kriterium in Kunstsachen.

---

[44] Büchner, "Lenz," 234–5.

[In all, I demand—life, the possibility of existence, and then all is well; we must not ask whether it is beautiful or ugly, the feeling that the work of art has life stands above these qualities and is the sole criterion of art.][45]

It is not beauty per se that matters in art; rather, it is the feeling of life, or animation that gives a work of art its power.

If it is motion, the endless capacity for one scene or a view to become another, that gives a work of art the feeling of life, then Lenz's unceasing journey and fluctuating perspectives give Büchner's text the very quality that its protagonist valorizes. As torturous as Lenz's madness is, it is, arising from the constant alternation between perspectives, the text's animating principle. Even Lenz's suicide attempts in the story represent not so much a desire to end life as a painful struggle to find one's place amidst shifting planes. In his suicide attempts, the window that was once a logical or legible frame comes to represent the impossible task that art must preserve motion and life.

Den Nachmittag wollte Oberlin in der Nähe einen Besuch machen; seine Frau war schon fort; er war im Begriff, wegzugehen, als es an seine Tür klopfte und Lenz hereintrat mit vorwärtsgebogenem Leib, niederwärts hängendem Haupt, das Gesicht über und über und das Kleid hie und da mit Asche bestreut, mit der rechten Hand den linken Arm haltend. Er bat Oberlin, ihm den Arm zu ziehen, er hätte ihn verrenkt, er hätte sich zum Fenster heruntergestürzt, weil es aber Niemand gesehen, wollte er es auch Niemand sagen.

[That afternoon, Oberlin wanted to pay a visit nearby; his wife had already left; he was just about to leave when there was a knock at his door and Lenz entered, his body bent forward, his head hanging down, ashes all over his face and here and there in his clothes, holding his left arm with his right hand. He asked Oberlin to pull on his arm, he had dislocated it, as he had thrown himself from the window, but since no one had seen it, he did not want to tell anyone.][46]

Throwing himself in despair out of the window, Lenz attempts to obliterate the divide between the expansive views of nature and the constrained space of the home that has plagued him. Is Lenz attempting to leave the

---

[45] Büchner, "Lenz," 234.
[46] Büchner, "Lenz," 245.

pictorial space, the realm of art, and attain "freedom?" Or is the "freedom" represented by the untamed mountains outside so terrifying that he feels he must submit to it in an act of self-erasure? The jump leaves Lenz literally dislocated, *verrenkt*—by jumping from the window and across the threshold from one perspectival realm into another, he inflicts on his body the injury that such crossing has previously inflicted on his mind.

After multiple attempts like this one, Oberlin decides the Lenz must leave the Steintal and return to Strasbourg—the village in the mountains can no longer contain Lenz or his madness. At the text's conclusion, it is as if Lenz has simply surrendered to his madness. Instead of finding beauty in the shifting of forms as he did earlier when the girls arose from braiding each other's hair and descended through the rocks, all shapes collapse into a blur that Lenz no longer struggles to parse. He sits in the wagon on the return journey to Strasbourg in utter indifference:

> Er saß mit kalter Resignation im Wagen, wie sie das Tal hervor nach Westen fuhren. Es war ihm einerlei, wohin man in führte; mehrmals wo der Wagen bei dem schlechten Wege in Gefahr geriet, blieb er ganz ruhig sitzen; er war vollkommen gleichgültig.
>
> [In cold resignation, he sat in the coach as they rode out of the valley toward the west. He did not care where they were taking him; several times when the coach was endangered by the bad road he remained sitting quite calmly; he was totally indifferent.]⁴⁷

Büchner indicates that although the struggle to move between locations and perspectives was torturous for Lenz, it was equally animating. No longer concerned with differentiating views, Lenz feels the deadened sense that everything is the same, "Es war ihm einerlei." To emphasize that Lenz's despondency is tied to the absence or rejection of perspective, Büchner offers the readers a final view of the mountains, receding from sight:

> Sie entfernten sich allmählig vom Gebirg, das nun wie eine tiefblaue Krystallwelle sich in das Abendrot hob, und auf deren warmer Flut die roten Strahlen des Abend[s] spielten; über die Ebene hin am Flusse des Gebirges lag ein schimmerndes bläuliches Gespinst.
>
> [Gradually, they left the mountains behind, which now rose up like a deep blue crystal wave into the sunset, and on its warm

---

⁴⁷ Büchner, "Lenz," 250.

flood the red rays of evening played; above the plain at the foot of the mountains lay a shimmering, bluish web.]⁴⁸

The mountains, flooded with the red light of dusk, disappear like a shimmering dream; only this time Lenz does not try to perceive or understand them. Instead, he simply stares calmly, with a numb angst rising inside him, out of the wagon window as the objects in his view "sich in der Finsterniss verloren" [became lost in the darkness].⁴⁹ The mountains in this passage tellingly shift from the *Gebirg*, the untamed, singular terrain that we encountered at the story's opening, to the *Gebirge*, that dissipates into the distance and into the textual past.

The text's strange conclusion, in which Lenz reaches Strasbourg and seems reasonable and wholly cured, feels strange in part because it is so hasty. Moreover, the resolution of Lenz's condition feels so dubious because it depends upon a disavowal of the animating struggle that has characterized Lenz and his story up until this point. In a final desiccated, almost clinical, paragraph, Büchner concludes:

> Am folgenden Morgen bei trübem regnerischem Wetter traf er in Straßburg ein. Er schien ganz vernünftig, sprach mit den Leuten; er tat Alles, wie es die Anderen taten, es war aber eine entsetzliche Leere in ihm, er fühlte keine Angst mehr, kein Verlangen; Sein Dasein war ihm eine notwendige Last. — So lebte er hin.

> [The next morning he arrived in Strassburg in dreary, rainy weather. He seemed quite rational, spoke with people; he acted like everyone else, yet there was a terrible void within him, he no longer felt any fear, any desire; his existence was a necessary burden.—So he lived on.]⁵⁰

Without the perspectival extremes, the *Verrückung*, that Lenz experienced in the mountains, he is perhaps sane. He can speak with others normally and do as they do without fear. But he is also without desire, utterly empty. He lives on—*So lebte er hin*—not as a maddened wanderer, an animate being, or a terrifying gorgon, but as one of the lifeless stone figures converted by the Medusa's gaze. He can live on, Büchner suggests, in this text, like an artifact in a museum display, devoid of both the madness and the beauty that defined his earlier, fluctuating actions.

---

⁴⁸ Büchner, "Lenz," 250.
⁴⁹ Büchner, "Lenz," 250.
⁵⁰ Büchner, "Lenz," 250.

MEDUSA IN THE MOUNTAINS

To conclude this discussion of "Lenz," I want to return to the enigmatic Medusa's head that has intrigued scholars for some time. In an early work of criticism, Ronald Hauser writes, "The Medusa's head [...] is meant as a symbol for the highest aspirations of the artist. Perfection in art is represented by an exact but frozen image of life."[51] But Büchner himself undermines such an idea when he has Lenz describe the girls' motion not as iconoclastic or destructive, but as the dynamism and vibrancy that gives the scene its beauty. When Paul Celan discusses this scene from "Lenz" in his acceptance speech for the Georg Büchner Prize, which he was awarded in 1960, he cites the Medusa's head as a metonymy for the anxiety over the artist's struggle with representation. Celan describes the possibility of freezing the girls in the mountains as the impulse of an art that attempts to efface its own difference from nature; to grasp the natural *as* the natural: "'Man möchte ein Medusenhaupt' sein, um ... das Natürliche als das Natürliche mittels der Kunst zu erfassen!" ["One wishes to be a Medusa's head" in order to ... grasp the natural as the natural with the help of art!]"[52] For Celan, this idea of art is one that is expansive and ultimately destructive in its aspirations:

> Das ist ein Hinaustreten aus dem Menschlichen, ein Sichhinausbegeben in einen dem Menschlichen zugewandten und unheimlichen Bereich—denselben, in dem die Affengestalt, die Automaten und damit ... ach, auch die Kunst zuhause zu sein scheinen.
>
> [This is a stepping beyond what is human, a stepping into an uncanny realm turned toward the human—the realm where the monkey, the automatons and with them ... oh, art too, seem to be at home.][53]

This kind of art causes estrangement and a loss of the self: human beings forget themselves in the forms that art represents, forms which might mimic the human but remain fundamentally unhuman and even, given the acute context in which Celan speaks, inhuman.

Celan of course goes on in the speech to articulate a poetic program that can work against such mimetic violence. The image of the Medusa's

---

[51] Ronald Hauser, *Georg Büchner* (New York: Twayne, 1974), 57.
[52] Celan, "Meridian," 38.
[53] Celan, "Meridian," 38.

head from Büchner's "Lenz" that turns to stone a beautiful moment in nature ultimately dissolves in Celan's critique of mimesis. But Celan himself makes a telling move in his discussion of the Gorgon's head. He stresses Büchner's language, pointing out that in Lenz's mention of the Medusa, he does not use the first person, but rather indicates that "one" would like to become a Medusa's head. Celan recalls that Büchner describes how "*Man* möchte heißt es hier freilich, nicht: *ich* möchte." [*One* wishes to does of course not mean here: *I* wish to.][54] Celan seems aware that Lenz himself disavows the totalizing gaze of the Medusa and instead lingers with the ever-changing form of the picture he sees. What's more, Celan acknowledges that rejecting the dominant, fixing grasp offered by the Medusa's head requires an abdication of the self, a self-estrangement that speaks pointedly to the experience Lenz has, as he shuttles between perspectives, never settling on or holding fast to a single view. It is worth reminding that it is they who look upon and lock eyes with the Gorgon that will turn to stone and not those who are looked at by the Medusa. Celan remarks:

> Wer Kunst vor Augen und im Sinn hat, der ist—ich bin hier bei der Lenz-Erzählung—der ist selbstvergessen. Kunst schafft Ich-Ferne. Kunst fordert hier in einer bestimmten Richtung eine bestimmte Richtung eine bestimmte Distanz, einen bestimmten Weg.

> [He who has art before his eyes and on his mind—I am with the Lenz narrative now—forgets himself. Art creates I-distance. Art here demands in a certain direction a certain distance, a certain route.][55]

Celan suggests that an encounter with art entails a distancing of the self; for Celan, absorption in an artistic work means a flight from individual concerns and preoccupations. In this description we hear echoes of the *Kunstgespräch* enumerated in Büchner's "Lenz." Perhaps Lenz is mad because he views the world with this distance, this self-estrangement. But Celan's notion that art makes for a "distance from the I," that it requires us to travel a certain distance in a certain direction, speaks even more forcefully of the reading I have offered here. When we understand "Lenz" as a text that depicts spatial disorientation as a form of madness and uses that madness to explore the possibilities of prose, we experience the forms of distance that Celan describes in his speech.

---

[54] Celan, "Meridian," 38; emphasis original.
[55] Celan, "Meridian," 44.

Celan's emphasis on perspective and on traveling is fitting for Büchner's text in which constant motion overturns and dissolves the familiar views of the sublime and of the still life. Büchner turns to the mountains not to draw upon existing conventions, but to look for new images and views that might illuminate uncertainty and transformation instead of annihilating life. By moving Lenz through the mountains, through unknown terrain that cannot be tamed but whose taming might in fact lead to a dulling or cessation of the artistic spirit, Büchner indicates that art must not freeze life in a moment of perfection, but rather re-present the vitality, the endless motion that comprises that beauty. Suspending the comprehensive grasp of the sublime, art, and especially literature, not only seeks out the realm of the uncertain, but precisely enters a dialogue with it. In "Lenz," we see that art may indeed "require that we travel," but the space, the direction, and the road may in fact be far from certain.

IV Folded Mountains—Paul Celan's "Gespräch im Gebirg"

MOUNTAINS VANISHED

In 1959, 120 years after Georg Büchner sent the despondent Lenz into the mountains, Paul Celan sets an unnamed Jewish man on a path through the Alps. A year after the publication of "Gespräch im Gebirg," Celan described his short, enigmatic text as a direct descendent of Büchner's "Lenz": "Vor einem Jahr, [. . .] brachte ich eine kleine Geschichte zu Papier, in der ich einen Menschen 'wie Lenz' durchs Gebirg gehen ließ." [A year ago [. . .] I wrote down a little story, in which I let a man walk 'like Lenz's' through the mountains.]¹ In the "Gespräch," Celan mentions Lenz explicitly, as his nameless traveler walks "wie Lenz" at the beginning and the conclusion of the story. The analogy appears at the end of the lengthy opening sentence, "[. . .] da ging er also und kam [. . .] wie Lenz, durchs Gebirg [. . .]" [[. . .] so he went off and came [. . .] like Lenz, through the mountains [. . .]], and at the story's end, in a nearly symmetric sentence, "[. . .] die da kamen, wie Lenz, durchs Gebirg [. . .]." [[. . .] those who came, like Lenz, through the mountains [. . .].]² These references would seem to suggest that someone—Lenz or Büchner—has already traversed the serpentine path that Celan constructs: "[. . .] kam er daher auf der Straße, der schönen, der unvergleichlichen, ging, wie Lenz, durchs Gebirg [. . .]." [[. . .] so he went off and came along this road, this beautiful, incomparable road, walked like Lenz through the mountains [. . .].]³ But the mountains that Celan writes into being in his "Gespräch" evoke an established topos of German literature only to diverge from that familiar terrain. The literary trajectory that runs from Solomon Gessner to Goethe, Jakob Michael Reinhold Lenz and *Sturm und Drang* on to the post-romantic work of Büchner serves as an origin from which Celan departs and sunders: "[. . .] ich, der ich da steh, auf dieser Straße hier, auf die ich nicht hingehör [. . .]." [[. . .] I who stand here on this road, here where I do not

---

1   Celan, "Meridian," 48.
2   Paul Celan, "Gespräch im Gebirg," *Prosa I: Zu Lebzeiten publizierte Prosa und Reden, Werke: Historisch-Kritische Ausgabe*, vol. 15.1, eds. Andreas Lohr and Heino Schmull (Frankfurt/Main: Suhrkamp, 2014), 27–31, 27, 31. Paul Celan, "Conversation in the Mountains," *Collected Prose*, trans. Rosemarie Waldrop (Manchester: Carcanet Press, 1983), 17–22.
3   Celan, "Gespräch," 27. Karin Lorenz-Lindemann outlines the close intertextual affinities of Celan's and Büchner's text in her "Paul Celan: Gespräch im Gebirg—ein Palimpsest zu Büchners Lenz," *Datum und Zitat bei Paul Celan. Akten des Internationalen Paul Celan-Colloquiums*, eds. Chaim Shoham and Bernd Witte (Bern: Peter Lang, 1987), 170–82.

belong [. . .].]⁴ The Jewish man should not be standing on this road. He concedes that he does not belong there, and his displacement is accentuated by the juxtaposition of his halting progression and the postpositive position of the adjectives "schön" and "unvergleichlich"—beautiful and incomparable. By forfeiting the man's right to stand on this street, the story also announces that the literary world from which the man comes and in which he felt familiar has vanished. Subsequently, Celan has the narrator renounce his literary kinship to the German tradition: "Eines Abends" [One evening], Celan begins, "*die Sonne und nicht nur sie, war untergegangen, da ging, trat aus seinem Häusel und ging der Jud,* [. . .] *durchs Gebirg* [. . .]" [*when the sun had gone down and not only the sun, the Jew* [. . .] *went off, left his house and went off* [. . .] *through the mountains* [. . .]].⁵

To better understand why the man no longer has a place in the world of mountains nor in the world of literature, I will briefly turn to Celan's "Ansprache anlässlich der Entgegennahme des Literaturpreises der Freien Hansestadt Bremen" [Speech on the Occasion of Receiving the Literature Prize of the Free Hanseatic City of Bremen]. In his 1958 "Bremen" speech, Celan makes palpable how important this literary world is to him, wherein books and men cohabitated—"in der Menschen und Bücher lebten."⁶ "Die Landschaft [. . .] aus der ich zu Ihnen komme, dürfte den meisten von Ihnen unbekannt sein." [The landscape from which I come to you [. . .] will be unfamiliar to most of you.] Celan speaks of the Bukowina, his home in Romania, and the reason why it is unfamiliar to the majority of its audience is because it vanished from history—"der Geschichtslosigkeit anheimgefallen."⁷ Celan no longer remembers the Bukowina as a politically, socially, or topographically identifiable region but as a literary

---

4   Celan, "Gespräch," 30. For a discussion of his trajectory, cf. Stéphane Mosès, "'Wege, auf denen die Sprache stimmhaft wird.' Paul Celans 'Gespräch im Gebirg'," *Argumentum e silentio: International Paul Celan Symposium*, ed. Amy Colin (Berlin: De Gruyter, 1987), 43–57, 48; and Arnd Bohm "Landscapes of Exile: Celan's 'Gespräch im Gebirg'," *Germanic Review* 78, no. 2 (2003): 99–111.
5   Celan, "Gespräch," 27; emphasis mine.
6   Paul Celan, "Ansprache anläßlich der Entgegennahme des Literaturpreises der Freien Hansestadt Bremen," *Prosa I: Zu Lebzeiten publizierte Prosa und Reden, Werke: Historisch-Kritische Ausgabe*, vol. 15.1, eds. Andreas Lohr and Heino Schmull (Frankfurt/Main: Suhrkamp, 2014), 23–5, 23. Paul Celan, "Speech on the Occasion of Receiving the Literature Prize of the Free Hanseatic City of Bremen," *Collected Prose*, trans. Rosemarie Waldrop (Manchester: Carcanet Press, 1983), 33–5.
7   Celan, "Ansprache Bremen," 23. About this landscape, Ulrich Baer writes, "The landscape from which Celan comes to us lies not only on the periphery of the history commonly termed 'European' but also constitutes the origin of a highly fragile and fragmented biography. It is an area where the Holocaust catastrophically eclipsed a community and culture and nearly terminated Celan's life [. . .]." Ulrich Baer, "Landscape and Memory," *Remnants of Song: Trauma and the Experience of Modernity in Charles Baudelaire and Paul Celan* (Stanford, CA: Stanford University Press, 2000), 210–55, 210.

and linguistic landscape—a "wordscape."[8] Books not only contain and create the wordscape Celan calls home, but through books, Celan was able to travel and reach distant places. Books took him to Bremen and Vienna—places either too far to travel or forbidden to reach:

> Aber Bremen, nähergebracht durch Bücher und die Namen derer, die Bücher schrieben und Bücher herausgaben, behielt den Klang des Unerreichbaren. Das Erreichbare, fern genug, das zu Erreichende hieß Wien. Sie wissen, wie es dann durch Jahre auch um diese Erreichbarkeit bestellt war.
>
> But though Bremen was brought closer through books, through the names of writers and publishers of books, it still had the sound of the unreachable. Within reach, though far enough, what I could aim to reach, was Vienna. You know what happened, in the years to come, even to this nearness.][9]

While geographical locations were suddenly inaccessible, the German language itself remained within reach and close by for Celan amidst all the losses brought about by the Nazi regime: "Erreichbar, nah und unverloren blieb inmitten der Verluste dies eine: die Sprache." [Only one thing remained within reach, close and secure amid all loss: language.][10] The language of which Celan speaks with the peculiar adjective "unverloren"—unlost—is the German language. Now, in 1958, thirteen years after the end of the Second World War, to Celan, German contains all the memories of a dark period of loss, of a deathly speech filled with a thousandfold darkness during the Third Reich that resulted in a lack of answers and horrible silence.[11] Celan outlines a double nature of German: on the one hand, the language is a propagandistic tool, conveying orders for deadly actions and heinous

---

8   In his preparatory notes for the "Meridian," Celan writes, "Gedichte als Wortlandschaften" [Poems as wordscapes]. Paul Celan, *Der Meridian: Endfassung, Vorstufen, Materialien*. Tübinger Ausgabe, eds. Bernhard Böschenstein and Heino Schmull (Frankfurt/Main: Suhrkamp, 1999), 102.
9   Celan, "Ansprache Bremen," 23.
10   Celan, "Ansprache Bremen," 23.
11   "Sie, die Sprache, bleib unverloren, ja trotz allem. Aber sie mußte nun hindurchgehen durch ihre eigenen Antwortlosigkeiten, hindurchgehen durch furchtbares Verstummen, hindurchgehen durch die tausend Finsternisse todbringender Rede. Sie ging hindurch und gab keine Worte her für das, was geschah; aber sie ging durch dieses Geschehen. Ging hindurch und durfte wieder zutage treten, 'angereichert' von all dem." [Yes, language. In spite of everything, it remained unlost. But it had to go through its own lack of answers, through horrifying silence, through the thousand darknesses of murderous speech. It went through. It gave me no words for what was happening, but it went through. Went through and could resurface, 'enriched' by it all.] Celan, "Ansprache Bremen," 24.

crimes, an instrument of abuse and obloquy. The results—
"Antwortlosigkeit" and "Verstummen," a lack of answers and silence—
are as devastating for the silenced victims of the Holocaust as they are
for the writers and historians trying to bring the atrocities into language.
On the other hand, language, instrumentalized by the Nazis, passed
through their crimes and emerged "enriched," full of the dark deeds of
a deadly daily life. It is within these parameters of language and
literature that Celan must place his writings and his poetics. It is within
these parameters that we must place "Gespräch im Gebirg."

A violent caesura—*when the sun had gone down and not only the sun*—
whose historical vanishing-point lies outside of the narrative itself,
traverses the story and severs it as early as the third parataxis of the text
from its invoked literary tradition. The atrocities of the Holocaust and
the cultural and linguistic devastations of Nazi Germany are cause not
only for the near-extinction of the European Jewry, but also for the
contamination of an entire literary tradition. The literary tradition I am
referring to here, however, is not the Jewish tradition, or that of Jewish
writers, but the consequential uselessness and unavailability of a
German literary tradition of the mountains to Celan after 1945.
Ostracized from his world and pushed to the margins of society, "der
Jud" has his place in the lower regions, "den Niederungen," and is a
foreigner to the glorious world of the mountains: "[. . .] ich, der ich das
steh, auf dieser Straße hier, auf der ich nicht hingehör, heute, jetzt, da sie
untergegangen ist, sie und ihr Licht [. . .]." [[. . .] I who stand here on
this road, here where I do not belong, today, now that is has set, the sun
and its light [. . .].][12] To write of luminous mountains in the wake of the
Holocaust is, for Celan, a treacherous undertaking. When Celan invokes
Lenz's mountains, identifies Alpine flora, or refers to the mountain trail
as the "road, this beautiful, incomparable road," he deploys topoi that
have lost their once-beautiful resonance. For Celan, the role and function
of mountains in literature must change from 1945 onward, as not only
the German language but also the romantic topoi of beautiful
mountainscapes have been made to serve Nazi ideologies. It is clear
why Celan can no longer refer to the mountainous topography of the
German literary tradition:

> The Romantic topos of [. . .] craggy mountains [. . .] is also tainted
> by the ideological uses of that tradition to link a specific group or a
> nation to a given geographic location. [. . .] The Landscape tradition
> [. . .] was co-opted and perverted with disastrous results in the
> ideologies leading to the Second World War. [. . .] Though not

---

[12] Celan, "Ansprache Bremen," 27, 30.

alone in this effort, fascist ideologues in particular relied on the myth of the landscape in order to turn genealogy and geographic origins into the exclusive foundations of group identity.[13]

A poet in exile, Celan is looking for a place within his work from which he can write of the atrocious experiences of the past. It cannot be found on a map or sketched topographically. "Ich suche das alles mit wohl sehr ungenauem, weil unruhigem Finger auf der Landkarte—auf einer Kinderlandkarte, wie ich gleich gestehen muß. Keiner dieser Orte ist zu finden [...]." [I am looking for all this with my imprecise, because nervous, finger on a map—a child's hild's map, I must admit. None of these places can be found. They do not exist [...].][14] Celan's searching is not for a place of belonging, as Ulrich Baer explains, but for "a place or position from which to address the radical unavailability of the very notions of native regions, of origin, and of the past itself. To find such a position from which to address this loss, Celan evokes a sense of actual space in his work."[15] Celan's mountains are not those figured in earlier works: neither a place of respite nor a figure of the sublime, the peaks of the "Gespräch" are emblems of uncertainty, amidst which a new poetics—layered and multiple—can unfold.

Celan's figurative leave-taking from the mountains of his literary predecessors corresponds to his actual departure from the mountains in July 1959, just months before the publication of the "Gespräch." Following an invitation by Peter Szondi, Celan came to Sils-Maria in the Engadin in early July of 1959, where Szondi had arranged for a meeting with Theodor Adorno. After several weeks spent traveling through the Alpine regions of Austria and Switzerland, Celan left the Swiss mountain resort of Sils on July 22, 1959 to return to Paris, one week prior to Adorno's arrival. It is unclear whether Celan's leaving was to avoid a meeting with Adorno or was motivated by other circumstances.[16] Yet if

---

[13] Baer, "Landscape and Memory," 219. For a discussion of landscape, power, and ideology, cf. W. J. T. Mitchell, *Landscape and Power* (Chicago: University of Chicago Press, 1995), and Simon Shama, *Landscape and Memory* (New York: Knopf, 1996).

[14] Celan, "Meridian," 50.

[15] Baer, "Landscape and Memory," 217–18. On the notion of exile in Celan, cf. Paul Auster, "The Poetry of Exile," *The Art of Hunger* (New York: Penguin, 1997), 90–103.

[16] Cf. Joachim Seng, "'Die wahre Flaschenpost' Zur Beziehung zwischen Theodor W. Adorno und Paul Celan," *Frankfurter Adorno Blätter VIII*, ed. Rolf Tiedemann (München: edition text + kritik, 2003), 151–76. *Paul Celan—Peter Szondi: Briefwechsel. Mit Briefen von Gisèle Celan-Lestrange an Peter Szondi und Auszügen aus dem Briefwechsel zwischen Peter Szondi und Jean und Mayotte Bollack*, ed. Christoph König (Frankfurt/Main: Suhrkamp, 2005), 10.

Celan's departure foregrounds the structure of the "Gespräch"—in which the mountains must be traversed in order to be reworked or even negated—the consequences of Celan's departure foreshadow the text's content: its meditations on the forms of communication that take shape and fail to take shape in a mountainous terrain. That the two men never met, that their conversation in the mountains never took place, has led to much speculation and interpretation on the part of critics. But while the existing scholarship illuminates some of the text's central themes— the attempt to achieve a stable subject through a dialogic structure and the instability of a precise language in the wake of the Holocaust—it does so without sufficient regard to the mountains that loom in the "Gespräch" and in Celan's life at the time when he was writing it.

Immediately after his departure from the mountains, Celan began to draft "Gespräch im Gebirg." He also spent time in August of 1959, while working on the "Gespräch," reading Leibniz's "Monadologie," which he had purchased in summer of the previous year. His reading and marginalia facilitate a meaningful link between the biographical and the literary. From his experience in the mountains to his encounters with Leibniz's ideas of simple and composite substances, Celan appears to have been immersed in the images of folded mountains that his "Gespräch" deploys as part of a poetics of the fold. As will become apparent, Celan discovers the fold as the geomorphological structure of the Alps as well as the organizing principle underlying Leibniz's monad.

The notion of the fold, which, Celan discovered in the mountains, in Leibniz, and develops in his "Gespräch im Gebirg," continues to engage him. In his notes to the "Meridian," Celan writes: "Das Gedicht involviert die Sprache: es faltet sich." [The poem involves language: it folds itself.][17] Celan now sees the poem as a folded structure, involving, that is enveloping, wrapping, entangling—folding language. Rather than a mere ironic inversion of the master discourse, Celan formally demonstrates how it is possible to refuse this hegemonic discourse while at the same time liberating oneself from it through writing. The radicality of the fold is further substantiated by the fact that the "Gespräch" is Celan's only fictional prose piece published during his lifetime. While he previously wrote himself into the long history of a European lyrical tradition, it is striking that he uses a different literary genre to explicate a radical, new literary form—the fold.

The fold, as represented by the geological structure of the mountains and the organizing structure of the monad, serves as a model for Celan's text. Bringing together historical and biographical work with a reading of Celan's prose, this chapter illustrates how the mountains' folded

---

[17] Celan, *Meridian*, Tübinger Ausgabe, 102.

structure shapes the form and content of the "Gespräch." The figure of the fold allows Celan to write an impossible conversation into existence: the fold represents a multiplicity, a layering that can conceal at the same time as it uncovers, a singular object or perspective that is also double, a structural entity which can contain opposing forms. Acknowledging the poetic force of the mountains in which Celan sets his text, my reading suggests that the "Gespräch," often described as paradoxical, oxymoronic, or undecided, in fact sets forth a distinctive poetics in which a mountainous topography offers a form for a conversation that succeeds through its very failure.

Put another way, in the "Gespräch," the fold confronts readers with the duality of language: its ability to point simultaneously to the singular and the collective; to reveal and to obscure; to establish ground that is always shifting. Rather than read these paradoxes as the result of the text's content—a conversation between two Jews in which they encounter one another and attempt to speak of the past—this chapter argues that such content arises *through* the story's form, through its use of the fold as a dominant paradigm through which Celan brings the contradictions of conversation and identity into being. In the "Gespräch" Celan uses the fold as a non-indexical linguistic device and as a poetic figure that collapses space and time in order to resist the harm and violence brought about through a language used for classification and delineation.

The halting, conflicted conversation between the man who sets out at the story's beginning "wie Lenz" and another nameless Jew whom he meets in the mountains proceeds through fits and starts, twists and turns that make the "Gespräch" feel rather like an oblique exchange than a productive dialogue. Several critics have suggested that in the "Gespräch" Celan attempts to create a stable subjectivity—an "I" that can stand alone, even if it does so through a process of negation and alienation.[18] But attention to the setting and its meaning for Celan indicates that the text's goal may be less to interrogate the possibility of subjecthood than to compose a poetics through which communication and its absence can be figured. Although its content seems evasive and its meaning obscure, communication does not fail but rather becomes implicit, transpiring through narrative form and movement rather than

---

[18] Cf. John E. Jackson, "Die Du-Anrede bei Paul Celan. Anmerkungen zu seinem 'Gespräch im Gebirg'." *Text und Kritik* 53/54 (1977): 62–68; Georg-Michael Schulz, "Individuation und Austauschbarkeit: Zu Paul Celans *Gespräch im Gebirg*," *Deutsche Vierteljahrsschrift für Literaturwissenschaft und Geistesgeschichte* 53, no. 3 (1979): 463–77; Bernhard Fassbind, *Poetik des Dialogs: Voraussetzungen dialogischer Poesie bei Paul Celan und Konzepte von Intersubjektivität bei Martin Buber, Martin Heidegger und Emmanuel Levinas* (München: Fink, 1995).

content. The fold's oscillation between the explicit and the implicit is inherent in its structure: implicit, explicit, and folded are—*plica ex plica*—united in their Latin and Greek etymological roots.

AUGUST 1959—READING LEIBNIZ

We have already encountered several different versions of the mountains and although Celan's *Gebirg* may have something in common with Hoffmann's transgressive, liminal space and Büchner's shifting terrain, Celan's mountains model the form of the fold. On a basic geological level, the mountain range of the Alps is formed through a process of folding: when two tectonic plates collide, shortening occurs along faults and the upper crust of the earth is thickened.[19] That Celan would think of mountains in such terms should come as no surprise: much has been said about his extensive geological knowledge.[20] But while Celan was looking to the geomorphologically-folded mountains for a literary and linguistic form that could adequately convey the perils of communication and the heaviness of loss, he also encountered generative models of a folded metaphysics in the pages of Leibniz's *Monadologie*. Though the fact has gone largely unremarked, Celan undertook an intensive reading of *Monadologie* in August of 1959, at the same time his manuscripts show that he was working on "Gespräch im Gebirg."[21] At the time of its writing, Celan's library contained a copy of the Felix

---

[19] John Whittow, *Dictionary of Physical Geography* (London: Penguin, 1984), 352.
[20] Interesting examples of such work on Celan's geological knowledge are James K. Lyon, "Paul Celan's Language of Stone: The Geology of the Poetic Landscape," *Colloquia germanica* 8 (1974): 298–317; Uta Werner, *Textgräber: Paul Celans geologische Lyrik* (München: Fink, 2002); Rochelle Tobias, *The Discourse of Nature in the Poetry of Paul Celan: The Unnatural World* (Baltimore, MD: Johns Hopkins University Press, 2006); Erika Schellenberger, "Von Gletschermühlen und Meermühlen: Geologische Motive in der Lyrik Paul Celans," *Wirkendes Wort* 38 (1988): 347–59; Sandro Zanetti, "Orte/Worte—Erde/Rede. Celans Geopoetik," *Geopoetiken: Geographische Entwürfe in den mittel- und osteuropäischen Literaturen*, eds. Magdalena Marszalek and Sylvia Sasse (Berlin: Kulturverlag Kadmos, 2010), 115–31.
[21] Much has already been said about the date and *Datum* in Celan's œuvre, but it is indeed noteworthy that the "Gespräch" is the only text actually dated by Celan. Following its final line, we read *"August 1959."* For Celan's notes in Leibniz, cf. Celan, *Meridian*, Tübinger Ausgabe, 204–5. Celan's Leibniz excerpts are collected in convolute F of the *Meridian* manuscript and dated August 19 and 20, 1959. Convolut F, though it was, according to Gisèle Celan-Lestrange, compiled by Celan himself, is a thematically and chronologically rather heterogeneous collection of notes. It includes texts from 1959 and 1960. Cf. the "Editorisches Vorwort," in Celan, *Meridian*, Tübinger Ausgabe, xi.

Meiner edition of Leibniz's *Vernunftprinzipien der Natur und der Gnade—Monadologie*. A date on the frontispiece shows that Celan purchased the book on January 24, 1958 in Cologne, and the copy, rife with dated excerpts, annotations, and markings testify that the days of August 19 and 20, 1959 were days of an immersed encounter with Leibniz's metaphysical work.[22]

Celan's notes from the time of the composition of the "Gespräch" reflect his engagement with Leibniz's ideas of becoming. It is in the second half of the *Monadologie* where Celan encounters Leibniz' notion of the structuring fold inside the monad. Of §61, Celan underlined and highlighted "elle ne sauroit *developper* tout d'un coup ses *replis*, car ils vont à l'infini" [it could never bring out all at once everything that is folded into it, because its folds go on to infinity].[23] In a series of infinite folds, the monad contains within it a multiplicity to be unfolded. What seems most compelling to Celan is Leibniz's conception of a substance that can contain within itself "virtually" or "potentially" all the properties of the entire universe. All these properties and temporalities are *"folded up"* within the monad; they unfold only when they have sufficient reason to do so, and slowly over time. The language that Leibniz uses to describe the monad evokes the geological structures that also interested Celan. Though structured and striated by peaks and valleys, the mountains are phenomenally as well as morphologically one infinite fold—peak following valley, fold upon fold. In Leibniz's extraordinary phrase, which appears frequently in his later work, the monad is "pregnant" with the future and "laden" with the past, lending it a dynamic structure of mutability and stability alike.[24] Like the mountain range of the Alps, the monad is a whole; in its foldedness, it

---

22   All annotations and markings in Celan's personal philosophical library have been transcribed in Paul Celan, *La Bibliothèque philosophique*, eds. Alexandra Richter et al. (Paris: Rue d'Ulm, 2004). For his notes on Leibniz, cf. 90–3.

23   Leibniz, *Monadologie* §61; emphasis mine. Though Celan worked in both the French and the German translation of *Monadologie*, I will refer to the French original only and provide an English translation. I draw my references from the French and German edition of *Monadologie* included in G. W. Leibniz, *Kleine Schriften zur Metaphysik, Philosophische Schriften 1, Französisch und deutsch*, ed. and trans. Hans Heinz Holz (Frankfurt/Main: Suhrkamp, 2000), 438–83. For English, I consulted Leibniz, *Philosophical Papers and Letters*, trans. and ed. L. E. Loemker, 2 vols. (Chicago: University of Chicago Press, 1956).

24   See, for example, Leibniz, *Monadologie*, §22: "Et comme tout present état d'une substance simple et naturellement une suite de son état precedant, tellement que le present y est gros de l'avenir." [And every momentary state of a simple substance is a natural consequence of the state immediately preceding it, so that the present is pregnant with the future.]

exists as a single, undivided, and singular structure. Celan likely recognized in reading the *Monadologie* that the fold is the organizing principle of the monad, and the excerpts and phrases that Celan isolates in his notes must be read with the fold in mind:

> causa formalis / immanentes Formprinzip // causa materialis / (Entelechie) [causa formalis / immanent principle of form // causa materialis / (entelechy)]
> Wird ein Gedicht "komponiert"? ("... das Zusammengesetzte hingegen entsteht aus Teilen und vergeht in Teile." Leibniz, Monadologie)
> [Is a poem "composed"? ("... the compound, however, comes into being by parts and dies away into parts." Leibniz, Monadologie]

> Denn es gibt niemals in der Natur zwei Wesen, die einander vollkommen gleichen und bei denen sich nicht ein innerer oder ein auf eine innere Bestimmtheit gegründeter Unterschied entdecken ließe'. (Leibniz, Mo)
> [For in nature there are never two beings which are perfectly alike and in which it is not possible to find an integral difference or at least a difference founded upon an intrinsic. (Leibniz, (Mo.)]

> Jeder noch so kleinen Zwischenraum ist ein "Teich voller Fische" (Leibniz). [Every between-space no matter how small is a "pond full of fish" (Leibniz).]²⁵

The implications of Celan's findings in Leibniz become evident when we turn to Gilles Deleuze's 1988 study, *Le pli: Leibniz et le baroque*, where he traces the concept of the fold through Leibniz's œuvre. From his reading of the *Monadologie*, Deleuze develops a phenomenology of the fold that "affects not only all kinds of materials [. . .] (*the mountains* and the waters [. . .]), but it also determines and brings form into being and into appearance, it makes of it a form of expression."²⁶ Celan's text is

---

[25] Celan, *Meridian*, Tübinger Ausgabe, 204–5.
[26] Gilles Deleuze, *The Fold: Leibniz and the Baroque*, trans. Tom Conley (Minneapolis: University of Minnesota Press, 1993). Deleuze's assumption that there is no one substance, only an always-differentiating process, resonates with Celan's overall poetic program in which "becoming" remains an infinitely incomplete and ongoing process. Gilles Deleuze, "The Fold," trans. Jonathan Strauss, *Yale French Studies* 80 (1991): 227–47, 242; emphasis mine.

neither a presentation of mountains, where phrases or images indicate valleys or peaks, nor is it a mimetic description, depicting impressive, beautiful, or sublime Alpine scenery. Nonetheless, the mountains feature prominently throughout the "Gespräch" and their folded nature structures the story and its poetics. Read considering Leibniz and Deleuze, the mountains of Celan's text can be understood as folded structures that give rise to the operative poetic principle of the "Gespräch."[27] In Celan's short text, the fold features in different forms. It is explicitly mentioned twice, once at the story's zenith, where, high in the mountains, the narrator announces that the earth is thrice folded—"hat sich gefaltet einmal und zweimal und dreimal" [folded once and twice and three times]—and once more towards the story's end, where the many folds are identified as the space in which conversation can develop "und geredet haben wir, viel, und die Falten dort" [and we talked, a lot, and those folds there].[28] The fold also appears implicitly in the opening phrase, as the protagonist's staggering hike through the mountains repeatedly folds back upon itself. The sentence describing this movement itself mirrors the structure of the fold. In its most fundamental form, the fold, as a tri-part configuration, structures the text, which, with its epic, dialogic, and monologic sections, appears as a fold. For Leibniz, the monad is a figure of development and envelopment, and Celan adopts the textile image of a folded veil when he describes the eyes of the Jewish man taking in the mountains. His eyes have veils that wrap themselves around and envelop entering images. These images then, as Celan underlined in his copy of Leibniz, "quite ou prenne des depouilles organiques" [take off or put on organic shells].[29]

Reading Celan's story in light of his engagement with Leibniz, we are prepared to encounter the "Gespräch" as a folded text in which the individual subject exists alongside, and only within, a collective, multiple constellation. The two men who meet and speak with one another in Celan's story seem simultaneously singular and entirely abstract. They traverse and observe the environment but also appear to be part of it. As the men wander a labyrinthine path through the mountains, their conversation echoes the folded structure of the mountain. Celan's "Gespräch" resonates not merely for its historical significance or evocative language; the text confounds the very notion of conversation by melding the speakers into a unity that assumes the characteristics of the fold. Here, Deleuze's work on Leibniz's fold is

---

[27] Deleuze calls the baroque fold an "operative function." Deleuze, *The Fold*, 3.
[28] Celan, "Gespräch," 28, 31.
[29] Leibniz, *Monadologie*, §77.

instructive. He explains that Leibniz's monad represents "a continuous labyrinth." It is "not a line dissolving into independent points, as flowing sand might dissolve into grains, but resembles a sheet of paper divided into infinite folds or separated into bending movements, each one determined by the consistent or conspiring surroundings."[30] This continuous movement between the whole and its parts, the individual and his environment, gives Celan's text its enigmatic, oscillating tenor, which Rochelle Tobias aptly describes:

> Two men go up into a mountain. Why? They don't know. Something draws them there. What? They don't really know that either. It could be the wish to talk, to talk with "mouth and tongue." But talking doesn't seem to bring them anywhere. What draws them there doesn't draw them out. The two men talk back and forth, exchanging phrases, swapping lines, as if the mere act of repeating what the other one says could insure that they have heard. After some time, the two men part. One goes on his way "accompanied by the love of the unloved." Which one? This time, we can't say. It could be the one or the other.[31]

LEAVING FOR THE MOUNTAINS

In *Monadologie*, Celan discovers the idea of a gradual development from dark to light, where previously indistinct shapes transform into more distinct figures, without ever reaching a state of complete discernment, or abandoning the multiplicity from which they stem. "Cet detail doit envelopper une multitude dans l'unité ou dans le simple. Car tout changement naturel se faisant par degrees, quelque chose change et quelque chose reste; [...]." [This detailed nature must envelop a multiplicity within the unity or within the simple substance. That is because every natural change happens by degrees, gradually, meaning that something changes while something else stays the same.][32]

---

[30] Deleuze, *The Fold*, 6.
[31] Rochelle Tobias, "The Ground Gives Way: Intimations of the Sacred in Celan's 'Gespräch im Gebirg'," *MLN* 114 (1999): 567–89, 567. Tobias' précis resonates strongly with Deleuze's explanation of the monad as a figure of compossibility: "Just as each monad conveys the entire world, so then a single notion can no longer pertain for one subject, and subject-monads will now be distinguished only by their inner manner of expressing the world: the principle of sufficient reason will become a principle of indiscernibles. Since there never exist two identical subjects, there can be no apparently identical individuals." Deleuze, *The Fold*, 50.
[32] Leibniz, "Monadologie," §13, 442.

Leibniz's notion of a "genetic process" of continual creation unsettles the possibility of distinct boundaries between the narrator, the men, and their surrounding environment.[33] The concept of "genetic process" can be said to establish a semiotics that allows for constant modulations and disturbs stable meanings. As Celan expounded in his "Bremen" speech, and as he shows in the "Gespräch," a violent semantic shift occurred from 1933 to 1945, whose repercussions are far reaching. The two Jews in the mountains, representative of Europe's Jewry, have been ousted from their language. They can now fall silent, adopt the hegemonic discourse, or find a third, folded in between. Turning now to the "Gespräch" itself, we can begin to uncover the relationship between the environment in which the story is set and its design; we can see the uncertain, multiple, and potential perspectives in the story as a product of its folded poetics. When Celan sends his hiker out at dusk, at twilight, he initiates a poetic version of the continuous variations encountered in Leibniz. The time of the day—*eines Abends*, twilight perhaps—is the first indicator that distinct contours will be dissolved. *Eines Abends* is that very period between light and dark when foreground and background blur into one another and clear delimitations are possible only momentarily:

> Eines Abends, die Sonne und nicht nur sie, war untergegangen, da ging, trat aus seinem Häusel und ging der Jud, der Jud und Sohn eines Juden, und mit ihm ging sein Name, der unaussprechliche, ging und kam, kam dahergezockelt, ließ sich hören, kam am Stock, kam über den Stein, hörst du mich, du hörst mich, ich bins, ich, ich und der, den du hörst, zu hören vermeinst, ich und der andre [. . .]

> [One evening, when the sun had gone down and not only the sun, the Jew went off, left his house and went off, the Jew and son of a Jew, and with him went his name, unspeakable, went and came, came shuffling along, made himself heard, came with his stick, came over the stone, do you hear me, you hear me, I'm the one, I, I and the one that you hear, that you think you hear, I and the other one [. . .].][34]

---

[33] "It is because for Leibniz clarity comes of obscurity and endlessly is plunging back into it." "Contrary to Descartes, Leibniz begins in darkness. Clarity emerges from obscurity by way of a genetic process [. . .]." Deleuze, *The Fold*, 89–90.

[34] Celan, "Gespräch," 27.

118 Writing the Mountains

The story itself begins with a single, paratactic sentence that spans an entire paragraph over fourteen lines. It describes the actions of a solitary hiker who progresses hesitantly through the mountains. Celan repeats words, inverts phrases, and protracts parenthetically to create the impression of a faltering journey. The lengthy sentence invokes a conventional story opening—one evening, a single protagonist sets out from home to begin his travels. But Celan's repetitions and inversions immediately subvert the linear narrative that such conventions establish. Through repetitive uses of "to come" and "to go," two verbs that indicate opposing directions, the prose folds back and in upon itself, so that even the movement described seems both progress and regress. The simple past forms, "ging" [walked or went] is used ten times in the first paragraph, while "kam" [came] appears seventeen times in the first two paragraphs. Celan also includes the present tense, "kommt" [is coming] and two modified forms of "gehen" [to go or to walk]. These verbs are occasionally paired: "ging und kam," "da ging er also und kam," which enforces the ambiguous or even static feel of the story's opening. Asyndetic constructions create a similar effect: "[. . .] da ging, trat aus seinem Häusel und ging [. . .], ging und kam, kam dahergezockelt, [. . .] kam am Stock, kam über den Stein" [[. . .] went off, left his house and went off [. . .], went and came, came shuffling along, [. . .] came with his stick, came over the stone]; "da ging er also und kam, kam daher auf der Straße [. . .], ging, wie Lenz durchs Gebirg, [. . .] er, der Jud, kam und kam" [so then he went and came, came down this road [. . .], went, like Lenz through the mountains, [. . .] he, the Jew, came and came]. The multiple alterations between coming and going— if followed with a pencil on a sheet of paper—would trace a zigzagged, folded line. With this elongated process of folding, the long sentence in its entirety resembles the geomorphosis of the Alps, as it is finally coming to a close by revealing the location of the Jewish man—"durchs Gebirg"—the mountains. While Büchner's opening phrase, "Am 20. ging Lenz durchs Gebirg," presupposes mountains to be traversed, Celan's first sentence suggests that his mountains must first be written into being. As the sentence slowly unfolds before the reader's eye with each parataxis and doubling back of *kommen* and *gehen*, so Celan's mountains take shape as well.

The sensation of uncertainty and indirection introduced in the opening sentence continues, as the unfinished and imperfect work throughout the story to emphasize the multiple possibilities inherent in the fold. Potentialities, subjunctives, and events to come are foretold, yet the perspective from which these are narrated is hardly stable, as predications are cast into doubt: "—ich hier, ich; ich, der ich dir all das sagen kann, sagen hätt können; der ich dirs nicht sag und nicht gesagt hab." [—I here, I; I, who can say, could have said, all that to you; who don't say and haven't said it to you]³⁵ The changing temporal flection throughout corroborates this sense of malleability, and the use of the simple past in the opening paragraph of Celan's piece is indicative of the temporal order of the fold, which is simultaneously finite and infinite.³⁶ The simple past is that tempus which emphasizes the imperfect, the unfinished, or not yet complete. Because it is difficult to determine whether the past is truly past or if it continues into the present, the imperfect allows for a strong fusion of present and past. After the first man sets out and wanders through the mountains in this process of approach and retreat, he comes upon another wanderer. At the moment when the Jews meet, the tempus switches to the present tense and the narrative voice announces their encounter: "Da stehn sie also, die Geschwisterkinder [...]." [So there they are, the cousins [...].]³⁷ Through the use of the present tense, the narrator begins to delineate the two men, as their plasticity gives way to discernable forms. Yet at the very moment when the narrator makes room for the two Jews to speak, the characters, in tempus and language, slip away into the past. "'Bist gekommen von weit, bist gekommen hierher...' 'Bin ich. Bin ich gekommen wie du.'" ["You've come from far, have come all the way here..." "I have. I've come, like you."]³⁸ In this way, the characters' place in both space and time elude the reader's grasp. Rather than finished forms awaiting discovery, the two appear as emanations from the fold, fluctuating between tempi and orders in a complementary relationship of actuality and potentiality, of presence and latency. Following the hike through the mountains, the reader is drawn into several indistinguishable orders of time, none of which are stable or differentiated. The changes in time and the condition of the imperfect evoke the men and the mountains as unformed entities that have yet to come to rest and achieve a finite form.

The character that sets out on this walk, who comes and goes, is of course named only as "der Jud." This designation marks him as both

---

35   Celan, "Gespräch," 31.
36   Deleuze describes the temporal order of the fold as an "equilibrium or disequilibrium," a coexistence of the finite and infinite. Deleuze, *The Fold*, 89; Gilles Deleuze, *Le pli: Leibniz et le baroque* (Paris: Les éditions de minuit, 1988), 119.
37   Celan, "Gespräch," 28. The switch in time happens on the diegetic level. On the extra-diegetic level, the narrative voice addresses the reader in the present tense—"Und wer, denkst du, kam ihm entgegen?" [And who do you think came to toward him?]—and continues to make generalizing remarks about the Jews in the present tense as well: "[...] den wenn der Jud daherkommt und begegnet einem zweiten [...]. [[...] because when a Jew comes along and meets another [...].] Celan, "Gespräch," 27.
38   Celan, "Gespräch," 28.

singular and anonymous, but more significantly, it speaks to the perspectival multiplicity that casts both narrative and subjective coherence into doubt from the story's outset. One the one hand, readers understand "the Jew" to be a single man who walks from his home into the mountains. But as Celan's language totters, doubles back, restarts, and circles around itself, "der Jud" comes to feel as if it might refer to many, rather than the singular that the phrase itself indicates.[39] The narrator begins anew, revisits and amends his statements, even addressing the reader directly with the second person at one point. This creates a sense of competing perspectives—either the narrator speaks from multiple positions or the man who walks through the mountains inhabits multiple times and spaces at once. This technique of reversal and revision is favored by Celan elsewhere, as in his *Meridian* and Bremen speeches, where he declares, "Es ist Zeit, umzukehren. Meine Damen und Herren, ich bin am Ende, ich bin wieder am Anfang." [It is time to turn around. Ladies and gentlemen, I am at the end—I am back at the beginning.][40] But here, at the beginning of the "Gespräch," this poetic strategy is oriented less toward a beginning or origin than toward an amalgamation of beginning and end that would otherwise be distinct in time and space.

WORDSCAPES

At the top of the winding trail, the two Jews finally meet, standing on an Alpine pasture surrounded by flowers. "Da stehn sie also, die Geschwisterkinder, links blüht der Türkenbund, blüht wie wild, blüht

---

[39] The namelessness of the two men has been read either as an instance of deprivation and extinction in anonymity, or in reference to the Judaic prohibition of pronouncing the name of God. The effacement through the loss of a name becomes palpable in the appellation of the two men as "Jud" and "Sohn eines Juden," the former propagating the derogatory, anti-Semitic collective-singular, while the latter refers to the Nuremberg Race Laws of 1935, where the Nazis switched the determination of Jewish parentage from the traditional Jewish matrilineal descendance to a patrilineal descent.

[40] Celan, "Merdian," 47. In his Bremen speech, Celan likewise intones, "Es war, Sie sehen es, Ereignis, Bewegung, Unterwegssein, es war der Versuch, Richtung zu gewinnen. Und wenn ich es nach seinem Sinn befrage, so glaub ich, mir sagen zu müssen, daß es in dieser Frage nach dem Uhrzeigersinn mitspricht." [It meant movement, you see, something happening, being *en route*, an attempt to find direction. Whenever I ask about the sense of it, I remind myself that this implies the question as to which sense is clockwise.] *Sinn* in this case alludes not to meaning but direction, the *sense* or movement around the clock always away and toward a beginning. Celan, "Ansprache Bremen," 24.

wie nirgends, und rechts, da steht die Rapunzel, und Dianthus superbus, die Prachtnelke, steht nicht weit davon." [So there they are, the cousins. On the left, the turk's-cap lily blooms, blooms wild, blooms like nowhere else. And on the right, lamb's lettuce, and *dianthus* superbus, the maiden-pink, not far off.]⁴¹ Presented from one stable point of view with detail, the text suddenly assumes a more rigid form. The positions of the men and the flowers with their common and Latinate names give the scene a sort of indexical clarity. This clarity, however, is superficial, marked only by the repeated use of the verb "stehen," as different taxonomic discourses—popular and scientific—are placed side by side. Just as it begins to take shape through distinct scientific names, the text begins to crumble instead of coalesce when the landscape reveals its semantic construction, and thematizes a lack of language: "Da stehn sie, [. . .] auf einer Straße stehn sie im Gebirg, [. . .] eine Pause ists bloß, eine Wortlücke ists, eine Leerstelle ists, du siehst alle Silben umherstehn." [There they stand [. . .] on a road in the mountains [. . .] it is nothing but a pause, and empty space between the words, a blank—you see all the syllables stand around.]⁴² In a twofold movement, Celan shows the desire for stable forms as well as the dangers that arise with their realization: "[. . .] es schweigt der Stock, es schweigt der Stein, und das Schweigen ist kein Schweigen, kein Wort ist da verstummt und kein Satz [. . .]." [[. . .] the stick silent, the stones silent, and the silence no silence at all. No word has come to an end and no phrase [. . .].]⁴³ Silence, as Celan indicates here, is not silence, as silence presupposes the possibility of speaking, and speaking the possibility of language. When Celan writes that not a single word has fallen silent, he does not mean that the chatter continues, but rather that the two Jews have no words that can fall silent. In this absence of language and silence, only pauses, word gaps, and ellipses are possible at best. And like the flowers and the Jews among them, syllables just stand about and fail to merge into meaningful words. The linguistic landscape sketched out by Celan disintegrates into its components instead of forming a coherent image. Gaps, indicating difference and separation between syntactical or phonetic units allow for meaning, yet they are in turn also the place where meaning and identity are most vulnerable. Since 1933, the relationship of an entire social group to language shifted violently. Forbidden to speak its language, banned from public discourse, renamed and reclassified, the Jewry of Germany and subsequently Europe suddenly finds itself in a relationship to language utterly

---

[41] Celan, "Gespräch," 28.
[42] Celan, "Gespräch," 28.
[43] Celan, "Gespräch," 28.

unfamiliar to it. Hebrew, Yiddish, and their use of German have become a marker of the identity for which they are persecuted. Through the image of the two men standing in a static landscape of crumbling language without a clear relationship to their surroundings, Celan seems to suggest that a wordscape more fluid and flexible, without rigid distinctions is not only far more hospitable, but, as we will see, much safer. The two men stand like foreign bodies in a landscape of taxonomic signifiers, yet their integration into a more coherent system would in turn again render the reader vulnerable. Re-entry, or entry into any symbolic order demands the positing of differences, of intervals and gaps that distinguish and consequently disband the multiform unity of the fold, which thus far has prevented delineation. The poetics of the fold has up to now denied permanent, stable forms but simultaneously provided protection against annihilation. Alternating between implication and explication, the fold reveals itself as a liminal structure, traversing the dichotomy of continuity and discontinuity as manifested by homogeneity and indifferentiation on one side, and heterogeneity and differentiation on the other.

When Celan considers acts of naming, he reflects upon the fact that between 1933 and 1945, millions of Jews were stripped of their individual names and forced to adopt names officially declared Jewish.[44] In everyday parlance, they were often assigned a single and undifferentiated derogatory marker—"der Jud." Celan never calls the two men by their name in "Gespräch," but addresses both as "der Jud," at times differentiated simply by size or age as "Klein" and "Groß." In fact, the man and his name seem not only disjointed from each other, as the name merely accompanies the man instead of being one with him—"und mit ihm ging sein Name, der unaussprechliche" [and with him his name, the unpronounceable name]—but moreover, his name is unspeakable.[45] The reasons for the unspeakability could be many. It is perhaps the German prohibition to use his proper, given name, or his refusal to use his imposed German name. Read through Celan's engagement with the fold, however, here the absence of, or liberation

---

[44] In 1938, Hitler passed a series of laws effecting drastic changes to Jewish names. The initial *Gesetz über die Änderung von Familiennamen und Vornamen*, of January 5, 1938, declared that Jewish Germans had to have a name deemed typically Jewish—"im deutschen Volk als typisch angesehen." The *Zweite Verordnung zur Durchführung des Gesetzes über die Änderung von Familiennamen und Vornamen* of August 17, 1938 amended the law. It included a list of officially sanctioned Jewish male and female names. Names for newborns had to be picked from this list. Jewish-Germans who did not have a name mentioned on the list were now required to add "Israel" or "Sarah" to their names.

[45] Celan, "Gespräch," 27.

from, names can also be a survival strategy. Rochelle Tobias has pointed out that "the unspeakability of the name guarantees that it can never be put to the service of representation."[46] To be without proper possessions—"denn der Jud, du weißts, was hat er schon, das ihm auch wirklich gehört, das nicht geborgt wär, ausgeliehen und nicht zurückgegeben" [because the Jew, you know, what does he have that is really his own, that is not borrowed, taken and not returned]—provides a degree of anonymity and flexibility, which, in the "Gespräch," may be positive.[47] The question underlying Celan's refusal to name the two men is one of surviving and operating in a system that places a high—and often fatal—value on naming and denominating. "Jud" and "Sohn eines Juden" are not individuating or unique names, but labels that originate from a classifying system that would eventually lead to great violence.

Celan goes so far as to suggest that once individuation takes place, it leads to death: "Auf dem Stein bin ich gelegen, damals, du weißt, auf den Steinfliesen; und neben mir, da sind sie gelegen, die anderen, die wie ich waren, die anderen, die anders waren als ich und genauso, die Geschwisterkinder." [I lay on the stone, back then, you know, on the stone tiles; and next to me the others who were like me, the others who were different and yet like me, my cousins.][48] In an allusion to concentration camps and gas chambers, an indefinite number of humans lie insensate on a floor of cold stone, as if asleep but showing no signs of life.[49] If the violence that Celan recalls is based simultaneously on a semantic order of individuality—the I who is differentiated—and on a ruthless disregard for that singularity, in the "Gespräch" he attempts to reanimate the possibility of both the individual and the collective through the poetics of the fold. This poetics is not based on identification in the service of violent amassing and segregation, but rather on gradual differentiation that can illuminate productive similarities. Rather than giving an identity or pointing to the thing itself, indexical names and designations are nothing but signifying tautologies, referring only to themselves. Celan knew of the desire to name things by their actual name, and a decade earlier, he exclaims in a passage from *Edgar Jené und der Traum vom Traume* that closely resembles the above-described scene from the *Gespräch*:

---

[46] Tobias, "The Ground," 583.
[47] Celan, "Gespräch," 27.
[48] Celan, "Gespräch," 30.
[49] Peter Szondi identifies the stone tiles as a German death camp. Peter Szondi, "Durch die Enge geführt. Versuch über die Verständlichkeit des modernen Gedichts," *Schriften*, vol. 2, ed. Jean Bollack (Frankfurt/Main: Suhrkamp, 1978), 345–89.

Alter Identitätskrämer! Was hast du erblickt und erkannt, tapferer Doktor der Tautologie? Was hast du erkannt, sag, am Rand dieser neuen Straße? Einen Auch-Baum oder Beinah-Baum, nicht wahr? Nun suchst du wohl dein Latein zusammen für einen Brief an den alten Linnaeus?

[Well, old identity-monger, what did you see and recognize, you brave doctor of tautology? What could you recognize, tell me, along this unfamiliar road? An also-tree or almost-tree, right? And now you are mustering your Latin for a letter to old Linnaeus.][50]

Definitions and denominations become impossible when one either does not have or does not want to have power over language. The Jews cannot name the trees around them as the discursive practices of sorting, ordering, and naming are also the violent discourses that contributed to the extermination of the Jews. The Linnaean system of nomenclature is rigid and elides all historical relations, yet by juxtaposing popular and scientific discourses, Celan dissolves the apparent homogeneity of a taxonomic system and renders visible its historical contingency when he folds different taxonomic nomenclatures into each other. If the use of such nomenclature is imprecise, and a return to a pre-lapsarian relationship of name and object naïve, as Celan says later in the same text, he must nonetheless draw upon a compromised language in order to give names to the characters and figures in his text.[51] To do this, Celan attempts to reduce language in the *Gespräch* to a kind of undelineated, embodied process. This strategy becomes evident when the narrator describes the language of the men: "Haben sich, auch jetzt, da die Zunge blöd gegen die Zähne stößt und die Lippe sich nicht ründet, etwas zu sagen!" [Even now, when their tongues stumble dumbly against the teeth and the lips won't round themselves, they have something to say to each other!][52] In a reduction of the interlocutors to three organs of the human vocal

---

[50] Paul Celan, "Edgar Jené und der Traum vom Traume," *Prosa I: Zu Lebzeiten publizierte Prosa und Reden, Werke: Historisch-Kritische Ausgabe*, vol. 15.1, eds. Andreas Lohr and Heino Schmull (Frankfurt/Main: Suhrkamp, 2014), 11–17, 11. Paul Celan, "Edgar Jené and The Dream About The Dream," *Collected Prose*, trans. Rosemarie Waldrop (Manchester: Carcanet Press, 1983), 3–10.

[51] "[. . .] wenn ich die Dinge bei ihrem richtigen Namen nannte. Ich wußte, daß ein solches Unternehmen die Rückkehr zu einer unbedingten Naivität voraussetzte." [[. . .] if I called things by their proper names. I knew that such an enterprise meant returning to absolute naïveté.] Celan, "Edgar Jené," 11–12.

[52] Celan, "Gespräch," 28.

apparatus—tongue, teeth, and lips—the narrator reminds us that the Jews do not speak in a signifying system based on difference. Their speech is cast as the physical production of sound yet with the delineation of phonemes—an aspirated stream of air, modulated and structured by a tongue—any tongue, teeth, and lips, fails. Yet despite their apparent inability to form the most basic meaning-making units, the two men succeed in communicating. They produce the linguistic material out of which the story develops.

As the Jews speak in this way, they share observations about the earth around them. Now high up in the mountains, they identify the peaks as being the result of a geological process of folding:

> Es hat sich die Erde gefaltet hier oben, hat sich gefaltet einmal und zweimal und dreimal, und hat sich aufgetan in der Mitte, und in der Mitte steht ein Wasser, und das Wasser ist grün, und das Grüne ist weiß, und das Weiße kommt von noch weiter oben, kommt von den Gletschern, man könnte, aber man solls nicht, sagen, das ist die Sprache, die hier gilt, das Grüne mit dem Weißen drin, eine Sprache [. . .].

> [The earth is folded up here, folded once and twice and three times, and opened up in the middle, and in the middle there is water, and the water is green, and the green is white, and the white comes from even farther up, from the glaciers, and one could say, but one shouldn't, that this is the language that counts here, the green with the white in it, a language [. . .].][53]

Three times, and hence multiple times, the earth folded itself, and this explicit discussion of the mountain's folds circles around a pool or a flow of water that stands in the middle of the peaks. The water, too, rather than appearing as an emblem of stasis or tranquility, is likewise folded. Like the strands of a plait, the green and the white of the water form yet another fold. In an infinite regression of green and white—the fact that white comes from higher up suggests that there is yet again green to follow upon white—Celan's braided prose oscillates between the green and white of the water, which stands in the middle of the folds but comes from an unknown source above. The reference here to a source of water becomes a figurative reference to the search for a source for language. The Jews suggest that the language spoken high up in the mountains is that of the folded water, "das Grüne mit dem Weißen drin." Mountains, glacial waters, and Celan's language itself

---

[53] Celan, "Gespräch," 28–9.

become here an endless series of folds, one in which no origin or endpoint can be easily localized. That an image from nature should be the most generative site for this folding comes as no surprise, given what Celan read in Leibniz:

> Mais la *raison suffisante*, se doit aussi trouver dans les *vérités contingentes ou de fait* [. . .] où la résolution en raisons particulières pourrait aller à un détail sans bornes à cause de la variété immense des choses de la Nature et de la division des corps à l'infini.
>
> [But a sufficient reason must also be found for contingent truths, truths of fact [. . .]. For truths of this sort reasons can be given in boundless detail, because of the immense variety of things in Nature and because of the infinite divisibility of bodies.]⁵⁴

The infinity of a reflective pool set amidst mountainous peaks demands a language, spoken by the Jews or written by Celan, that proceeds without linear or terminal logic. At the same time, this language denies taxonomic principles of denomination and annulation. It is a language without grounding, a language that signifies, just as the fold, implicitly and explicitly. Though imaginable but in no way definitive, green and white could be water in different states of aggregation—cold snow, ice, viscous glaciers, or snowmelt. To be able to call this a language but better not to do so—"man könnte, aber man solls nicht, sagen" [one could say, but one shouldn't]—is the refusal, as a gesture to the identity-monger Linnaeus, of scientific or geological taxonomies. Celan has the Jews name the water as distinct from rock, the green as different from the white, the heights distant from the valleys. But he simultaneously insists on the imbrication of these categories, dissolving their neat separation—"sans bornes" [boundless]—by folding them into one another. Simultaneously separating and combining, the fold preserves difference without suspending the continuity of its structure.

---

54 Celan finds the images of an emanating source, of a chain of infinite regress, and of a steady flow of water in Leibniz. "[. . .] dans la quelle le detail des changemens ne soit qu'eminemment, comme dans la source [. . .]." [[. . .] The details of all the contingent changes are contained in him only eminently, as in their source.] "[. . .] et il faut que la raison suffisante ou dernière soit hors de la suite ou *series* de ce detail des contingences, quelqu'infini, qu'il porroit être." [[. . .] the train of detailed facts about contingencies [. . .] doesn't contain the sufficient reason, the ultimate reason, for any contingent fact. For that we must look outside the sequence of contingencies.] "Car tous les corps sont dans un flux perpetuel comme des riviéres [. . .]." [[. . .] because all bodies are in a perpetual state of flux, like rivers] Leibniz, *Monadologie*, §36, §37, §38, §71.

In this passage of Celan's text, the fold appears in three variations. The fold, as Deleuze reminds us, is a tripartite formation, a structure of a fold between two folds: "the fold from preformation is a Zweifalt, not a fold in two—since every fold can be thus—but a 'fold-of-two,' an *entre-deux*, something 'between' in the sense that a difference is being differentiated."[55] This tripartite structure, as well as a geomorphologically accurate description of folded mountains, is mimetically contained in this passage through the graded listing of numerals—"hat sich gefaltet einmal und zweimal und dreimal" [folded once and twice and three times]—and the tripartite climax "Es hat sich [. . .] gefaltet hier oben, hat sich gefaltet [. . .], und hat sich aufgetan [. . .]." [The earth folded up here, folded [. . .] and opened up in the middle [. . .]][56] In its structure, the passage also replicates the structure of the *Gespräch* as a triple-folded text, with a narrative or epic first section describing the hike of the Jew up until the encounter with his interlocutor, a dialogic middle piece, and a third, monologic part.

The figure of the third is relevant once more regarding the *Gespräch*. Celan himself, in notes about the *Gespräch* collected in convolute F of the *Meridian* materials, speaks of the presence of a third, a witness, who, through language is always present in any narration: "Es ist noch ein Dritter dabei, le témoin, von Gnaden der Sprache. Ein wider willen und malgré lui. Er sagt, lauter Blondheiten grauhaarig wie er da steht, noch immer lauter Blondheiten." [There is a third one standing by, le témoin, by the grace of language. An aversion and malgré lui. He speaks, only blondnesses gray-haired as he stands there, still nothing but blondnesses.][57] Language may have aged and turned gray, yet it still carries with it the sins of its youth. Only through the third voice of the narrator can the conversation of the two men enter the first part of the story, then transform into its dialogic form in the second, and thirdly, into its monologic form. Literature, in this third, monologic form, as a medium of a different order, can render transparent the dynamics inherent to its epistemological structure. This third includes both language itself and the narrative voice. The witness, rooted in language, is the narrative voice reporting the unfolding of the events to the reader, but he is also, in the form of language, witness to the atrocities and crimes committed against language and against the Jews. His speaking

---

55 "Epxlication. implication-complication form the triad of the fold, following the varioations of the relation of the One-Multiple." Deleuze, *The Fold*, 10, 24.
56 Cf. also Arnim Burckhardt,"'. . . als die Lippe mir blutet vor Sprache.' Zum Problem des Sprachzerfalls in Büchners 'Lenz' und Celans 'Gespräch im Gebirg'." In *Die Fremdheit der Sprache. Studien zur Literatur der Moderne*, eds. Jochen C. Schütze, Hans-Ulrich Treichel, and Dietmar Voss (Hamburg: Argument-Verlag, 1988), 135–55, 149.
57 Celan, *Meridian*, Tübinger Ausgabe, 129.

in "Blondheiten" is testimony to language being enriched—"angereichert"—by German forms and phrases. This phrase reveals the difficulty of not only speaking about language through language, but moreover, of leveling a critique of language through language. This third voice still knows of the "Straße, der schönen, der unvergleichlichen" [beautiful, incomparable road] as a topos of bucolic mountain roads, but it is also as a means for conveying knowledge of atrocities.

THE FOLDED EYE

We recall that through the perspective of the narrative voice, the two Jews are shown meeting on a road through a mountain meadow. Though the text brings the Jews and the flowers before the reader's eye, the Jews themselves are unable to see the floral world around them as the reader does: "Aber sie, [. . .], sie haben keine Augen." [But they, [. . .], they have no eyes.][58] The reason why the flowers remain invisible to the Jews is because they have, metaphorically speaking, a different set of eyes. The visual sensorium of the two men is as strange as it is simplistic in its conception: an image enters the eye and is caught by a veil hanging behind it. The exact nature of the image remains unspecified, but the union of the veil with the image not only precludes the idea of an image as a window to the world, but in form also repeats the Leibniz windowless monad.[59]

> Genauer: sie haben, auch sie, Augen, aber da hängt ein Schleier davor, nein, dahinter, ein beweglicher Schleier; kaum tritt ein Bild ein, so bleibts hängen im Geweb, und schon ist ein Faden zur Stelle, der sich da spinnt, sich herumspinnt ums Bild, ein Schleierfaden; spinnt sich ums Bild herum und zeugt ein Kind mit ihm, halb Bild und halb Schleier.

> [Or, more precisely: they have, even they have eyes, but with a veil hanging in front of them, no, not in front, behind them, a movable veil. No sooner does an image enter than it gets caught in the web, and a thread starts spinning, spinning itself around the image, a veil-thread; spins itself around the image and begets a child with it, half image, half veil.][60]

---

[58] Celan, "Gespräch," 28.
[59] Christine Buci-Glucksmann, "Barock und Komplexität: Eine Ästhetik des Virtuellen," *Barock: Neue Sichtweisen einer Epoche*, ed. Peter J. Burgard (Wien: Böhlau, 2001), 205–12, 211.
[60] Celan, "Gespräch," 28.

In the image of a veiled eye, the text provides an instrument with which the writerly operation of the text itself can be rendered visible. Though a visual organ, the eye steps back behind speech and writing, and becomes an instrument of writing and speaking. The veiled eye allows for a new perspective, one that makes it possible, in a shifted view, to see nature, the Jews, and the form of the fold. The layered visual construction that Celan offers consequently criticizes notions of objective representation and fixed perspective. When the text positions the flowers to the left and right of the Jews, and subsequently announces that the Jews have no eyes, or better, a different set of eyes, it suggests that the men are oblivious to the flowers as "Türkenbund," "Rapunzel," "Prachtnelke," and "Dianthus superbus." The two are blind to the flowers as represented by signifiers: the generic and scientific names of plants. The text does not indicate that the two men fail to see the plants at all, only that they cannot see them according to this indexical scheme. Despite their Latinate names, the flowers remain ambiguous forms that lack clear attributes: "[...] blüht wie wild, blüht wie nirgends [...]." [[...] blooms wild, blooms like nowhere else.][61]

Here, the flowers, are ambivalent, implacable visual data and exemplify what Celan communicates about sight. The veiled eye cannot receive and process images objectively, sorting and classifying their details. The eye is rather another fold, one that may perceive and illuminate reality, but only through its contortion and layering. What Celan describes in the metaphor of an eye with a movable veil before and behind it is not a contrastive grid that overlays the sensory organ and hence arranges perspective and perception, but yet another fold.[62] The notion that objects will appear differently depending on perspective, and moreover, that the perceiving subject will change as well in relation to the object he perceives, is an idea Celan noted in Leibniz:

> Et comme une même ville regardée de différents côtés paraît toute autre et est comme multipliée perspectivement; il arrive de même, que par la multitude infinie des substances simples, il y a comme

---

[61] Celan, "Gespräch," 28.
[62] Alberti writes about the veil before used as a structural medium between object and canvas: "[...] I think one cannot find anything more convenient than that veil [...] a veil woven of very thin threads and loosely intertwined, dyed with any color, subdivided with thicker threads according to parallel partitions, in as many squares as you like, and held stretched by a frame; which [veil] I place, indeed, between the object to be represented and the eye, so that the visual penetrates through the thinness of the veil. This cut of the veil [...] always presents the same surfaces unchanged." Alberti, *On Painting*, 50–1.

autant de différents univers, qui ne sont pourtant que les perspectives d'un seul selon les différents points de vue de chaque Monade.

[And as the same town, looked at from various sides, appears quite different and becomes as it were numerous in perspectives; even so, as a result of the infinite number of simple substances, it is as if there were so many different universes, which, nevertheless are nothing but perspectives of a single universe, according to the special point of view of each Monad.][63]

The image that enters the eye will not be sutured into the story but integrated in a more elastic manner into the text's pleats: "Folding and unfolding, wrapping and unwrapping are the constants of this operation [. . .]."[64] The transitory position of the veil—first before, then behind the eye—underlines the nature of the fold as a structure always in motion. The two positions of the veil around the eye echoes the fold's double nature, offering at least two perspectives on whatever is seen. While the contradictory vectors of "kommen" and "gehen" of the opening sentence initially undermined the stable position of the narrator, we can now imagine that it is the veiled eye that receives and refracts the image of this fraught journey. At the same time, the veil shows something yet envelops it, and moreover, it shows its process of enveloping and developing. The veiled eye does not yield clarity or singularity as much as a vision of "entanglement."[65] What previously

---

[63] Leibniz, "Monadologie," §57.
[64] Deleuze, *The Fold*, 123–4.
[65] Cf. Mieke Bal, "Auf die Haut/Unter die Haut: Barrockes steigt an die Oberfläche," *Barock: Neue Sichtweisen einer Epoche*, ed. Peter J. Burgard (Wien: Böhlau, 2001), 17–51, 30. Rochelle Tobias reads the abdication of the narrative voice as an indication of negated representability in the conversation: "All representation, in fact, seems to come to a halt at this moment, for the shift from narration to conversation is not merely a shift from representation by another to representation by and for oneself. The absence of both a subject matter and two clearly identifiable subjects makes this conversation unrepresentable; it also forecloses the possibility that this conversation could represent anything." Tobias, "The Ground," 568. "If the status of the object is profoundly changed, so also is that of the subject. [. . .] It is not exactly a point but a place [. . .]. To the degree it represents variation or inflection, it can be called *point of view*. Such is the basis of perspectivism, which does not mean a dependence in respect to a pregiven or defined subject; to the contrary, a subject will be what comes to the point of view, or rather what remains in the point of view. That is why the transformation of the object refers to a correlative transformation of the subject [. . .]." Deleuze, *The Fold*, 20.

has been read with the dual yet separate images of a caterpillar's metamorphosis into a butterfly, or the death of a spider's prey caught in a web, can now productively be united in the figure of the fold.[66] This metamorphic development uniting creation and death again has its origins in Leibniz: "Et ce que nous appellons *Generations* sont des developpmens et des accroissmens; comme ce que nous appellons *Morts*, sont des Envellopmens et Diminutions." [What we call births [generations] are developments and growths, while what we call deaths are envelopments and diminutions.][67] Rather than a disappearance in extinction, the fold is a withdrawal and return to potentiality.

The metaphor underlying the veiled eye, however, is that of a birth: "und zeugt ein Kind mit ihm" [and begets a child with it]. In his essay, "Die Du-Anrede bei Paul Celan," John E. Jackson describes the slow coming into being and assumption of a name in the first section of the conversation as "die Geburt der zwei jüdischen Namen aus der rein wörtlichen Materie des Satzes" [the birth of two Jewish names from the purely literal matter of the sentence], yet the two men never receive a name other than the "Jud" given by the narrator.[68] Hence, the completion of the birth referred to by Jackson, in this case, must take place beyond the text. When neither the act of naming nor, consequently, that of the birth takes place within the text, we should then further question the nature of the child born from a union of image and veil. "[H]alf image, half veil," the progeny is more half-born than hybrid. The child begotten by the eye will continue, like the two Jews in the story, to envelop and develop, to explicate itself—"ich und kein andrer, ich und nicht er [. . .] ich, den's getroffen hat, ich, den's nicht getroffen hat" [me and no other, me and not him [. . .] me who has been hit, me, who has not been hit]— without ever reaching a defined state of being.[69] The metamorphoses of the two men will not end in clear and distinct beings; their outlines dissolve as they return into the dark of the night and into the text's folded prose. The dystopian reading of the fold-born half-child would be the catastrophic reversal of a movement from dark to light. A failed unfolding and development out of the dark questions the teleological notion of the form-matter binary he excerpted from Leibniz: "causa formalis / immanentes Formprinzip // causa materialis /

---

[66] Cf. Hermann Burger, *Paul Celan: Auf der Suche nach der verlorenen Sprache* (Frankfurt/Main: Fischer Taschenbuch Verlag, 1989), 19. Leibniz himself refers to a butterfly's metamorphosis from a caterpillar: "les chenilles deviennent papillons" [and caterpillars become butterflies]. Leibniz, "Monadologie," §74.
[67] Leibniz, "Monadologie," §73.
[68] Jackson, "Die Du-Anrede," 64.
[69] Celan, "Gespräch," 29.

(Entelechie)."⁷⁰ Celan's marginalia in Leibniz indicate that the idea of perfectability, the idea of bringing a being to its completion and of realizing its full potential, was of great concern to him. In §18 of the *Monadologie*, Celan reads that monads are entelechies, already containing a certain degree of perfection and self-sufficiency—"a certain perfection [. . .] a certain self-sufficiency," or as the French has it, "une certain perfection [. . .] une suffisance."⁷¹ He marks the passage with two lines of pencil in the margins, and a few paragraphs later recalls Hermolaus Barbarus' translation of entelechies as "perfectihabies"—perfection havers—a Heideggerian neologism.⁷² A utopian reading strengthens the *causa formalis* and allows for a productive fold that holds the promise of virtuality in the linguistic material at hand that can come to its realization when one abandons the rigidity of binary dualisms. The continued use of the imperfect is neither the denial of perfectable forms, nor a despondent resignation on behalf of Celan. Instead of creating neologisms or bridging between what is and what can be said through paradoxical constructions, Celan unites them in the figure of the fold.

On page 69 of Celan's copy of *Monadologie*, following the final paragraph of Leibniz's treaty, an entry in pencil marks the *Lektüreschluß*, the date of Celan's last reading as August 19, 1959. Celan amended the date with a short remark about his mood upon completing the reading: "19.8.59 (Nicht ohne Beklommenheit. . .)"—not without trepidation.⁷³ §90 contains the statement that if man was able to understand the order of the universe, he would recognize that it is impossible to improve upon it.⁷⁴ Considering what Celan endured and witnessed during the years of the Nazi regime, his trepidation concerning Leibniz's ultimate thesis is understandable. If the order and form of the universe, and with it also the world in which Celan lives, cannot be improved upon, then it must already contain a form in which it and its atrocities can be represented. Celan finds this form in the fold. "Laden" with past, and "pregnant" with the future, only the fold can adequately deal with the burden of the past and bring about the previous and the prospective in the now. The unspeakability of the historical trauma that pervades the

---

70   Celan, *Meridian*, Tübinger Ausgabe, 204.
71   Leibniz, *Monadologie*, §18.
72   Leibniz, *Monadologie*, §48. Celan, *Bibliothèque*, 90.
73   Celan, *Bibliothèque*, 92.
74   "que si nous pouvions entendre assez l'ordre de l'Univers, nous trouverions [. . .] qu'il est impossible de le render meilleur qu'il est." [if we could sufficiently understand the order of the universe, we should find [. . .] that it is impossible to make it better than it is.] Leibniz, *Monadologie*, §90.

text recalls historical and cultural memories that can no longer be accessed. Through the fold, Celan can say what no longer can be said. Celan sounds out the poetological possibilities of the fold in a poetically charged piece of prose and not in poetry. In the poetics of the fold, the impossibility of a historical encounter becomes a historical event by not speaking, by not meeting, by not taking place.

At the end, in a final fold of the text, the speaker of the monologue reiterates for a last time the potentialities within the text:

> —ich hier, ich; ich, der ich dir all das sagen kann, hätt sagen können; der ich dirs nicht sag und nicht gesagt hab; ich mit dem Türkenbund links, ich mit der Rapunzel [. . .] ich hier und ich dort, ich [. . .] ich auf dem Weg hier zu mir, oben.
>
> [[. . .] me here, me, who can tell you all this, could have and don't and didn't tell you; me with a turk-cap's lily on my left; me with the lamb's lettuce [. . .] me here and there, me [. . .] me here on the way to myself, up here.][75]

As the text draws to a close, it folds itself, not in circular fashion but in a layering movement of implication and explication, to its beginning. Still "auf dem Weg hier zu mir, oben" [on the way to myself, up here], we see how the folded structure of the opening sentence pervades the entire text, and how, in its path, the folded shape of the mountains structured the poetics of the *Gespräch*. But to say that this structure has enabled the successful representation of a conversation would be as inadequate as to claim that it has failed. Although concrete forms arise from the text's images and landscape, they remain ungraspable, fleeting, or unnamable. But their implicit emergence, as brief or vacillating as it may be, resists disappearance. Celan's words and images leave resonant traces that ask readers to reckon with the singularity—of a star, for instance—as it becomes just one element in the constellation of the fold:

> [. . .] und in meinem Aug [. . .] da hängen die Schleier, die beweglichen [. . .] und der Stern—denn ja, der steht jetzt überm Gebirg—, wenn er da hineinwill, so wird er Hochzeit halten müssen und bald nicht mehr er sein, sondern halb Schleier und halb Stern [. . .] ich weiß, ich bin dir begegnet, hier, [. . .] und die Falten dort [. . .].

---

[75] Celan, "Gespräch," 31.

[[. . .] and in my eye [. . .] there are the veils, the movable veils [. . .] and the star—yes, it is up there now, above the mountains—if it wants to enter it will have to wed and soon it won't be itself, but half veil and half star [. . .] I know, I've met you here [. . .] and those folds there [. . .].][76]

---

[76] Celan, "Gespräch," 31.

V Liquid Mountains—Elfriede Jelinek's *Die Kinder der Toten*

MOUNTAIN GRAVES

"Seht, diese Landschaft lebt, da sie doch mehr als fünfzig Jahre tot war oder sich zumindest totgestellt hat! Jetzt schlägt sie die Augen auf und empfängt ihren Blutzoll an Individuen, die dem Verkehr geopfert wurden." [Look! This landscape is alive, now that it's been dead for fifty years or at least feigned death! Now its opening its eyes and collecting its butcher's bill in individuals, sacrificed to traffic.][1] In 1995, the year of the 50th anniversary of the end of World War Two and the victory over Nazi Germany, the Austrian mountains awaken in Elfriede Jelinek's *Die Kinder der Toten*. The ground has been in motion for quite some time in Jelinek's œuvre—"Die Kruste der Erde wölbt sich, ein Berg tritt im Abendschein auf" [The crust of the earth begins to camber, a mountain appears in the sunset], she write in her 1985 *Oh Wildnis, oh Schutz vor ihr*, "Herr Doktor, dieser Boden lebt ja förmlich [. . .]" [Herr Doktor, this ground is really alive [. . .]—yet in *Die Kinder der Toten*, the mineral hardness of the Austrian Alps gives way to hair, flesh, and bone.[2] "Der Fels öffnet sich jetzt, Achtung!" [The rock is opening now, look out!][3]

It is the many deaths of the Holocaust that cause this gruesome transformation. Hastily buried in the ground and conveniently forgotten or repressed, the victims' bodies have been hidden as Austria's constitutional transition from the First to the Second Republic attempted to dissociate from a troubled a past. But the slow decay of the victims' bodies begins to soften the foundations of the Austrian nation after 1945. In an infernal allegory, Jelinek explicates the failures of an Austrian society that thought it possible to reground itself on a soil containing crimes of the past by depicting the collapse of its physical foundations. The idea of soil—German or Austrian—and those buried therein becomes a metonymy for the resurrection of a whole nation, an idea whose foundations Jelinek unsettles throughout her oeuvre. In the acknowledgments of her 1990 play *Wolken. Heim*, Jelinek references Leonhard Schmeiser's essay "Das Gedächtnis des Bodens," where

---

[1] Elfriede Jelinek, *Die Kinder der Toten* (Reinbek: Rohwolt, 1995), 449.
[2] *Oh Wildnis, oh Schutz vor ihr* contains moments of anthropomorphization of rocks, mineralizations of man, and similes between rock and man: "Seine Haut ist wie Gestein." [His skin is like rock.] "Der Mann ist von Brüchen durchzogen, er ist eine tektonische Verwerfung ersten Ranges. [. . .] Er ist aber auch kein Mineral. Er ist kein unfühlender Stein." [This man is riven by fissures, he is a tectonic distortion of the first degree. [. . .] But he is not a mineral. He is not an insensitive mineral.] Elfriede Jelinek, *Oh Wildnis, oh Schutz vor ihr* (Reinbek: Rowohlt, 1985), 35, 38, 52–3.
[3] Jelinek, *Die Kinder*, 17.

Schmeiser points out the importance of the notion of an afterlife of the buried dead to the nationalistic discourse of the late eighteenth and early nineteenth century. Remembering the soil with its dead is a requisite act for the nation's rebirth.[4] In *Die Kinder der Toten*, post-1945 Austrian acts of founding and foundation are undermined in an imagery of maceration and subsidence: "Die Pension scheint ein wenig im Humus versunken. [...] Ist dies Haus nicht niedriger als gestern?" [The inn seems to have sunk into the humus. [...] Isn't this house today lower than yesterday?][5] And an almost obsessive iteration of the adjective "weich" throughout the novel begins to dissolve the soil, the characters, and even the text itself, to a point at which they all become indistinguishable:

> Edgars weiches Fleisch wird genutzt wie ein Gottesacker, in den sich die Schaufeln bis zum Ellenbogen, bis auf den Grundton des Bodens einsinken. Es war unausweichlich, daß die Erde ihn sich schließlich geholt hat, ein jeder gehe zu seinem Erzeuger [...] Das Fleischliche und Irdische aber gehört der Erde.

> [Edgar's soft flesh is used like a churchyard, into which the shovels sink deep down to the elbows, down to the very foundation of the ground. It was inevitable that the ground finally grabbed him—each must go to his maker [...] But the carnal and the terrestrial belong to the ground.][6]

In Elfriede Jelinek's iconoclastic and highly regarded novel—Jelinek received the 2004 Nobel Prize in literature—the mountains are anything

---

[4] Leonhard Schmeiser, "Das Gedächtis des Bodens," *Tumult. Zeitschrift für Verkehrswissenschaft* 10 (1987): 38–56. Elfriede Jelinek, *Wolken.Heim.* (Göttingen: Steidl, 1990), text unpaginated.

[5] Jelinek, *Die Kinder*, 315. Cf. Juliane Vogel: "In einer gigantischen Allegorie der österreichischen Nachkriegskultur führt Jelinek am Totalversagen des Bodens das Totalversagen einer Gesellschaft vor, die sich auf einem von 'Maische' aufgeweichten Grund neu zu verankern zu können glaubte (*Kinder* 273). In Bildern der Erweichung und des Einsinkens stellt sie die Legitimität österreichischer Gründungsakte nach 1945 in Frage, sowie die Möglichkeit leugnet, durch Gründung 'Umstrukturiertes in Strukturiertes' zu überführen." Juliane Vogel, "'Keine Leere der Unterbrechung'—*Die Kinder der Toten* oder der Schrecken der Falte," *Modern Austrian Literature* 39, no. 3–4 (2006): 15–26, 16. Cf. also Juliane Vogel, "Elfriede Jelineks Kinder der Toten," *manuskripte* 132 (1996): 110–11; and Juliane Vogel, "Wasser hinunter, wohin? Elfriede Jelineks Roman *Kinder der Toten*—ein Flüssigtext," *"Other" Austrians: Post-1945 Austrian Women's Writing*, ed. and intro. Allyson Fiddler (Bern: Lang, 1998), 235–42.

[6] Jelinek, *Die Kinder*, 305–6; emphasis mine.

but sublime.[7] They serve as the repository of Austria's gruesome past, the denial of its all too-willing participation in the atrocities of the Third Reich. The novel, described as "an experimental ghost story of remembrance" as well as a "postmodern horror novel," depicts a truly terrifying mountainscape over its 666-page span.[8] Much has been written by scholars about the novel as an interrogation of how literature can represent the atrocities of the Holocaust, yet none have paid sufficient attention to the role of the mountains through which this interrogation is made possible.[9]

Jelinek's novel, as difficult in content and in form as it is, presents us with an extremely compelling example of how the mountains in twentieth-century German-language literature serve as figures through which questions of history, of memory, and of narrative form are addressed. Mountains are literary historical forms—that is, when we encounter the mountains in a German text, we recall the many representations of mountains that occur throughout the long history of German literature. Much more than a mere formal and representational problem, the aesthetic engagement with mountains has always connected issues of form and narration to radical questionings of subjectivity and historicity. Jelinek activates the historical lineage of literary tradition to insist upon a persistence and material obduracy of the past. Her treatment of the mountains in *Die Kinder der Toten* evokes paradigms we traditionally associate with German literature on the mountains in order to pervert or dispose of them entirely as obsolete forms.

When we arrive at the foothills of Jelinek's mountains, we have traveled a great distance from Enlightenment rationalism and romantic

---

[7] Since its publication, *Die Kinder der Toten* has often been grouped with Döblin's *Berline Alexanderplatz*, Franz Kafka's *Prozeß*, Kluge's *Chronik der Gefühle*, but also Joyce's *Finnegan's Wake* or Josè Lezama Limas' *Paradiso*. Cf. Ralf Schnell, "Stoffwechselprozesse. Oberfläche und Tiefe in Elfriede Jelineks Roman *Die Kinder der Toten.*" *Lob der Oberfläche. Zum Werk von Elfriede Jelinek*, eds. Thomas Eder and Juliane Vogel (München: Wilhelm Fink, 2010), 169–79, 169.

[8] Jutta Gsoels-Lorensen, "Elfriede Jelinek's *Die Kinder der Toten:* Representing the Holocaust as an Austrian Ghost Story," *Germanic Review* 81, no. 4 (2006): 360–82, 360.

[9] Cf. Ian Wilson, "Greeting the Holocaust's Dead? Narrative Strategies and the Undead in Elfriede Jelinek's *Die Kinder der Toten*," *Modern Austrian Literature* 39, no. 3–4 (2006): 27–55; Maria Regina Kecht, "The Polyphony of Remembrance: Reading *Die Kinder der Toten*," *Elfriede Jelinek: Writing Woman, Nation, and Identity*, eds. Matthias Konzet and Margarete Lamb-Faffelberger (Madison, NJ: Fairleigh Dickinson University Press, 2007), 189–220; Jessica Ortner, "Aspekte des Untoten in Elfriede Jelinek's Roman *Die Kinder der Toten*: Erinnerungsästhetische und narratologische Überlegungen," *Jelinek[jahr]buch 2012*, ed. Pia Janke (Wien: Praesens, 2012), 83–103.

subjectivity. Jelinek confronts readers with the Austrian Alps as abject masses of undead, shifting matter. As bodies erupt and emerge from the mountains, only to vanish again, Jelinek gives us an utterly transformed—and transforming—view of the mountains. Through her daring, alienating prose, Jelinek's mountains collapse the living and the dead, the here and the there, the past and the present. The mountains become a space where history is confronted in the present and retold in new forms. Jelinek makes the wounds of the past visible and tangible; denying the reader the safe distance, she refuses to confine the past to the past or make it wholly legible or knowable. Material chaos and linguistic strangeness work together in this postmodern novel where mountains lead us to the vertiginous height of uncertainty:

> Der Berg ist schon wieder ein Streicheltier geworden, besänftigt, Achtung, ducken Sie sich, es beginnt der vorliegende Text. Er rutscht unter Ihren Händen weg, aber das macht nichts, muß mich halt ein anderer zu Vollendung tragen, ein Bergführer, nicht Sie!

> [Once again the mountain has become an animal in a petting zoo, domesticated, look out, duck down, the text at hand is about to begin. It will slip out from under your hands, but that won't matter, then someone else will just have to bring me to completion, a mountain guide, not you!][10]

Dispensing with the illusion that the mountain can be fully conquered, domesticated like an animal in a petting zoo, Jelinek also declares that her novel, which is about to begin, will be a text in motion. A narrative voice cautions the reader to duck as the text commences, suggesting a threat from above, only to then inform him that the novel will slip from his hands. This strange warning disorients the reader; the text immediately refuses a linear reading and further thwarts a reader's desire for completion: "muß mich halt ein anderer zu Vollendung tragen." [then someone else will just have to bring me to completion] As the narrative voice shifts, the text seems to recede, retracting from the reader's grasp.

Who is the mountain guide that could navigate the landscape as well as the twists and turns of the novel? If a guide's perspective is unavailable to the readers, perhaps they are meant to adopt the perspective of the undead protagonists, who will lead them haphazardly through a deformed Alpine landscape. The novel itself comes to mirror the mountain—both shift, dissolve, and evade the reader's grasp in

---

[10] Jelinek, *Die Kinder*, 15.

their excess and their inscrutability. Juliane Vogel describes the material (in)consistency of the text that lends it this elusive character:

> Die Instabilität des Wortes, seine unbestimmte Pluralisierung in ähnlichen Wörtern, seine Weichheit, bildet die Grundlage der Jelinekschen *poiesis*. Der Roman handelt von den semiotischen Konvulsionen einer Sprache, die nur noch für Momente zum Distinkten vordringt, einer Sprache, die wie der Boden keine Festigkeit besitzt [...].
>
> [The instability of the word, the unsettled pluralization in similar words, its plasticity, form the basis of Jelinek's *poiesis*. The novel depicts the semiotic convulsions of a language which connects with the distinct only for brief moments—a language that lacks firmness as does the ground below.][11]

Convulsions and softness dominate the landscape and the language, so that readers and critics wishing to "make sense" of Jelinek's text must grapple with a setting, a language, and a history that erupt and recede.

The mountains in *Die Kinder der Toten* are central to Jelinek's unflinching interrogation of Austria's Nazi past and its subsequent historical amnesia. But rather than just an exposition of history as it appears in the mountains, the formal innovations that Jelinek develops render the Austrian Alps a cite of trauma, unresolved and unavailable to dominant, teleological historical narratives that would place the dead squarely in the past. Jelinek narratively embeds sedimented layers of obscured histories in the novel's mountains, which then rupture violently into the open. Her linguistic strategies dissolve the boundaries of time and space that are central to a linear and progressive sense of history; the history that emerges from the mountains for Jelinek is, like Celan's, one of folding, re-emergence, and dissolution.[12] In fact, Jelinek

---

[11] Vogel, "Keine Leere," 23.
[12] Juliane Vogel reads *Die Kinder der Toten* as manifesting a superficial aesthetic, and identifies Jelinek's rhetoric as a baroque semiotic, which denies stable forms and permits modulations only. "Statt aus der Tiefe kommen die Wiedergänger aus der Tiefe der Oberfläche, deren aktuelle Variante, Modulation, Entwicklung und Realisierung sie sind. Das Fundament des Bodens verhält sich als Komplexität – d.h. als eine 'Tausendfältigkeit' von Schichtungen, Stoffen und Hüllen, aus deren Bewegungen, Überlappungen und Stülpungen eine groteske und transitorische Population hervorgeht." [Instead of coming from the depths, the revenants come from the depths of the surface, whose current variant, modulation, development, and realization they are. The foundation of the soil behaves as a complexity - i.e. as a 'thousand-fold' of layers, materials, and shells, from whose movements, overlappings, and inversions emerges a grotesque and transitory population.] Vogel, "Keine Leere," 22.

pays homage to Celan's "Gespräch im Gebirg" in her 2002 play *In den Alpen*, where the dead of a gruesome cable car accident converse with paramedics and the returning dead of older atrocities. In the midst of all of this, the stage directions specify that a man named Celan is called to the phone. "Man hört von überallher, immer mit Unterbrechungen, kreischen, schreien: 'Celan, Telefon!'—'Celan! [. . .].'" [From everywhere at once can be heard, with interruptions, screaming, yelling: 'Celan, phone!'—'Celan! [. . .].']"[13] Jelinek recounts the events of a horrible accident from November 2000, when 155 skiers burned to death in a tunnel of the glacier cable car on the Kitzsteinhorn. She juxtaposes the magnitude of today's sport culture with early documents of Alpinism, when mountain sports were not only reserved for the elite but were also a domain of anti-Semitic exclusion.[14] In *In den Alpen*, Jelinek interweaves her text with citations from Celan:

"[. . .] denn da bin ich ja, hier, auf dieser Straße, von der sie sagen, daß sie schön ist, bin ich ja, beim Türkenbund und bei der Rapunzel [. . .] da drüben [. . .] da geht das Lärchenholzkästchen in Flammen auf da entzündet sich das hölzerne Dämmaterial [. . .] da rasen die Flammen mit der Zugluft davon, den Kamin hinauf [. . .] ich seh's, ich seh es und seh's nicht [. . .]."

[Now there I am, here, on this road, of which they say that it is beautiful, here I am, next to the turk-cap's lily and the lamb's lettuce [. . .] over there [. . .] there the larch wood box is going up in flames and there the wooden insulation catches fire [. . .] there the flames are racing away with the draft, up the chimney [. . .] I see it, I see it and don't see it [. . .].][15]

---

[13] Elfriede Jelinek, *In den Alpen* (Berlin: Berlin Verlag, 2002), 41.
[14] Volker Mergenthaler, "Was es heißt, von den 'Opfern der Berge' zu sprechen. Elfriede Jelinkes *In den Alpen*." *Literatur für Leser* 13, no. 4 (2013): 211–20. Cf. also Wolfgang Straub, "Jelineks 'Bergstücke'—Ein neuer Mythos?," *Elfriede Jelinek: Stücke für oder gegen das Theater?*, eds. Inge Arteel and Heidy Margrit Müller (Brussels: Koninklijke Vlaamse Academie van Belgie voor Wetenschappen en Kunsten, 2008), 175–82.
[15] Jelinek, *In den Alpen*, 57–8. Cf. also Nancy Erickson, "Echoes of Celan and Heidegger in Jelinek's *In den Alpen*," *Elfriede Jelinek: Writing Woman, Nation, and Identity*, eds. Matthias Konzet and Margarete Lamb-Faffelberger (Madison, NJ: Fairleigh Dickinson University Press, 2007), 174–88; Pia Janke, "Der Mythos Kaprun in *In den Alpen* und *Das Werk*," *Jelinek, une répétition? A propos des pieces "In den Alpen" et "Das Werk."* / *Jelinek, eine Wiederholung? Zu den Theaterstücken "In den Alpen" und "Das Werk,"* eds. Françoise Lartillot and Dieter Honig (Bern: Peter Lang, 2009), 127–41.

HISTORICAL MATTERS

To give a neat summary of *Die Kinder der Toten* is nearly impossible. In many looping and repeated narrative strands, the three main characters—all of them undead, decomposing, and mute—engage in brutal acts of sex and violence. These three main characters are Edgar Gstranz, a minor ski star who died when he crashed his car into a wall; Gudrun Bichler, a failed philosophy student who cannot remember committing suicide; and Karin Frenzel, a middle-aged widow and former secretary in the sales department of an office supply company who dies in a bus accident that takes place in the novel's prologue. The three characters watch and partake in what have been called "amorphoses" or "defigurations"—destructive metamorphoses:

> Gudrun verkrümmt sich, und plötzlich steckt sie mit der ganzen Hand in sich selbst drinnen! [. . .] Gudrun Bichler steckt bis zum Ellenbogen in ihrem eigenen Körper, sie öffnet sogar die Hand darin. Eine Kaverne. Ein Loch. Ein ziehender Schmerz im Handgelenk, als wäre Gudrun aus ihrem Leib heraus, von einem uneinsichtigen Tier gebissen worden [. . .].
>
> [Gudrun twists and suddenly she is stuck with her entire hand inside herself! [. . .] Down to the elbow, Gudrun Bichler is stuck in her own body; she even opens her hand inside herself. A cavern. A hole. A dragging pain in her wrist, as if Gudrun had been bitten by an unregenerate animal from out of her own body.][16]

Just as three revenants modulate and transform only to remain unchanged, so does the text itself as passages and episodes are repeated and return throughout. The novel is replete with intertextual and intratextual references and it would be a daunting task for any reader or philologist to try to list every allusion and reference in Jelinek's novel. A vast polyphony, if not cacophony, ensues because of the novel's omnivorous literary metabolism. It feeds off anything. Textual recycling becomes the dominant principle of the text. Linguistic trash and human waste are reprocessed.

---

[16] Jelinek, *Die Kinder*, 548. Juliane Vogel writes that "Jelineks Metamorphosen sind vor allem destruktive Prozesse und deshalb eher als 'Amorphosen', bzw. als 'Defigurationen' (Rosenkranz) zu lesen, da sie ihren Gegenstand weniger verwandeln als zersetzen bzw. liquidieren." [Jelinek's metamorphoses are above all destructive processes and are therefore better read as "amorphoses" or as "defigurations" (Rosenkranz), since they do not so much transform their subject as decompose or liquidate and liquify them.] Vogel, "Wasser hinunter," 240.

What already has been produced is enough: make it new, rework the old. Recycling is full of iterations—revenants—and it seems as if all the texts, as well as their characters, are afflicted by an uncanny drive to repetition: "Edgar ist zumute, als erlebte er etwas, das bereits stattgefunden hat, ein zweites Mal, in einem Wiederholungszwang, wie eine Melodie, die einem nicht aus dem Kopf gehen will." [Edgar feels like he is experiencing something that already took place for a second time in a repetition compulsion, like a melody one just can't get out of one's head.][17]

However, it is as if *Die Kinder der Toten* could be entered at any place and at any line. Every phrase centrifugally points to the novel's center of death and decay. The text is dominated by the principle of metamorphosis, as everything dissolves, is unable or unwilling to maintain form, or be retained by language at any stage of its transformation. When one begins to move along the thin textual soil provided by the novel, the ground breaks open and everything begins to dissolve. Narration here results in dissolution and liquefaction instead of instantiating causality. The novel is filled with attempts at narration that blossom up only to dissolve. In this suspension, the banal and quotidian takes on a quality of the uncanny and horrific as a hotel room takes on a sinister life of its own, a car accident congeals into an outgrowth of flesh, and the dead appear on TV to participate in the popular Saturday evening game show "Wetten Dass." The novel stages these metamorphoses in the Austrian Alps, and the text centrally features the mountain vistas, rustic inns, and tourist attractions that have come to define Austria's leisure industry since the end of the Second World War. As the narrative evolves, Jelinek exposes the Austrian idyll as a deeply troubling façade—a kind of theme park simulacrum, a rotten and rotting terrain hidden behind the glossy surface of postcard sceneries, in which the mountainscape and the untranslateable "Gemütlichkeit" have been rendered a valuable commodity that attracts millions of travelers to Austria every year:

> Alle Augen richten sich immer nur auf die Bauchladen mit den bunten Ansichtskarten, kein Mensch schaut nach, ob es hinter den Menschen, die ihre Heimat verkaufen, auch wirklich so aussieht, wie es, die lügen ja wie gedruckt, hier so bunt abgebildet ist.
>
> [All eyes are always only on the vendor's trays with their colorful postcards, but nobody ever checks, if, behind these people, who sell their "home," it really looks like this—like the lies so colorfully printed here.][18]

---

[17] Jelinek, *Die Kinder*, 89.
[18] Jelinek, *Die Kinder*, 148.

The familiar images of Austrian scenery are so enticing and dominant that it becomes Jelinek's task to expose them as colorful, printed, lies. Several critics have discussed how the novel engages the specifically Austrian history of the Holocaust. As has been discussed in more detail, the novel takes issue with the peculiar absence, or at least belatedness, with which Austria has tackled the collaborative conflictions of its past.[19] While it is a wildly held belief that Germany has been confronting its past through the much-discussed notion of "Vergangenheitsbewältigung," Austria has long hidden behind the notion that the country was "Hitler's first victim," and evaded both the pressures of Allied "Denazification" and self-scrutiny by forestalling any public discourse about the Holocaust for decades. Austrian popular discourse held that the Anschluss of 1938, which annexed Austria to Germany's Third Reich, occurred under conditions of military force—an official narrative that obscured the fact that much of the Austrian population either supported or was indifferent to the incorporation of Austria into the Third Reich. The so-called Moscow Declaration, from November 1, 1943, drafted following a conference of the Secretaries of State of the Allied Forces on October 30, 1943 in Moscow, states that Austria shall be regarded as the first victim of Hitler's aggression. However, the declaration also clearly proclaims that Austria sided with Hitlter during the war and will therefore be held accountable. It further asserts that Austria is to actively participate in liberation from Hitler-Germany. The latter, unfortunately, did not happen, and after 1945, Austria merely clung to the unfortunate title of having been Hitler's first victim. The first-victim theory also shaped the Austrian government's reluctance to aid in the Allies' efforts after the war to bring Nazi leaders to trial.[20]

---

[19] Cf. Marlies Janz, "'Die Geschichte hat sich nach 45 entschlossen, noch einmal ganz von vorne zu beginnen ...' Elfriede Jelineks Destruktion des Mythos historischer 'Unschuld'," *Elfriede Jelinek—Die international Rezeption*, eds. Daniela Bartens and Paul Pechmann (Graz: Droschl, 1997), 225–38. Sabine Treude, "*Die Kinder der Toten* oder: Eine Verwicklung der Geschichten mit einer Geschichte, die fehlt," *Text+Kritik* 117 (2007): 100–9.

[20] Cf. Judith Beniston "'Hitler's First Victim?'—Memory and Representation in Post-War Austria: Introduction," *Austrian Studies* 11 (2003): 1–13. "The governments of the United Kingdom, the Soviet Union and the United States of America are agreed that Austria, the first free country to fall victim to Hitlerite aggression, shall be liberated from German domination. They regard the annexation imposed on Austria by Germany on March 15, 1938, as null and void. [...] Austria is reminded, however that she has a responsibility, which she cannot evade, for participation in the war at the side of Hitlerite Germany, and that in the final settlement account will inevitably be taken of her own contribution to her liberation." The original English and its official German translation can be found in Gerald Stourzh, *Einheit und Freiheit. Staatsvertrag, Neutralität und das Ende der Ost-West Besetzung Österreichs* (Wien: Böhlau, 1998), 607–8.

It was not until the late 1980s and 1990s, during the time when Jelinek was presumably working on *Die Kinder der Toten*, that a long-overdue public discussion of Austria's past began to take place. The discussion was generated in part by the increasing popularity and success of the right-wing Austrian Freedom Party. Public conversations and debates led to the first official acknowledgments of guilt, most notably in a speech delivered by Chancellor Franz Vranitzky to the Austrian parliament. In that speech, given in 1991, Vranitzky said:

> Wir bekennen uns zu allen Taten unserer Geschichte und zu den Taten aller Teile unseres Volkes, zu den guten wie zu den bösen. Und so wie wir die guten für uns in Anspruch nehmen, haben wir uns für die bösen zu entschuldigen, bei den Überlebenden und bei den Nachkommen der Toten.
>
> [We admit to all the deeds of our history and the deeds of our people, to the good and to the evil. As we seek to claim the good for ourselves, so too must we apologize for the evil, here among the survivors and the descendants of the dead.][21]

Vranitzky's gesture toward the "Nachkommen der Toten" echos in the title of Jelinek's novel and even more so in its many allusions to "der Kanzler" and his speech: "[. . .] in die Hände des Vaters Franz, des Bundeskanzlers, der über ein paar Millionen weiteren Toten jetzt seine berühmte gelenkige Rede hält." [[. . .] in the hands of father Franz, the Chancellor, who will now give his famous, articulated speech about a few additional million dead.][22] The novel criticizes the government's belated apologizing, commemorating, and memorializing by suggesting that such acts attempt to place "the evils" of the past too neatly in the past—where they remain safely out of sight, hidden from the eyes of what Jelinek calls "das Ausland" [from abroad] and its many tourists who come to visit every year.[23] The Austrian mountains, then, become an unruly, material manifestation of the grim history that refuses to be tamed or relegated to the past.

Jelinek's Austria is a giant necropolis, populated by zombies that are dying at one moment, rising from the dead the next, then coalescing

---

[21] Franz Vranitzky, Stenographisches Protokoll, 35. Sitzung des Nationalrats der Republik Österreich, XVIII Gesetzgebungsperiode, Montag, 8., und Dienstag, 9.7.1991, 3268–408, 3282.
[22] Jelinek, *Die Kinder*, 178.
[23] Jelinek, *Die Kinder*, 16.

with one another and with their environment.[24] Revenants appear in no fewer than twenty of her pieces, spanning thematic clusters of fascism and holocaust, terrorism, sports, and war, to depression and ennui. In a preface to the 2010 Japanese translation of *Die Kinder der Toten*, Jelinek makes explicit the link between the undead, the crimes commited during Austria's fascist period, and its reluctance to process them:

> Da ich die Untoten schon immer als eine Metapher für die österreichische Geschichte gelesen habe, eine eben gespenstische Geschichte, die, [. . .] mit diesem: 'Es muß endlich einmal schluß sein!', die nie enden, nie sterben kann [. . .] weil überall, wo man gräbt, die Knochen aus dem Boden kommen, war es für mich immer klar, daß ich [. . .] einen Gespensterroman schreiben würde. [. . .] Dieses Auftauchen der Toten, denen man ihr Leben gestohlen hat, dieses Zombiehafte des Landes, das [. . .] nie ganz da ist und nie ganz fort, so wie seine Toten eben nie ganz sterben können, solange man ihnen nicht gibt, was ihnen genommen wurde, ist willkürlich, denn Österreich hat es nicht in der Hand, seine Geschichte für tot und abgeschlossen zu erklären. Sie kommt immer wieder zurück.

> [Since I have always read the undead as a metaphor for Austrian history, for a haunting history, [. . .] with this "It has to be finally done and over with at some point!," which can never end, never die [. . .] because everywhere, where you dig, the bones come out of the ground, it was always clear to me, that I [. . .] would write a haunted novel. [. . .] This appearance of the dead, whose life was stolen, this zombielike nature of the country, which [. . .] is never fully there and never fully gone, just like its dead simply cannot fully die whilst one does not give them what was taken from them, is arbitrary, because it is not up to Austria to declare its history dead and closed. History will always return.][25]

---

24   Elfriede Jelinek herself refers to Austria as a necropolis in an interview: "Dieses Nichts, das unsere nationale Identität, diese Nekropolis [. . .]." [This nothing, that our national identy, this necropolis [. . .]] Adolf-Ernst Meyer, "Elfriede Jelinek im Gesräch mit Alfred-Ernst Meyer," *Sturm und Zwang. Schreiben als Geschlechterkampf* (Hamburg: Klein, 1995), 9–74, 49.

25   Elfriede Jelinek, "Ich als Toten-Ausgräberin," *Jelinek[jahr]buch 2012*, ed. Pia Janke (Wien: Praesens, 2012), 17–19. The undead, vampires, and zombies have been haunting Jelinek's œuvre since 1969, when vampires first appeared in *DER FREMDE! störenfried der ruhe eines sommerabends der ruhe eines friedhofs*. Cf. also Moira Mertens and Elisabeth Günther, "'Ich will kein Leben,' Elfriede Jelinek's Ästhetik des Untoten," *Jelinek[jahr]buch 2012*, ed. Pia Janke (Wien: Praesens, 2012), 104–26.

In short, Jelinek transforms the Austrian Alps into a splatter-film worthy space defined by the materiality of corpses and the horror of their reawakening. The novel's opening line prepares readers for this horror with bitter irony: "Das Land braucht oben viel Platz, damit seine seligen Geister über dem Wasser ordentlich schweben können." [The country needs much space up above, so that its blessed spirits can float neatly upon the water.] [26] "Das Land," the country of *Die Kinder der Toten*, indeed needs ample space for its many ghosts. Yet these ghosts are not the spirits of the illustrious minds like Schubert and Mozart that Jelinek goes on to name, but the victims of past persecution and genocide. Much less esoterically and much more viscerally, space is occupied not by the spirits but by the bodies of victims, supposedly "safely" buried and concealed in the Alps. The play on "Land" here, meaning both country and ground, is telling, as the nation proves to be founded—grounded—on grotesque, shifting terrain. The violent "unheard-of event" that opens the story is in fact its ending, when a landslide tears open the shallow grave of the mountainside, rupturing the fabric of a manufactured idyll and exposing the gruesome foundations of its historic underside. That the narrative's end is also, in this sense, its beginning effects the dissolution of linear historical time from the novel's outset. The "Land" is immediately transformed into an uncanny Alpine space of return that dominates the novel throughout.

The traumatic event of the Holocaust that returns as a linguistic and structural trauma throughout the novel lies outside the plot itself and thus suspends a linear progression of time that could bring the events to some kind of resolution—"die Zeit sprudelt nur so dahin in ihrem Flußbett, daß der Zukunft entgegenfließt, doch sie löscht das Menschenfeuer nicht." [time sputters along in its riverbed, which is flowing towards the future, but it can't put out the human pyre.][27] No matter how much water flows happily down the riverbed, it cannot extinguish the pyre of the Holocaust, so that the past continues to haunt the present and the future alike. The novel's three temporal orders of the past—"das Menschenfeuer"; the present—"sprudelt so dahin"; and the future—"der Zukunft entgegen" coalesce in a series of repetitions.

The novel focuses relentlessly on death and the undead so that it seems not to progress along a temporal axis but instead to describe only one single moment. Time barely proceeds, or does so in fits and starts, returning readers repeatedly to the same moments. This poses a great problem for any reader trying to establish order and coherence. As with Fredric Jameson's analysis of postmodern art, *Die Kinder der Toten* is a text of space but not of time:

---

[26] Jelinek, *Die Kinder*, 7.
[27] Jelinek, *Die Kinder*, 199.

Edgars Aufbrechen soll sich vor dem, was da in endlos dunkler Wolke auf ihn zukommt: der Zeitlosigkeit! verwahren. Was heißt das, schlimmer kann es doch nicht mehr kommen, den Edgar ist ja vielleicht schon tot. Was kann ihm da noch passieren. In einer Zipfelhaube lässt sich die Zeit nicht fangen.

[Edgar's departure should beware of what awaits him in the infinitely dark clouds: timelessness! What does it mean, it can't get any worse, because Edgar is perhaps already dead. Time can't be captured in a sleeping cap.][28]

In an image of eternal return and everlasting presence, every day is the same: "So ist für Gudrun immer alles Gegenwart [. . .] den es gibt ja keine Zukunft [. . .] und es gibt auch keinen Aufbruchsort." [Everything is always the present for Gudrun [. . .] because there is no future [. . .] and because there is no point of departure.][29] Edgar was warned not to launch into the timeless void—the launch is made literal by his occupation as a professional grass-ski tester who launches himself downhill. And Gudrun no longer has a point of departure—an *Aufbruchsort*—into her future. For travelers, *Aufbruch* is simple departure, a beginning, the starting point of a journey; in the language of miners, *Aufbruch* is a geological breaking open, a break-up, a penetration of the soil to open a new mine; in the language of hunters, *Aufbruch* is a disembowelment and refers to the internal organs of freshly slain prey. The novel seizes upon all three meanings, so that departure is also a geological rupture, out of which emerge bodies and flesh. But in spite of this *Aufbruch*, time remains static. Jelinek opens her sentence about Gudruns's relationship to time emphatically, only to complete the sentence with an ironic repartee: "Es ist jeder Tag derselbe Tag, am Abend enden still die Gedanken, nur um am nächsten Morgen wiederzukehren, unversehrt, ungeklärt, aber von Gudrun mal wieder tüchtig gequält und geschunden." [Every day is the same day, in the evening, the thoughts calmly quiet down, only to return the next morning, unexplained, unscathed, but once again well flayed and tortured by Gudrun.][30] To be precise, a twenty-four-hour day with a morning and an evening does not do justice to the temporal structure of the novel. It is in fact one single moment, decelerated to expand across 666 infernal pages. In a layering of myriad stills, the reader witnesses the final moment prior to Karin's, Edgar's, and Gudrun's suicides. He

---

[28] Jelinek, *Die Kinder*, 34.
[29] Jelinek, *Die Kinder*, 36.
[30] Jelinek, *Die Kinder*, 36.

is given a glimpse of the elongated *Augenblick* just before Gudrun opens her wrists, Karin throws herself into a water basin, and Edgar slams into a wall. Jelinek's alternative history operates outside any "normal" chronology and the mountains play a central role in establishing the novel's suspended, iterative time.

INTO THE MOUNTAINS

Not long after the opening sentence, Jelinek writes more explicitly of the mountains:

> Im Gebirge, wo die Beschaulichkeit leicht von Blitzen zerrissen werden kann, diesen vorübergehenden Schrecken, die im Grunde wenig hervorbringen, aber viel kaputtmachen, im Gebirge sind ein paar Menschen verschwunden. Dafür sind andere wiedergekommen, die wir gar nicht vermißt hatten.
>
> [In the mountains, where tranquility can be easily torn asunder by lightning, these temporary horrors that produce a little but destroy a lot, in the mountains, a couple of people have disappeared. Yet others came back in their place, those we had not missed at all.][31]

This passage introduces the mountains as a space defined by the tension of disappearance and reemergence, a landscape where the now of a leisurely tourist experience is interrupted by a past replete with repressed and unspeakable violence.

The issue of tourism here is not unimportant and Jelinek insists from the novel's opening that the mountains thwart the romantic ideas of nature and the picturesque that inspire Austrian tourism. Because the mountains contain the grim history that *Die Kinder der Toten* unearths, Alpine tourism quickly becomes a grisly affair. The charms of the alpine Pension Alpenrose have attracted various visitors, including the novels' three protagonists, to Styria in the summertime. In the prologue, a minivan carrying Karin, her mother, and other guests sets out from the pension to visit quintessential mountain sites: "das Wildalpengebiet mit seinen Seen und das Schlößchen des Erzherzogs der Habsburger" [the mountain meadows with its lakes and the small palace of the Habsburgs' archduke].[32] But the mountain itself revolts, turning the

---

[31] Jelinek, *Die Kinder*, 14.
[32] Jelinek, *Die Kinder*, 8.

tourists' bucolic nature excursion into a nightmarish scene. The twists and turns of the mountain roads cause a gruesome accident: the minivan plunges off the mountainside and its passengers are killed. Jelinek is explicit in describing how the mountain itself is in large part responsible for the accident:

> Wo früher ein festfrohes Bankett war und man stets grade noch ausweichen konnte, wenn einem ein größerer PKW entgegenkam, ist jetzt ein jäher Abbruch, eine gezackte Wunde in den Seiten der Straße. Man muß nichts, keine Lanze, hineintauchen, um zu sehen, daß die Wunde echt ist.

> [Where previously there had been a happy embankment where one could just avoid larger, oncoming traffic, now there is a sudden drop-off, a jagged wound in the side of the road. One must do nothing, insert no lance, to see that the wound is real.]³³

In the German, the "happy embankment" or curb—"festfrohes Bankett"—also evokes a joyous banquet, introducing the sinister images of eating and ingestion that Jelinek plays out extensively later in the scene. In place of the curb, the mountain now bears a wound, a gash that forces the travelers off the road to their deaths. The mountain—Jelinek's figure for repressed and returning history—is itself figured frequently as a wound. For instance, when Karin accompanies her mother on a hike through the mountains, she comes across a spot whose center is the black eye of a dark, inscrutable water basin. The characters often come upon gory chasms in the rock and Jelinek goes to great lengths to depict the mountain as an organic, throbbing thing—a wound that refuses to heal. Here, for instance, much later in the novel, Gudrun and Edgar happen upon an "alten Graben," "an old ravine," that Jelinek describes in vivid detail:

> Die Steine, die sich vorhin noch dicht zusammenzuschieben schienen, kaum einen Saumpfad freigeben, weichen plötzlich auseinander. Sie haben einen feuchten Belag, erscheinen viel dunkler als die helle, mit Mettalladern durchzogene Wundwand, die dringend ein Pflaster bräuchte (sie wird es schon noch kriegen!), sie wurde ja ohne Rücksicht auf dessen tektonische Verwerfungen aus dem Gebirge einfach herausgesprengt. Wunden im Fels, ein steinernes Gemetzel.

---

³³ Jelinek, *Die Kinder*, 10.

[The rocks, which earlier seemed to push against each other so tightly that there was hardly room left for a narrow track through, are suddenly parting. They are covered with a moist film and seem much darker than the bright, wound-wall striated with metallic veins that they expose, the wound that urgently needs a bandage (it will still get one!), the wound that simply exploded out of the mountain without regard for tectonic warpage. Wounds in the rock, a stony carnage.]³⁴

Here, the mountain that earlier has concealed history is torn open, freshly bleeding, awaiting a dressing that Jelinek gestures toward but refuses to provide. The mountain assumes a strange form of agency—stones push, pull, and erupt without regard for geological norms; the earth becomes an animate, birthing organ and just as it gives way to new, bright shapes, the mountain collapses back into "stony carnage." This passage is revealing, because it shows how Jelinek insists upon the presence of history throughout the novel. Although it gives us an explanation of how the mountain has come to be this living, wounded thing, it also suspends us between that past, the present in which the characters encounter it, and the strange future tense in which the wounded mountain will perhaps one day be bandaged. Vacillating between verb tenses, we can never be sure which events have concluded and which continue. The poetic, verbless phrases, such the one that ends this passage, "Wunden im Fels, ein steinernes Gemetzel," work like eerie still-life paintings. Readers face the wounded rocks, the stony carnage, in a time that is out of joint.

Jelinek keeps history from becoming a closed, distant past by shifting tenses and writing about the past most often in the present tense. She also turns to the mountains themselves to embody this temporal blurring. Although we think of mountains as immovable forms shaped by slow geological time, in *Die Kinder der Toten* the layers of earth seem to be the products of ancient history, the more recent past, and the present. The Pension Alpenrose is perched on a mountain that turns out to be made of wounded stones, human remains, and masses of human hair. But even this debris, which clearly evokes Austria's Holocaust victims, is difficult to locate in time. Of the dead that begin to emerge from the mountains, Jelinek writes:

Sie sind so gründlich verschwunden, als wären ihre Hinterlassenschaften Fossilien in Stein, Urwesen, deren Bewegungen vor Jahrtausenden verwischt worden sind, und nur

---

³⁴ Jelinek, *Die Kinder*, 442.

mehr die Knochen, diese vernünftigen himmlischen Seelen, füllen noch den pneumatischen Markt mit nichts als Luft. Die aus einem Mund kommt und höchstens dünne Streifen Papier bewegt. Sogar die Negative dieser Wesen sind vernichtet, und die Negative ihrer Namen im Tausendgründe-Buch (warum wir ständig und daher nie an sie denken) dazu.

[They disappeared so thoroughly, as if their residues were stone fossils, ur-beings whose movements were obliterated thousands of years ago, and now they are just bones, those reasonable heavenly souls, and fill the pneumatic market with nothing but air. Air that comes from a mouth and moves, at most, only thin strips of paper. Even the negatives of these beings were destroyed, as are the negatives of their names in the book of one thousand reasons (this is why we think of them constantly and also never think of them).][35]

While certainly, as other critics have remarked, this scene resurrects the disappeared Holocaust dead so that Jelinek's readers must, as the passage concludes, think of them, I am interested in the way that the Alpine space establishes new relations of time through the bodies, objects, and words with which the mountain is riddled. Here, the past is expunged so fully from Austrian consciousness that it seems entirely lost—the dead are so "thoroughly disappeared" that not even "the negatives of their names" remain available to us. Jelinek addresses the disappearance of the dead in her customary laconic fashion and asks to see their graves: "[. . .] bitte wo sind diese Gräber? Wir wollen sie besichtigen!" ["[. . .] where are these graves now? We want to visit them!][36] Because of their complete extermination, the dead are not even capable of materializing as revenants or undead like the three protagonists Edgar Gstranz, Karin Frenzel, and Gurdun Bichler. And yet, the mountains cough up residue that resembles fossils, so that the past of genocide seems both pre-historic—Jelinek describes the remnants as the bones of "ur-beings"—*and* utterly present. She reverts to the present tense and incorporates us readers in her second-person address. The bones lend the text an archaeological weight before they are transformed into air. In the course of the sentence, the air turns to paper, and the paper into a mysterious book that we simultaneously read and ignore. Through the movement of the passage, from solid bones to immaterial souls to printed matter, Jelinek suggests that the

---

[35] Jelinek, *Die Kinder*, 163.
[36] Jelinek, *Die Kinder*, 451.

novel—her novel—can record both the total disappearance of Austria's victims *and* the persistence of that loss. The "Tausendgründe-Buch" alludes to the thousands of hidden, neglected stories that make up the mountainous ground—*den Grund*—of contemporary Austria.

METAMORPHOSES—DIE MURIE. DIE FURIE

Other stories also inform Jelinek's novel, in particular those that tell of transformations and material changes. As in Hoffmann's *Bergwerke von Falun*, it is once more the aspect of unstable, transforming matter that connects the depiction of mountains to the malleable human body. Ovid's *Metamorphosis*, the *locus classicus* for the concept of *fingere* and its derivations, is a clear reference for Jelinek's novel. The classical text displays poetically the various meaning of *fingere* and *fictio*. Ovid's text commences with all the bodies changed into new forms—"In nova fert animus mutatas dicere formas corpora"—and tells how the world was created out of chaos.[37] To populate this world, Prometheus, the son of Titans, completes the creation by mixing the seeds of the Gods with clear fresh water to bring about man. The waters in Jelinek, however, are no longer clear. In fact, the liquids are highly viscous, muddied waters— "dunkle Flüssigkeit" [dark liquids], "blutiger Schaum" [bloody foam], "Biomasse" [biomass]—that turn into massive landslides: "Und das Wasser der Massen verbindet sich mit den Wassermassen zu einem einzigen Lebensborn-Brei, der schäumend in die Täler rast und alles mit sich reißt, was sich ihm in den Weg stellt." [And the water of the masses joins the masses of water to form one "spring-of-life" mush that rushes churning into the valley and sweeps everything with it that crosses its path.][38] In the gory image of a *Lebensborn-Brei* avalanche, destroying everything in its path, Jelinek yokes together processes of destruction and creation, of destruction and remembrance.

Jelinek's project of destruction and remembrance resonates with how in 1726 Thomas Burnet describes the origins of the mountains. Burnet claims that prior to the biblical deluge, the earth was entirely smooth:

> The Face of the Earth before the Deluge was smooth, regular, and uniform; without Mountains, and without a Sea. [. . .] if you travel it all over, you will not meet a Mountain or a Rock, yet well provided of all requisite things for an habitable World; [. . .] it had

---

[37] Ovid, *Metamorphoses*, lib. I: 1–2.
[38] Jelinek, *Die Kinder*, 403, 434, 379.

the Beauty of Youth and blooming Nature, fresh and fruitful, and not a Wrinkle, Scar or Fracture in all its Body; no Rocks nor Mountains, no hollow Caves, nor gaping Channels, but even and uniform all over.[39]

After the deluge, the mountains come into being as the "Ruins of a broken World," and Burnet asks, "What can have more the Figure and Mien of a Ruin, than Crags, and Rocks, and Cliffs?" He offers a portrait of the mountains as formations that are created by a sacred form of "creative destruction." Jelinek draws upon *The Metamorphoses* in her treatment of the changing states of the human body and the way that these changes reflect and refract their surrounding environment. In Ovid's work, the Gods destroy the earth and obliterate the entire human population, leaving only one man and one woman alive. New humans emerge from rock that turns to flesh. In Jelinek's novel, rock also turns to flesh, but the mountains give birth to corpses and the undead, rather than new beings. The dead emerge from the Alps not to generate a new race but to annihilate the old one. Where Ovid's metamorphoses stage a genesis of new orders and new beings, Jelinek rather offers an apocalyptical story: if there is to be a new order, it can come about only through the thorough destruction of the existing world. This destruction must paradoxically entail previously neglected acts of remembrance.[40] Ovid here serves as a literary historical gesture to such remembrance—Jelinek draws upon *The Metamorphoses* only to invert the text and depart from its conventions.

Chaos and order, fecundity and death remain in close contact throughout *Die Kinder der Toten*, and various acts of procreation and recreation are rehearsed over and over without result.[41] Unlike its

---

[39] Burnet, *The Sacred Theory*, 82.
[40] Burnet, *The Sacred Theory*, 90, 43.
[41] Juliane Vogel also reads the metaphor or birth and birthing as central to Jelinek's novel: "Die prototypischen Falten in *Die Kinder der Toten* sind Geburtsfalten, aus denen heraus das 'vielfältige[] Geschlecht[]' (230) neue 'Wesenheiten' (164, 165) gebiert. [...] Jelineks Boden besitzt damit nicht zwei Geschlechter, sondern nur eins, sofern es sich wie in den Geschlechterlehren der Antike und bis in die Neuzeit durch Ein und Ausstülpung, Erregung und Erschlaffung, d.h. einmal männlich—als zeugendes und/oder geborenes—und einmal weiblich—als gebärendes—verhält." [The prototypical folds in *Die Kinder der Toten* are birth folds out of which the "manifold[] sex []" (230) gives birth to new "entities" (164, 165). [...] Jelinek's ground therefore possess not two genders, but one, insofar as it acts, as is written in the gender theories from antiquity to modern-times, through invagination and protrusion, arousal and flaccidity, as at times male—procreative and/or born—and as at times female—as giving birth.] Vogel, "Keine Leere der Unterbrechung," 19–20.

Ovidian intertext, Jelinek's novel begins with attempts at creation and ends in destruction. Jelinek's deluge of liquefied rock and human remains at the end of the novel echoes book one of *The Metamorphoses*, in which Jupiter floods the earth to punish the outrageous humans, after Lycaon's iniquity has provided incontrovertible proof of man's wickedness. After the brief but devastating flood, which ends as suddenly as it begins, only Deucalion and Pyrrha survive. The two consult the oracle of the Goddess Themis and are told to descend from the temple and cast the bones of the great mother: "'discedite temple / et velate caput cinctasque resolvite vestes / ossaque post tergum magnae iactate parentis!" [Depart hence, and with veiled heads and loosened robes throw behind you as you go the bones of your great mother.][42] Afraid of committing sacrilege by taking the pronouncement of the oracle literally and disturbing their ancestors' peace, Deucalion and Pyrrha first hesitate and Pyrrha begs the oracle for clemency. It is not until Deucalion realizes that the oracle is to be understood metaphorically that they can begin creation amidst chaos: "'aut fallax ait' est sollertia nobis, / aut [. . .] / magna parens tera est: lapis in corpora terrae / ossa reor dici; iacere hos post terga iubemur." [Either my wit is at fault, or else [. . .] our great mother is the earth, and I think that the bones which the goddess speaks of are the stones in the earth's body. 'Tis these that we are bidden to throw behind us.][43] The bones that they are meant to cast are in fact stones. As is the case in Jelinek's *Die Kinder der Toten*, the rocks thrown by Deucalion and Pyrrha become malleable. However, in Ovid they assume a sweet, soft form before slowly turning into human shapes. The outcome of the oracle's mandate and this process is initially unclear:

> saxa [. . .] / ponere duritiem coepere suumque rigorem / mollirique ora mollitaque ducere formam. / mox ubi creverunt naturaque mitior illis / contigit, ut quaedam, sic non manifesta videri / forma potest hominis [. . .]

> [And the stones [. . .] began at once to lose their hardness and stiffness, to grow soft slowly, and softened take on form. Then, when they had grown in size and become milder in their nature, a certain likeness to the human form, indeed, could be seen, still not very clear [. . .].][44]

---

[42] Ovid, *Metamorphoses*, lib. I: 381–3.
[43] Ovid, *Metamorphoses*, lib. I: 391–4.
[44] Ovid, *Metamorphoses*, lib. I: 400–5.

In Jelinek the earth also softens and the mountains—stone—turn into flesh. But in the novel, this is not a genesis so much as a resurrection of those already and still dead. The bones have not been willingly cast into space but buried, repressed, and forgotten. The bones and human remains in *Die Kinder der Toten* are suspended in a liminal state—they do not that reassemble into fully living beings nor do they lie inert in their mountainous graves.

Ovid emphasizes more a transition and flow than the realization of anthropomorphic form.[45] Despite the toughness of the human character that stems from his rocky origins—"inde genus durum sumus experiencesque laborum / et documenta damus qua simus origine nati" [Hence come the hardness of our race and our endurance of toil; and we give proof to what origin we are sprung]—the supple nature of softening rock is of greater importance in the formation of a human being.[46] Moreover, heterosexual reproduction is also still central to the metamorphosis from rock to man in Ovid's work. The stones cast by Pyrrha become female, while those thrown by Deucalion are male: "missa viri minibus faciem traxere viorum / et de femineo reparta est femina iactu." [the stones thrown by man's hand took on the form of men, and the women were made from the stones the women threw.][47] So, although it is formed from stones and rocks, what springs forth nonetheless becomes human through the intervention of gendered beings. Only through active, human aid can the stones become bones, the geological veins vital, human ones: "quae tamen ex illis aliquot pars umda suco / et terrena fuit, versa est in corporis usum; / quod solidum est flectique nequit, mutatur in ossa, / quae modo vena fuit, sub eodem nomine mansit [. . .]." [That part of them, however, which was earthy and damp with slight moisture, was changed to flesh; but what was solid and incapable of bending became bone; that which was but now veins remained under the same name.][48] When the oracle tells Pyrrha and Deucalion to cast the bones of the great mother, they are ordered to "induce labor" and to help repopulate the ancient world. For Jelinek, there is no such generative reproduction, and coupling only returns readers to the sole kind of birth possible in the novel—that of the earth disgorging its victims:

> Der Leib dieses jungen Mannes könnte zwar gestorben sein [. . .] doch der Strahl seiner Kraft ist wieder über ihn gekommen, so

---

[45] Leonard Barkan, *The Gods made Flesh* (New Haven, CT: Yale University Press, 1986), 32.
[46] Ovid, *Metamorphoses*, lib. I: 414–15.
[47] Ovid, *Metamorphoses*, lib. I: 411–12.
[48] Ovid, *Metamorphoses*, lib. I: 407–10.

sieht es aus, und er schickt seinen gut durchfleischten, etwas holzigen Stengel in Gudruns Mund hinein [. . .] Es ist das weiche Fleisch, bäh, Tiefgefrorenes! Fertiggekauftes! [. . .] Der schwärzliche, nicht sehr saubere Tote ist zwischen seinen Schenkeln unmäßig angeschwollen, weil sein Fleisch nicht mehr so recht zusammenhält [. . .] Der Getötete hat seine Seele abgelegt, ablegen müssen, dafür erhält diese Frau jetzt ihren Bräutigam. [. . .] Keine Grenze zwischen Ja zum Tod und Nein zum Tod. [. . .].

[The body of this young man could have been dead [. . .] but it looks like the beam of his force came over him again, and he is sending his well-fleshed, somewhat woody stalk into Gudrun's mouth [. . .] it is the soft flesh, eww, deep-frozen! ready-bought! [. . .] The blackish, not very clean corpse is swollen excessively between his thighs, because his flesh will no longer really stick together [. . .] The murdered discarded his soul, had to discard it, in return this woman now receives her groom. [. . .] There is no boundary between a Yes to death and a No to death.][49]

At the end of the novel, the ground revolts. The long process of disinterment, of unearthing the history within the mountains, cannot be stopped and culminates in a massive avalanche. The mountain collapses, and "Die Mure. Die Furie"—the mudslide, the fury—Jelinek tells us, descends upon the Pension Alpenrose and all of its inhabitants. "Die Mure"—an avalanche, a mudslide, a natural disaster—is deified and elevated through contiguity and assonance to the status of chtonic deities, half-human, half-inhuman monsters. Also invoking Hegel's "*Furie* des Verschwindens" [*fury* of disappearance], Jelinek indicates that the disappearance of the dead and the persistence of their loss can only be preserved in a negative gesture.[50] Mixed in with the mud and debris of the avalanche descending upon the bucolic guesthouse, however, is human hair: "Haar. Menschliches Haar. Es wird ausgegraben. [. . .] Nur: Es ist einfach zuviel Haar da für die geschätzte Anzahl der Verschütteten." [Hair. Human hair. It is being dug up [. . .]. However: There is simply too much hair for the estimated number of

---

[49] Jelinek, *Die Kinder*, 175–9.
[50] "Kein positives Werk noch Tat kann also die allgemeine Freiheit hervorbringen; es bleibt ihr nur das *negative Tun*; sie ist nur die *Furie* des Verschwindens." [Universal freedom, therefore, can bring forth neither a positive work nor a deed; there is left for it only *negative action*; it is merely the *fury* of disappearance.] Georg Willhelm Friedrich Hegel, *Phänomenologie des Geistes*, *Werke*, eds. Eva Moldenhauer and Karl Markus Michel, vol. 3 (Frankfurt/Main: Suhrkamp, 1986), 435–6; emphasis original.

Elfriede Jelinek's *Die Kinder der Toten* 159

victims.]⁵¹ It is tempting to read this conclusion as either the forgotten dead taking their long-awaited vengeance or as the inevitable descent of utter chaos. But a closer look at this ending reveals that Jelinek's focus on the mountains suggests something more complex. The concluding chapter in which the mudslide obliterates the Pension Alpenrose begins with this paragraph:

> Es sind im Gebirge ungeheure Materialströme vorhanden, welche nur der ordnenden Hand eines Helfers, der, leidenschaftlos, sich niemals von Vorliebe oder Abneigungen leiten ließe, bedürfen, um ihr Geröll, Geschiebe, Erdreich und ihren Schlamm loszulassen, diese Leckerein, die das Gebirg eigentlich ganz allein essen wollte. Es hat uns nichts davon abgeben wollen. Doch jetzt überreicht uns die Bergwelt mit einer leichten Verbeugung sich selbst sowie die ganze Umgebung dazu. So hat der Urlauber es sich nicht vorgestellt. Daß er, lüstern, begeistert, einem Verhältnis zur Natur auf der Spur, nicht sie, diese Umgebung, betrachtet, sondern daß vielmehr sie auf ihn fliegt!

> [In the mountains, there are immense streams of flowing material, which require only the ordering hand of a helper, who, without passion, never influenced by preference or animus, can release the mountains' gravel, their soil, their mud, their rubble, these tasty morsels which the mountains would have wanted to eat all by themselves. The mountains did not want to share any of it with us. But now, the mountains, with a curtsy, are offering themselves and their surroundings to us. The tourist imagined it otherwise. He did not imagine that he, ardently lustful, longing to discover his relationship to nature, would himself be pursued. Nature, this environment—she launches herself onto him, instead of allowing him to observe her from a distance.]⁵²

In the mountains, as we have seen, there are streams of material—dynamic, animate flows that contain the remnants of the past. And here, they are set loose, turned into a furious mudslide, by the "ordnenden Hand eines Helfers," the ordering hand of a helper, who puts the mud and rocks in motion with a disinterested gesture. With this phrasing, Jelinek indicates that the avalanche brings "order" by initiating or restoring material chaos. The mountain, she suggests, is neither static nor inanimate. The mountains, as figures of history,

---

51   Jelinek, *Die Kinder*, 665.
52   Jelinek, *Die Kinder*, 653.

conceal their secrets and then, willingly share them, once provoked by the ordering hand, which we may think of here as Jelinek's. But, as the passage goes on to illustrate, the dimensions of the past may become quickly overwhelming. Those who wish to observe from a distance quickly have that distance destroyed. Austrian history, Jelinek tells us, cannot be viewed from a safe, disinterested vantage point. The mountains resist the kind of perspective or reading that would keep them at a distance, that would render them sublime. In complete opposition to the Kantian observer who views something beautiful in a disinterested manner or views the sublime mountains from a distance, the characters and the whole of the novel are subsumed by the sliding mountains. Once seen for what they are—repositories of a violent, unacknowledged past—the mountains rupture and overpower everything in their path.

The only process of sublimation at work in *Die Kinder der Toten* is one of reversal and return, reflected in the changes in states of aggregation: all that is solid does not melt into air, but rather liquefies, as the mountains turns to mud and mortified flesh decays. Jelinek's narrative is a narrative of perpetual change, of vicissitude and alteration. However, Jelinek does not use clear, analytical language that can be readily translated into precise political messages. It is not her primary aim to illustrate how Germans and Austrians carelessly dealt with their past but instead to demonstrate how such a critique may be embedded in a new poetics that emphasizes remembrance over political practice. Jelinek wrestles with the way that literary images and language may be used to depict the burdens of the past even when a benevolent use or redress of that past is impossible. Her prose attempts to document the return of a painfully unusable, unloveable history: "Auf einmal, völlig zwecklos, ist die Vergangenheit wieder da, unmöglich sie zu lieben." [All at once and entirely useless, the past is back, and impossible to be loved.]⁵³

The avalanche at the novel's conclusion returns us to its opening. It turns out that the avalanche happens because the bus accident in the prologue has "disturbed" the bedrock of a mountain stream. The contingency of the accident instigates a moment in which present and past concur. The accident in the mountains is the entry point for the crimes of the past to appear in the conscience of the present.

Die Sprengungen damals in Mauthausen haben unseren gigantischen Berghang ein für allemal ins Rutschen gebracht; es sind zu unterlassen [. . .] die Beseitigung der Vegetationsdecke

---

⁵³ Jelinek, *Die Kinder*, 5.

und eben jegliche Sprengarbeiten: Tschinn. Bumms. Krach. Jörg. Tragende Grundpfeiler bums. Tschinda. Rassa. Die tragenden Grundpfeiler unseres Wiederaufbaus, der ein Neubau ist, befinden sich im ganzen Oberkrain, und unsere Aufgabe ist ritsch! Ratsch! Umrissen.

[Those explosions, back then, in Mauthausen caused our gigantic mountain slope to slide off once and for all; one should refrain from [. . .] any removal of vegetation cover and precisely these blasting operations: Bang. Boom. Crash. Jörg. Load-bearing foundation pillars thunk. Boom. Boom. Cchhh. The load-bearing pillars of our reconstruction, which is a new construction, are located in the entire Oberkrain, and our task is rip! Rap! Outlined and torn down.]⁵⁴

Over fifty years ago, the blasts in the brutal quarries of Mauthausen shook the mountains and began to set the avalanche in motion. In 1995, the accident unleashed the avalanche fully. The foundational pillars on which the Second Republic is to be built, however, have by then already been unsettled and knocked over. Here at the novel's end, Jelinek evokes the novel's own history. The mountains, within the temporality of the novel, are therefore both a constant—a site to which readers return—*and* the site of chaos, of change. History then, as embodied by the mountains, is neither cyclical nor teleological. It cannot be said to be a neat circle nor a straight line that progresses from the past toward the future. The history of *Die Kinder der Toten* located "im Gebirge," in Jelinek's mountains, comes into view only to dissolve.

---

[54] Jelinek, *Die Kinder*, 564.

Coda—Mountains Immaterial

Our journey has taken us from Kant's sublime peaks to Jelinek's abject avalanches, and it might appear that the trajectory of the book leads readers to an endpoint of dissolution and total negation. But recent years have seen the persistence of mountains in German-language literature—not only as sites of terror or destruction, but as sites of intrigue and wonder. The mountain remains a powerful trope and continues to speak to the intimate relationship between familiar subject matter and innovative technique. Like the authors discussed in the preceding chapters, contemporary Austrian, Swiss, and German writers continue turning to the mountains in order to evoke a national literary history and to revise it. But rather than focus on the materiality of the mountains, as did Simmel in his treatment of "Massenmoment," Hoffmann with his stony miner, or Celan in his text of folded forms, contemporary authors depict elusive mountains that evoke something of the present moment's immateriality. Mountains become emblems of the current longing for substance and contact in a world that seems increasingly mediated and immaterial. While the previous chapters have focused on representations of mountains that express history and its overturning, contemporary texts convey a longing for tangible experience as well as the impossibility of satisfying such desires.

Mountains feature prominently in recent texts by Austrian writers Christoph Ransmayr and Thomas Glavinic, and by Swiss author Christian Kracht.[1] In their novels, the writers turn to the mountains in order to explore assumptions about external reality and about narrative norms. In Ransmayr's *Der fliegende Berg* from 2006, a 350-page epic poem, for instance, two Irish brothers attempt to scale the heights of Phur-Ri, a Tibetan mountain that is said to occasionally vanish by flying upward before returning again to earth. In Glavinic's 2013 fairytale-like coming-of-age novel *Das größere Wunder*, alternating chapters narrate the story of a young man's development and his dangerous expedition on Mount Everest. The novel leaves us wondering whether its protagonist Jonas has reached the summit and, as a corollary, whether he has in fact come of age. In the novel, Mount Everest is a bizarre place of existential sub-zero temperatures, where eyeballs burst in the extreme cold, and a curious euphoria runs rampant. It smells of sweaty feet and one must drink tea all the time so as not to go mad. The ascent of Mount Everest provides the frame through which we learn what lead Jonas, the protagonist, to climb the mountain in the first place. In cutbacks, we

---

[1] Christoph Ransmayr, *Der Fliegende Berg* (Frankfurt/Main: Fischer, 2006); Thomas Glavinic, *Das größere Wunder* (München: Carl Hanser, 2013); Christian Kracht, *Ich werde hier sein im Sonnenschein und im Schatten* (Köln: Kiepenheuer & Witsch, 2008).

encounter Jonas as a Wunderkind, a highly gifted boy, who writes postcards to himself and grows up with his mentally disabled brother in the care of a man named Picco. Picco, a kind of Mafioso and infinitely wealthy, not only provides shelter and education for the two boys, but also gives Jonas the motto for his life, which can also serve as the narrative program of the novel: "Antworten werden überschätzt." ["Answers are overrated."][2] Here is a look at the novel's final scene:

> "Jonas? Seid ihr da drin?"
> Er schaute aus dem Zelt. Hadan hielt ihm eine Kanne Tee hin.
> Jonas bedankte sich und stellte sie vor sich auf einem flachen Stein ab.
> "Eine Frage muss ich dir noch stellen," sagte Hadan. "Nicht dass das jetzt noch eine Rolle spielte, aber warst du eigentlich auf dem Gipfel?"
> Jonas warf Marie einen Blick zu. Sie lächelte und wandte das Gesicht ab. Er holte tief Luft und schloss die Augen.
> "Nein," sagte er.
>
> ["Jonas? Are you in there?"
> He looked out from the tent. Hadan gave him a pot of tea. Jonas thanked him and set it down on a flat rock.
> "I have to ask you one last question," Hadan said. "Not that it really matters now, but did you actually make it to the summit?"
> Jonas looked at Marie. She smiled and turned her head. He took a deep breath and closed his eyes. "No," he said.][3]

In this final passage, Jonas undoes, in a sense, the 500 pages that have come before. If he has not made it to the summit, what then are readers to make of the preceding chapters in which his successful expedition is described? The "no" with which Glavinic leaves his readers might be just the answer of an exhausted climber whose recollection of the summit is blurred by the physical conditions he faced at the summit. Glavinic describes the dizzy, fluctuating mind of Jonas as he trudges through vertiginous, oxygen-scarce heights. Or perhaps the reply is a figurative rejection—Jonas succeeded in climbing Everest, but the physical feat failed to meet the mythical dimensions that summiting should have. Or perhaps Jonas' answer indicates only that the expedition was a failure insofar as it did not bring with it the personal transformation that he expected. In any case, the reader is left in a state

---

[2] Glavinic, *Wunder*, 36.
[3] Glavinic, *Wunder*, 523.

of suspension—a state of confusion in which he must contend with the undoing of the very goal that the novel has driven toward from its opening. We, as readers, must concede that the mountain—imposing, intriguing, physically and formally dominating throughout the novel—is the matter that somehow, as the mountain guide says, "doesn't matter."

Christian Kracht's novel, *Ich werde hier sein im Sonnenschein und im Schatten* from 2008, takes readers deep into the Swiss mountains, which are, in Kracht's dystopian future, the fortress of the Soviet Republic of Switzerland. Lenin had never left Switzerland, and the Swiss army retreats into the mountain fortress as a Third World War with Germany rages outside and threatens to destroy the entire planet. Deep inside the Réduit lives the painter Nicolas Roerich:

> Später, später. Unser Freund Roerich ist Kunsthandwerker, wissen Sie, er hilft dabei, das Réduit zu entbergen. Das, was die Griechen Techne nennen, also das Hervorbringen, schafft nur das Kunstwerk. In ihr, in Roerichs Gemälden, geschieht auf diese Art und Weise Wahrheit; die griechische Aletheia, das koreanische Wu, das hinduistische Samadhi. Hierin verstehen wir das Hervorbringen von Nichtanwesendem ins Anwesende. Also das Experiment und die Erkenntnis, genauso wie die Bearbeitung der Natur, die Erzeugung von Produkten, das Aufstellen von Theorien, das Sammeln neuer Einfälle und Ideen.
>
> [Later. Later. Our friend Roerich is an artist, you know, he is helping to uncover the réduit. That, what the Greeks call techne, that is, the bringing forth, can only be accomplished by a work of art. In it, in Roerich's painting, truth comes about in this way; the Greek aletheia, the Korean wu, the Hinu samadhi. Herein, we understand the bringing forth of the non-present in the present. That is, the experiment and the recognition, just as the processing of nature, the making of products, the advancing of theories, the collecting of new thoughts and ideas.][4]

"Roerich hilft das Réduit zu entbergen"—literally, the artist helps to remove, to take away the mountains—*ent- bergen*—as the German prefix *ent-* suggests. *Entbergen* also means to uncover or to reveal, very much in the sense of how Heidegger used the term in relation to *aletheia*, the coming forth of truth. *Aletheia*, the revelation of truth in a world of

---

[4] Kracht, *Sonnenschein und Schatten*, 118–19.

relations, happens in a *Lichtung*, a clearing or place of light.[5] All these engagements with mountains then remain at once contingent upon and questioning of media's capacities to "reveal"—just as the subtitle of George Soulier's first photo of the summit of Mont Blanc suggestively probed: "What is it that reveals itself to our gaze?"[6]

In these recent texts, the mountains offer heights that characters long to reach—summits that motivate journeys and structure narratives. But the authors make the mountains unconquerable. They remain beyond reach and perspective. Readers are left to track vanishing peaks, question the outcome of an expedition, or enter the mountains as a counterfactual space in which real and alternate history collide. While Jelinek uses her shifting prose and wordplay to depict the mountain as a material record of a violent history that is both immediate and elusive, the contemporary authors whose work I have just briefly described make the mountains themselves elusive. The mountains in these books change hands, escape memory, and even vanish. They seem therefore suited to the current moment in which readers understand that history cannot be dismissed but also confront a world that seems increasingly immaterial and transient. These recent texts illustrate how existing literary genres and forms can be adapted, expanded, and revised in order to tell new stories about mountains in the twenty-first century.

The mountains, then, allow us to trace an arc through German-language literature. This arc tells us about changes in perspective, form, and notions of subject and object from the nineteenth century into the twenty-first. And moreover, the mountains point us to the past—to literary and material histories that cannot be overlooked or concealed. But they also lead us into the present, into an uncertain time ahead in which these histories may take on new meanings and forms; or in which they might dissolve altogether.

These new novels set in the mountains tell stories of expedition and adventure—but they narrate impossible quests whose goals cannot be reached. Moreover, these novels deploy the mountains in narratives that are less decidedly national in focus and instead take place against

---

[5] Martin Heidegger, "Die Frage nach der Technik," *Vorträge und Aufsätze* (Stuttgart: Clett-Kotta, 2004), 9–41. For an interesting application of the Heideggerian concepts and etymologies of "Berg," "bergen," "entbergen," and "verbergen" in the interpretation of Ludwig Tieck's 1802 *Der Runenberg*, see Peter Arnds, "From Eros to Thanatos: Hiking and Spelunking in Ludwig Tieck's *Der Runenberg*," *Heights of Reflection: Mountains in the German Imagination from the Middle Ages to the Twenty-First Century*, eds. Sean Ireton and Caroline Schaumann (Rochester: Camden House, 2012), 176–92.

[6] Felsch, "Mountains of Sublimity," 352.

an expanding, more global horizon. This current trend in contemporary fiction can perhaps be summed up as follows:

> It is possible to identify, I think, something like a world community of writers, an emerging canon of international literary fiction. [...] Where the story of the novel has tended in the past to be told in terms of discrete national traditions, it is increasingly the case [...] that the novel comes into being in an international, cosmopolitan space, which exceeds the boundaries of any single cultural domain.[7]

The mountains then become a kind of newly wrought terrain, one which is ideal for investigating the tensions between "German," "Austrian," or "Swiss" literature and "contemporary" literature as it is being written and read on a global stage. The mountains are no longer a trope through which authors confront and rewrite aesthetic traditions or history based solely on national identity, but are sites through which that history and identity are cast into dialogue, and into question, with the world. Mountains seem therefore suited to the current moment in which readers understand that history cannot be dismissed but also confront a world that seems increasingly immaterial and transient. In short, these contemporary novels demonstrate that mountains, far from being stable, static masses, are shifting entities. Literary genres and forms are likewise shifting, ready to be adapted in order to tell new stories about mountains in the twenty-first century. Georg Simmel's claim about the trouble of representing mountains remains vexing to contemporary artists, and this problem is more than simply an impasse. As Hartmut Böhme suggests, the mountains, unattainable and recalcitrant, retreat productively into the realm of literature and the imagination:

> Das archaisch Unverfügbare der Berge hat sich ins Imaginäre, in Metaphern und bildnerische Vergegenwärtigung zurückgezogen und begleitet den Prozeß der technischen Verfügbarmachung des Montanen als eine Reflexionsebene, die die unumkehrbare Säkularisierung der Berge mit ästhetischer Achtung und zunehmend auch ökologisch mit Schonung einer Naturzone verbindet, vor der sich die Menschen jahrtausendlang zu schützen hatten, während die Berge nun ihrerseits vor den Menschen geschützt werden.

---

[7] Peter Boxall, *Twenty-First Century Fiction: A Critical Introduction* (New York: Cambridge University Press, 2013), 6–7.

[The archaic unobtainability of the mountains has retreated into the imaginary, into metaphors and pictorial visualizations. They accompany the process of making technically available the mountainous as a reflective plane, which links the irrevocable secularization of the mountains to aesthetic attention and increasingly also in an ecological sense to the protection of a natural habitat. For thousands of years humanity had to keep itself safe from the mountains, whereas now the mountains are protected from humans.][8]

It remains questionable whether the mountains, as Böhme suggests, actually become a protected sanctuary or if they remain the realm of the dangerous and the extreme, where economic and ecological catastrophes indicate that the domestication of the mountains is at best human hubris and an illusion of domination. In sum, the mountains—transforming and transformative—prove to be fertile ground for writers whose poetic innovations break literary terrain and leave it shifting, thrillingly, beneath their readers' feet.

---

[8] Böhme, "Berg," 59.

Bibliography

Adelung, Johann Christoph. "Verrückung." In *Grammatisch-kritisches Wörterbuch der Hochdeutschen Mundart*. Volume 4. Wien: Bauer, 1808, 1111.
Agamben, Giorgio. "§7 Privation is Like a Face." In *The Man Without Content*. Translated by Georgia Albert. Stanford, CA: Stanford University Press, 1999, 59–67.
Agamben, Giorgio. "§8 Poiesis and Praxis." In *The Man Without Content*. Translated by Georgia Albert. Stanford, CA: Stanford University Press, 1999, 68–94.
Alberti, Leon Battista. *On Painting: A New Translation and Critical Edition*. Translated by Rocco Sinsigalli. Cambridge: Cambridge University Press, 2011.
Alewyn, Richard. "Ein Wort über Eichendorf." In *Eichendorf heute: Stimmen der Forschung mit einer Bibliographie*. Edited by Paul Stöcklein. Darmstadt: Wissenschaftliche Buchgesellschaft, 1966.
Aristotle. "Physics." Translated by R. P. Hardie and R. K. Gaye. In *The Complete Works of Aristotle. The Revised Oxford Translation*. Edited by Jonathan Barnes. Volume 1. Princeton, NJ: Princeton University Press, 1995, 315–446.
Arnds, Peter. "From Eros to Thanatos: Hiking and Spelunking in Ludwig Tieck's *Der Runenberg*." In *Heights of Reflection: Mountains in the German Imagination from the Middle Ages to the Twenty-First Century*. Edited by Sean Ireton and Caroline Schaumann. Rochester, NY: Camden House, 2012, 176–92.
Auerbach, Erich. "Figura." Translated by Ralph Manheim. In *Scenes from the Drama of European Literature*. Minneapolis: University of Minnesota Press, 1984, 11–78.
Auster, Paul. "The Poetry of Exile." In *The Art of Hunger*. New York: Penguin, 1997, 90–103.
Bachmann, Vera. *Stille Wasser—Tiefe Texte? Zur Ästhetik der Oberfläche in der Literatur des 19. Jahrhunderts*. Bielefeld: Transcript, 2013.
Baer, Ulrich. "Landscape and Memory." In *Remnants of Song: Trauma and the Experience of Modernity in Charles Baudelaire and Paul Celan*. Stanford, CA: Stanford University Press, 2000, 210–55.
Bal, Mieke. "Auf die Haut/Unter die Haut: Barrockes steigt an die Oberfläche." In *Barock: Neue Sichtweisen einer Epoche*. Edited by Peter J. Burgard. Wien: Böhlau, 2001, 17–51.
Barkan, Leonard. "Living Sculptures and The Winter's Tale." *English Literary History* 48 (1981): 639–67.
Barkan, Leonard. *The Gods Made Flesh*. New Haven, CT: Yale University Press, 1986.
Barkan, Leonard. *Unearthing the Past: Archaeology and Aesthetics in the Making of Renaissance Culture*. New Haven, CT: Yale University Press, 1999.

Begemann, Christian. "Erhabene Natur. Zur Übertragung des Begriffs des Erhabenen auf Gegenstände der äußeren Natur in den deutschen Kunsttheorien des 18. Jahrhunderts." *Deutsche Vierteljahrschrift für Literaturwissenschaft und Geistesgeschichte* 58 (1984): 74–110.

Begemann, Christian. *Furcht und Angst im Prozeß der Aufklärung: Zu Literatur und Bewußtseinsgeschichte des 18. Jahrhunderts.* Frankfurt/Main: Athenäum Verlag, 1987.

Bell, Gerda. "Windows: A study of a Symbol in Georg Büchner's Work." *Germanic Review* 46 (1972): 95–108.

Beniston, Judith. "'Hitler's First Victim?'—Memory and Representation in Post-War Austria: Introduction." *Austrian Studies* 11 (2003): 1–13.

Bennett, Jane. *Vibrant Matter: A Political Ecology of Things.* Durham, NC: Duke University Press, 2010.

Bialek, Edward and Jan Pacholski, eds. *"Über allen Gipfeln . . . ": Bergmotive in der deutschsprachigen Literatur des 18. bis 21. Jahrhunderts.* Dresden: Neisse Verlag, 2008.

Bird, Friedrich and Franz Amelung. *Beiträge zur Lehre von den Geisteswissenschaften.* Darmstadt and Leipzig: Carl Willhelm Keske, 1836.

Boehm, Gottfried. *Studien zur Perspektivität: Philosophie und Kunst in der Frühen Neuzeit.* Heidelberg: Carl Winter, 1969.

Bohm, Arnd. "Landscapes of Exile: Celan's 'Gespräch im Gebirg'." *Germanic Review* 78, no. 2 (2003): 99–111.

Böhme, Gernot. "Pyramiden und Berge." In *Kants "Kritik der Urteilskraft" in neuer Sicht.* Frankfurt/Main: Suhrkamp, 1999, 83–107.

Böhme, Hartmut. "Geheime Macht im Schoß der Erde. Das Symbolfeld des Bergbaus zwischen Sozialgeschichte und Psychohistorie." In *Natur und Subjekt.* Frankfurt/Main: Suhrkamp, 1988, 67–144.

Böhme, Hartmut. "Das Steinerne: Anmerkungen zur Theorie des Erhabenen aus dem Blick des 'Menschenfremdesten'." In *Das Erhabene. Zwischen Grenzerfahrung und Größenwahn.* Edited by Christine Pries. Weinheim: VCH Acta Humaniora, 1989, 119–41.

Böhme, Hartmut. "Berg." In *Wörterbuch der philosophischen Metaphern.* Edited by Ralf Konsermann. Darmstadt: Wissenschaftliche Buchgesellschaft, 2007, 46–61.

Borgards, Roland. "'Wie in Verzweiflung stürzten beide aufeinander los!' Büchner's Lenz is encountering a cat." In *Animal Encounters. Mensch-Tier-Kontakte in Kunst, Literatur, Kultur und Wissenschaft.* Edited by Alexandra Böhm and Jessica Ullrich. Stuttgart: J. B. Metzler, 2019, 85–100.

Böschenstein-Schäfer, Renate. "Anmerkungen zu Paul Celans 'Gespräch im Gebirg'." In *Über Paul Celan.* Edited by Dietlind Meinecke. Frankfurt/Main: Suhrkamp, 1970, 226–38.

Boxall, Peter. *Twenty-First Century Fiction: A Critical Introduction.* New York: Cambridge University Press, 2013.

Büchner, Georg. "Lenz". *Complete Works and Letters.* Edited by Walter Hinderer and Henry J. Schmidt. Translated by Henry J. Schmidt. New York: Continuum, 1968, 139–59.

Büchner, Georg. *Lenz. Dichtungen, Sämtliche Werke, Briefe und Dokumente.* Volume 1. Edited by Henri Poschmann. Frankfurt/Main: Deutscher Klassiker Verlag, 1992, 223–50.

Büchner, Georg. *Woyzeck. Dichtungen, Sämtliche Werke und Briefe.* Volume 1. Edited by Henri Poschmann. Frankfurt/Main: Deutscher Klassiker Verlag, 1992, 143–219.

Bibliography 173

Büchner, Georg. *Georg Büchner: Werke und Briefe (Münchner Ausgabe)*. Edited by Karl Pörnbacher et al. München: Hanser, 2007.

Buci-Glucksmann, Christine. "Barock und Komplexität: Eine Ästhetik des Virtuellen." In *Barock: Neue Sichtweisen einer Epoche*. Edited by Peter J. Burgard. Wien: Böhlau, 2001, 205–12.

Burckhardt, Arnim. "'. . . als die Lippe mir blutet vor Sprache.' Zum Problem des Sprachzerfalls in Büchners 'Lenz' und Celans 'Gespräch im Gebirg'." In *Die Fremdheit der Sprache. Studien zur Literatur der Moderne*. Edited by Jochen C. Schütze, Hans-Ulrich Treichel, and Dietmar Voss. Hamburg: Argument-Verlag, 1988, 135–55.

Burger, Hermann. *Paul Celan: Auf der Suche nach der verlorenen Sprache*. Frankfurt/Main: Fischer Taschenbuch Verlag, 1989.

Burnet, Thomas. *The Sacred Theory of the Earth: Containing an Account of the Original of the Earth, and of all of the General Changes which it hath already undergone, or is to undergo, till the Consummation of all Things*. London: J. Hooke, 1726.

Celan, Paul. "Conversation in the Mountains." In *Collected Prose*. Translated by Rosemarie Waldrop. Manchester: Carcanet Press, 1983, 33–5.

Celan, Paul. "Edgar Jené and The Dream About The Dream." In *Collected Prose*. Translated by Rosemarie Waldrop. Manchester: Carcanet Press, 1983. 3–10.

Celan, Paul. "Speech on the Occasion of Receiving the Literature Prize of the Free Hanseatic City of Bremen." In *Collected Prose*. Translated by Rosemarie Waldrop. Manchester: Carcanet Press, 1983, 33–5.

Celan, Paul. *Der Meridian: Endfassung, Vorstufen, Materialien*. Tübinger Ausgabe. Edited by Bernhard Böschenstein and Heino Schmull. Frankfurt/Main: Suhrkamp, 1999.

Celan, Paul. "Ansprache anläßlich der Entgegennahme des Literaturpreises der Freien Hansestadt Bremen." In *Gesammelte Werke in sieben Bänden*. Volume 3. Edited by Beda Allemann and Stefan Reichert. Frankfurt/Main: Suhrkamp, 2000, 185–6.

Celan, Paul. "Der Meridian." In *Gesammelte Werke in sieben Bänden*. Volume 3. Edited by Beda Allemann and Stefan Reichert. Frankfurt/Main: Suhrkamp, 2000, 187–202.

Celan, Paul. "Edgar Jené und der Traum vom Traume." In *Gesammelte Werke in sieben Bänden*. Volume 3. Edited by Beda Allemann and Stefan Reichert. Frankfurt/Main: Suhrkamp, 2000, 155–61.

Celan, Paul. "Gespräch im Gebirg." In *Gesammelte Werke in sieben Bänden*. Edited by Beda Allemann and Stefan Reichert. Volume 3. Frankfurt/Main: Suhrkamp, 2000, 169–73.

Celan, Paul. *La Bibliothèque philosophique*. Edited by Alexandra Richter et al. Paris: Rue d'Ulm, 2004.

Celan, Paul. *Mikrolithen sinds, Steinchen: Die Prosa aus dem Nachlaß*. Edited by Barbara Wiedemann and Bertrand Badiou. Frankfurt/Main: Suhrkamp, 2005.

Celan, Paul. *The Meridian. Final Version—Drafts—Materials*. Edited by Bernhard Böschenstein and Heino Schmull. Translated by Pierre Joris. Stanford, CA: Stanford University Press, 2011.

Celan, Paul. "Ansprache anläßlich der Entgegennahme des Literaturpreises der Freien Hansestadt Bremen." In *Prosa I: Zu Lebzeiten publizierte Prosa und Reden*. *Werke: Historisch-Kritische Ausgabe*. Volume 15.1. Edited by Andreas Lohr and Heino Schmull. Frankfurt/Main: Suhrkamp, 2014, 23–5.

Celan, Paul. "Der Meridian." In *Prosa I: Zu Lebzeiten publizierte Prosa und Reden. Werke: Historisch-Kritische Ausgabe*. Volume 15.1. Edited by Andreas Lohr and Heino Schmull. Frankfurt/Main: Suhrkamp, 2014, 33–51.

Celan, Paul. "Edgar Jené und der Traum vom Traume," In *Prosa I: Zu Lebzeiten publizierte Prosa und Reden. Werke: Historisch-Kritische Ausgabe*. Volume 15.1. Edited by Andreas Lohr and Heino Schmull. Frankfurt/Main: Suhrkamp, 2014, 11–17.

Celan, Paul. "Gespräch im Gebirg." In *Prosa I: Zu Lebzeiten publizierte Prosa und Reden. Werke: Historisch-Kritische Ausgabe*. Volume 15.1. Edited by Andreas Lohr and Heino Schmull. Frankfurt/Main: Suhrkamp, 2014, 27–31.

Cohen, Jeffrey Jerome. *Stone: An Ecology of the Inhuman*. Minneapolis: University of Minnesota Press, 2015.

Cronon, William. "Foreword to the 1997 Paperback Edition." In Marjorie Hope Nicolson, *Mountain Gloom and Mountain Glory: The Development of the Aesthetics of the Infinite*. Seattle: University of Washington Press, 1997. vii–xii.

Daiber, Jürgen. "Fenster-Metaphorik: Zum historischen Spannungsfeld von Text-Bild-Relationen." In *Grenzen der Germanistik: Rephilologisierung oder Erweiterung?* Edited by Walter Erhart. Stuttgart: Metzler, 2004, 392–409.

Dannenberg, Hillary P. *The Changing Heavens: Major Recurrent Images in the Poetic Writings of Georg Büchner*. Rheinbach: H. P. Dannenberg Verlag, 1994.

Darbieux, Bernard and Gilles Rudaz. *The Mountain: A Political History from the Enlightenment to the Present*. Chicago: University of Chicago Press, 2015.

Decurvières, Benedikt. "Der Wahnsinn als Kraftfeld: Eine symptomatische Lektüre zu Georg Büchners Erzählung *Lenz*." *Weimarer Beiträge* 52 (2006): 203–26.

Dedner, Burghard. "Büchners 'Lenz.' Rekonstruktion der Textgenese." *Georg Büchner Jahrbuch* 8 (1990–4), 1995: 3–68.

Dedner, Burghard. "Textgenese." In Georg Büchner, *Sämtliche Werke und Schriften. Historisch-kritische Ausgabe mit Quellendokumentationen und Kommentar*. Volume 5. Edited by Burghard Dedner et al. Darmstadt: Wissenschaftliche Buchgesellschaft, 2001, 127–65.

Dedner, Burghard et al., eds. *"Lenzens Verrückung" Chronik und Dokumente zu J.M.R. Lenz von Herbst 1777 bis Frühjahr 1778*. Tübingen: Max Niemeyer, 1999.

Deleuze, Gilles. *Le pli: Leibniz et le baroque*. Paris: Les éditions de minuit, 1988.

Deleuze, Gilles. "The Simulacrum and Ancient Philosoph." In *The Logic of Sense*. Translated by Mark Lester. Edited by Constantin V. Boundas. New York: Columbia University Press, 1990, 253–79.

Deleuze, Gilles. "The Fold." Translated by Jonathan Strauss. *Yale French Studies* 80 (1991): 227–47.

Deleuze, Gilles. *The Fold: Leibniz and the Baroque*. Translated by Tom Conley. Minneapolis: University of Minnesota Press, 1993.

Dennis, John. *Miscellanies in Verse and Prose*. London: James Knapton, 1693.

"Dichter-Aufgabe." *Jason. Eine Zeitschrift. Herausgegeben vom Verfasser des goldenen Kalbes*. Volume1 (January–April), Gotha: n.p., 1809, 394–6.

Eicher, Thomas, ed. *Das Bergwerk von Falun: Varianten eines literarischen Stoffes*. Münster: Lit Verlag, 1996.

Elkins, James. *The Poetics of Perspective*. Ithaca, NY: Cornell University Press, 1994.

Engel, Manfred. "Naturphilosophisches Wissen und romantische Literatur—am Beispiel von Traumtheorie und Traumdichtung der Romantik." In *Wissen in Literatur im 19. Jahrhundert*. Edited by Lutz Danneberg et al. Berlin: De Gruyter, 2002, 65–91.

Bibliography 175

Erickson, Nancy. "Echoes of Celan and Heidegger in Jelinek's *In den Alpen*." In *Elfriede Jelinek. Writing Woman, Nation, and Identity*. Edited by Matthias Konzet and Margarete Lamb-Faffelberger. Madison, NJ: Fairleigh Dickinson University Press, 2007, 174–88.

Eshel, Amir. "Paul Celan's Other: History, Poetics, and Ethics." *New German Critique* 91 (2004): 57–77.

Fassbind, Bernhard. *Poetik des Dialogs: Voraussetzungen dialogischer Poesie bei Paul Celan und Konzepte von Intersubjektivität bei Martin Buber, Martin Heidegger und Emmanuel Levinas*. München: Fink, 1995.

Felsch, Phillipp. "Mountains of Sublimity, Mountains of Fatigue: Towards a History of Speechlessness in the Alps," *Science in Context* 22, no. 3 (2009): 341–64.

Felstiner, John. *Paul Celan: Poet, Survivor, Jew*. New Haven, CT: Yale University Press, 1995.

Franzel, Sean. "Time and Narrative in the Mountain Sublime around 1800." In *Heights of Reflection: Mountains in the German Imagination from the Middle Ages to the Twenty-First Century*. Edited by Sean Ireton and Caroline Schaumann. Rochester, NY: Camden House, 2012, 98–115.

Friedmann, Georg. "Die Bearbeitung der Geschichte von dem Bergmann von Fahlun." Dissertation, Königliche Friedrich-Wilhelms-Universität Berlin, 1887. Berlin: Druckerei der Berliner Börsenzeitung, 1887.

Frühsorge, Gotthart. "Fenster: Augenblicke der Aufklärung über Leben und Arbeit. Zur Funktionsgeschichte eines literartischen Motivs." *Euphorion* 77 (1983): 346–58.

Geist, Kathrin. *Berg—Sehn—Sucht: Der Alpenraum in der deutschsprachigen Literatur*. Paderborn: Wilhelm Fink, 2018.

Gennep, Arnold van. *Les rites de passage*. Paris: É. Nourry, 1909.

Gersch, Hubert. *Der Text, der (produktive) Unverstand des Abschreibers und die Literaturgeschichte*. Tübingen: Max Niemeyer, 1998.

Gessner, Konrad. "Beschreibung des Frakmont, oder Pilatus mit dem gewöhnlichen Namen, bei Luzern in der Schweiz. 20. August 1555." In *Die Entdeckung der Alpen. Eine Sammlung schweizerischer und deutscher Alpenliteratur bis zum Jahr 1800*. Edited by Richard Weiss. Frauenfeld: Huber, 1934, 13–14.

Gessner, Konrad. "Brief über die Bewunderung der Berge, geschrieben vom Arzt Konrad Geßner and Jakob Vogel." In *Die Entdeckung der Alpen. Eine Sammlung schweizerischer und deutscher Alpenliteratur bis zum Jahr 1800*. Edited by Richard Weiss. Frauenfeld: Huber, 1934. 6–12.

Glavinic, Thomas. *Das größere Wunder*. München: Carl Hanser, 2013.

Goethe, Johann Wolfgang von. "Briefe aus der Schweiz. Erste Abteilung." In *Campagne in Frankreich, Belagerung von Mainz, Reiseschriften. Sämtliche Werke, Briefe, Tagebücher und Gespräche*. Volume 16. Edited by Klaus-Detlef Müller. Frankfurt/Main: Deutscher Klassiker Verlag, 1994.

Goethe, Johann Wolfgang von. "Briefe aus der Schweiz. Zweite Abteilung." In *Campagne in Frankreich, Belagerung von Mainz, Reiseschriften. Sämtliche Werke, Briefe, Tagebücher und Gespräche*. Volume 16. Edited by Klaus-Detlef Müller. Frankfurt/Main: Deutscher Klassiker Verlag, 1994.

Goethe, Johann Wolfgang von. "Aus Makariens Archiv." In *Wilhelm Meisters Wanderjahre. Werke, Kommentare, und Register, Hamburger Ausgabe in 14 Bänden*. Volume 8. Edited by Erich Trunz. München: C. H. Beck, 1999.

Goethe, Johann Wolfgang von. *Aus meinem Leben: Dichtung und Wahrheit. Werke, Kommentare und Register: Hamburger Ausgabe in 14 Bänden.* Volume 10. Edited by Erich Trunz. München: C. H. Beck, 1999.

Gold, Helmut. *Erkenntnis unter Tage: Bergbaumotive in der Literatur der Romantik.* Opladen: Westdeutscher Verlag, 1990.

Grave, Johannes. "Reframing the *finestra aperta*: Venetian Variations on the Comparison of Picture and Window." *Zeitschrift für Kunstgeschicte* 72 (2009): 49–68.

Groves, Jason. *The Geological Unconscious: German Literature and the Mineral Imaginary.* New York: Fordham University Press, 2020.

Gsoels-Lorensen, Jutta. "Elfriede Jelinek's *Die Kinder der Toten:* Representing the Holocaust as an Austrian Ghost Story." *Germanic Review* 81, no. 4 (2006): 360–82.

Guichonnet, Paul et al., eds. *Mont-Blanc: Conquête de l'imaginaire.* Chambéry: La Fontaine de Siloé, 2002.

Haberkorn, Michaela. *Naturhistoriker und Zeitenseher. Geologie und Poesie um 1800. Der Kreis um A.G. Werner (Goethe, A.v. Humboldt, Novalis, Steffens, G. H. Schubert).* Frankfurt/Main: Peter Lang, 2004.

Haller, Albrecht von. *Die Alpen.* Edited by Harold T. Betteridge. Berlin: Akademie-Verlag, 1959.

Hansen, Peter. H. *The Summits of Modern Man: Mountaineering after the Enlightenment.* Cambridge, MA: Harvard University Press, 2013.

Hardie, Philip. *Ovid's Poetics of Illusion.* Cambridge: Cambridge University Press, 2002.

Hartmann, Regina. "Technischer Fortschritt als menschheitlicher Progress? Reiseberichte über das Bergwerk von Falun zwischen Aufklärungshoffnung und Aufklärungsskepsis." *Zeitschrift für deutsche Philologie* 122 (2003): 184–99.

Hasubeck, Peter. "'Ruhe' und 'Bewegung': Versuch einer Stilanalyse von Georg Büchners 'Lenz'." *Germanisch-Romanische Monatsschrift* (1969): 33–59.

Hauser, Ronald. *Georg Büchner.* New York: Twayne, 1974.

Hausmann, Johann Friedrich Ludwig. *Reise durch Skandinavien in den Jahren 1806 und 1807.* Göttingen: Johann Friedrich Römer, 1818.

Hebel, Johann Peter. "Unverhofftes Wiedersehen." In *Die Kalendergeschichten. Sämtliche Erzählungen aus dem Rheinländischen Hausfreund.* Edited by Hannelore Schlaffer and Harald Zils. München: Hanser, 1999, 328–32.

Hegel, Willhelm Friedrich. *Phänomenologie des Geistes. Werke.* Volume 3. Edited by Eva Moldenhauer and Karl Markus Michel. Frankfurt/Main: Suhrkamp, 1986.

Heidegger, Martin. "Die Frage nach der Technik." In *Vorträge und Aufsätze.* Stuttgart: Clett-Kotta, 2004, 9–41.

Henke, Adolph. *Lehrbuch der gerichtlichen Medicin. Zum Behuf academischer Vorlesungen und zum Gebrauch für gerichtliche Ärzte und Rechtsgelehrte.* Berlin: Ferdinand Dümmler, 1832.

Herder, Johann Gottfried. "Kalligone: Vom Angenehmen und Schönen." In *Schriften zur Literatur und Philosophie 1792–1800. Werke.* Volume 8. Edited by Hans Dietrich Irmscher. Frankfurt/Main: Deutscher Klassiker Verlag, 1998, 641–964.

Heringman, Noah. *Romantic Rocks, Aesthetic Geology.* Ithaca, NY: Cornell University Press, 2004.

Hinderer, Walter. "Pathos der Passion: Die Leiddarstellung in Büchners *Lenz.*" In *Wissen aus Erfahrungen: Werkbegriff und Interpretation heute; Festschrift für*

Hermann Mayer zum 65. Geburtstag. Edited by Alexander von Bormann. Tübingen: Max Niemeyer Verlag, 1976, 474–94.

Hinderer, Walter. *Büchner—Kommentar zum dichterischen Werk.* München: Winkler, 1977.

Hoffmann, E. T. A. "The Mines of Falun." In *Tales.* Translated by L. J. Kent and E. C. Knight. Edited by Victor Lange. New York: Continuum, 1982, 163–87.

Hoffmann, E. T. A. "Die Bergwerke zu Falun." In *Die Serapions-Brüder. Sämtliche Werke in sechs Bänden.* Volume 4. Edited by Wulf Segebrecht. Frankfurt/Main: Deutscher Klassiker Verlag, 2001, 208–41.

Hoffmann, E. T. A. "Des Vetters Eckfenster." In *Späte Prosa, Briefe, Tagebücher und Aufzeichnungen, Juristische Schriften, Werke 1814–1822. Sämtliche Werke in sechs Bänden.* Volume 6. Edited by Gerhard Allroggen et al. Frankfurt/Main: Deutscher Kassiker Verlag, 2004, 468–97.

Hollis, Dawn L. "*Mountain Gloom and Mountain Glory*: The Genealogy of an Idea." *ISLE: Interdisciplinary Studies in Literature and Environment* 26, no. 4 (Autumn 2019): 1038–61.

Hollis, Dawn L. and Jason Köng, eds. *Mountain Dialogues from Antiquity to Modernity.* New York: Bloomsbury Academic, 2021.

Holub, Robert C. "The Paradoxes of Realism. An Examination of the Kunstgespräch in Büchner's Lenz." *Deutsche Vierteljahrsschrift für Literaturwissenschaft und Geistesgeschichte* 59 (1985): 102–24.

Hooley, Dan. "Gessner's Mountain Sublime." In *Mountain Dialogues from Antiquity to Modernity.* Edited by Dawn Hollis and Jason König. London: Bloomsbury Academic, 2021, 21–36.

Hope Nicolson, Marjorie. *Mountain Gloom and Mountain Glory: The Development of the Aesthetics of the Infinite.* New York: W. W. Norton, 1959.

Hutcheon, Linda. *A Poetics of Postmodernism: History, Theory, Fiction.* New York: Routledge, 1988.

Hutcheon, Linda. "Historiographic Metafiction: Parody and the Intertexts of History." In *Intertextuality and Contemporary American Fiction.* Edited by P. O'Donnell and Robert Con Davis. Baltimore, MD: Johns Hopkins University Press, 1989, 3–32.

Ireton, Sean and Caroline Schaumann, eds. *Heights of Reflection: Mountains in the German Imagination from the Middle Ages to the Twenty-First Century.* Rochester, NY: Camden House, 2012.

Ireton, Sean and Caroline Schaumann, eds. *Mountains and the German Mind: Translations from Gessner to Messner, 1541–2009.* Rochester, NY: Camden House, 2020.

Issa, Hoda. *Das "Niederländische" und die "Autopsie": Die Bedeutung der Vorlage für Georg Büchners Werke.* Frankfurt/Main: Peter Lang, 1988.

Jackson, John E. "Die Du-Anrede bei Paul Celan. Anmerkungen zu seinem 'Gespräch im Gebirg'." *Text und Kritik* 53–4 (1977): 62–8.

Janke, Pia. "Der Mythos Kaprun in *In den Alpen* und *Das Werk*." In *Jelinek, une répétition? A propos des pieces "In den Alpen" et "Das Werk." / Jelinek, eine Wiederholung? Zu den Theaterstücken "In den Alpen" und "Das Werk."* Edited by Françoise Lartillot and Dieter Honig. Bern: Peter Lang, 2009, 127–41.

Jansen, Peter K. "The Stuctural Function of the *Kunstgespräch* in Büchner's *Lenz*." *Monatshefte* 67, no. 2 (1975): 145–56.

Janz, Marlies. *Vom Engagement absoluter Poesie: Zur Lyrik und Ästhetik Paul Celans.* Frankfurt/Main: Syndikat, 1976.

Janz, Marlies. "'Die Geschichte hat sich nach 45 entschlossen, noch einmal ganz von vorne zu beginnen . . .' Elfriede Jelineks Destruktion des Mythos historischer 'Unschuld'." In *Elfriede Jelinek—Die international Rezeption*. Edited by Daniela Bartens and Paul Pechmann. Graz: Droschl, 1997, 225–38.

Japp, Uwe. "Das Erhabene in den Bergwerken von Falun." In *Nördlichkeit— Romantik—Erhabenheit. Apperzeption der Nord/Süd –Differenz (1750–2000)*. Edited by Andreas Fülberth et al. Frankfurt/Main: Peter Lang, 2007, 205–14.

Jelinek, Elfriede. *Oh Wildnis, oh Schutz vor ihr*. Reinbek: Rowohlt, 1985.

Jelinek, Elfriede. *Wolken.Heim*. Göttingen: Steidl, 1990.

Jelinek, Elfriede. *Die Kinder der Toten*. Reinbek: Rohwolt, 1995.

Jelinek, Elfriede. *In den Alpen*. Berlin: Berlin Verlag, 2002.

Jelinek, Elfriede. "Ich als Toten-Ausgräberin." In *Jelinek[jahr]buch 2012*. Edited by Pia Janke. Wien: Praesens, 2012, 17–19.

Jens, Walter. *Euripides. Büchner*. Pfullingen: Neske, 1964.

Kant, Immanuel. *Kritik der Urteilskraft. Werkausgabe*. Volume 10. Edited by Wilhelm Weischedel. Frankfurt/Main: Suhrkamp, 1974.

Kant, Immanuel. "Beobachtungen über das Gefühl des Schönen und Erhabenen." In *Vorkritische Schriften bis 1768, Band 2. Werkausgabe*. Volume 2. Edited by Wilhelm Weischedel. Frankfurt/Main: Suhrkamp, 1977.

Kant, Immanuel. *Anthropologie in pragmatischer Hinsicht. Werkausgabe*. Volume 12. Edited by Wilhelm Weischedel. Frankfurt/Main: Suhrkamp, 2000.

Kant, Immanuel. *Critique of the Power of Judgement*. Translated by Paul Guyer. Cambridge: Cambridge University Press, 2000.

Kecht, Maria-Regina. "The Polyphony of Remembrance: Reading *Die Kinder der Toten*." In *Elfriede Jelinek. Writing Woman, Nation, and Identity*. Edited by Matthias Konzet and Margarete Lamb-Faffelberger. Madison, NJ: Fairleigh Dickinson University Press, 2007, 189–220.

Kleese, Marc. "Oszillationsfiguren. Zu einer Poetik des Traums bei E. T. A. Hoffmanns *Die Bergwerke zu Falun*." *E. T. A. Hoffmann-Jahrbuch* 18 (2010): 25–41.

König, Christoph, ed. *Paul Celan—Peter Szondi: Briefwechsel. Mit Briefen von Gisèle Celan-Lestrange an Peter Szondi und Auszügen aus dem Briefwechsel zwischen Peter Szondi und Jean und Mayotte Bollack*. Frankfurt/Main: Suhrkamp, 2005.

Kopf, Martina. *Alpinismus—Andinismus: Gebirgslandschaften in europäischer und lateinamerikanischer Literatur*. Stuttgart: J. B. Metzler 2016.

Koschorke, Albrecht. *Die Geschichte des Horizonts*. Frankfurt/Main: Suhrkamp, 1990.

Kracht, Christian. *Ich werde hier sein im Sonnenschein und im Schatten*. Köln: Kiepenheuer & Witsch, 2008.

Kritisch Neuse, Erna. "Büchners *Lenz*. Zur Struktur der Novelle." *German Quarterly* 43 (1970): 199–209.

Kubik, Sabine. *Krankheit und Medizin im literarischen Werk Büchners*. Stuttgart: Metzler, 1994.

Küchler Williams, Christiane. "Was konserviert den Bergmann zu Falun— Kupfer- oder Eisenvitriol? Eine chemische Fußnote zu den Variationen des 'Bergwerks zu Falun'." *Athenäum* 10 (2000): 191–7.

Lachmann, Renate. *Erzählte Phantastik: Zur Phantasiegeschichte und Semantik phantastischer Texte*. Frankfurt/Main: Suhrkamp, 2002.

Langen, August. *Anschauungsformen in der deutschen Dichtung des 18. Jahrhunderts (Rahmenschau und Rationalismus)*. Jena: Wissenschaftliche Buchgesellschaft, 1934.

Leibniz, G. W. *Philosophical Papers and Letters.* Volume 2. Edited and translated by L. E. Loemker. Chicago: University of Chicago Press, 1956.
Leibniz, G. W. "Monadologie." In *Kleine Schriften zu Metaphysik, Philosophische Schriften 1, französisch und deutsch.* Edited and translated by Hans Heinz Holz. Frankfurt/Main: Suhrkamp, 2000, 438–83.
Leyel, Adam. "Narratio accurata de cadavere humano in fodina cuprimontana ante duos annos reperto." *Acta litteraria Sveciae publicita* 1 (1722): 250–4.
Lindenberger, Herbert. *Georg Büchner.* Carbondale: Southern Illinois University Press, 1964.
Loewy, Hanno and Gerhard Milchram, eds. *Hast du meine Alpen gesehen? Eine jüdische Beziehungsgeschichte.* Hohenhems: Bucher Verlag, 2009.
Longinus. *On the Sublime.* Translated by W. H. Fyfe. *The Loeb Classical Library.* Volume 199. Edited by Jeffrey Henderson. Cambridge, MA: Harvard University Press, 2005.
Lorenz-Lindemann, Karin. "Paul Celan: Gespräch im Gebirg—ein Palimpsest zu Büchners Lenz." In *Datum und Zitat bei Paul Celan. Akten des Internationalen Paul Celan-Colloquiums.* Edited by Chaim Shoham and Bernd Witte. Bern: Peter Lang, 1987, 170–82.
Lotman, Jurij. *Die Struktur literarischer Texte.* Translated by Rolf-Dietrich Keil. München: Fink, 1972.
Lughofer, Johann Georg, ed. *Das Erschreiben der Berge: Die Alpen in der deutschsprachigen Literatur.* Innsbruck: Innsbruck University Press, 2014.
Lyon, James K. "Paul Celan's Language of Stone: The Geology of the Poetic Landscape." *Colloquia germanica* 8 (1974): 298–317.
Mahoney, Dennis F. "The Sufferings of Young Lenz: The Function of Parody in Büchner's *Lenz.*" *Monatshefte* 76, no. 4 (1984): 396–408.
Marti, Benedikt. "Lob der Berge." In *Die Entdeckung der Alpen. Eine Sammlung schweizerischer und deutscher Alpenliteratur bis zum Jahr 1800.* Edited by Richard Weiss. Frauenfeld: Huber, 1934, 1–5.
Mersch, Dieter. *Posthermeneutik.* Oldenbourg: Akademieverlag, 2010.
Mertens, Moira and Elisabeth Günther. "'Ich will kein Leben,' Elfriede Jelinek's Ästhetik des Untoten." In *Jelinek[jahr]buch 2012.* Edited by Pia Janke. Wien: Praesens, 2012, 104–26.
Meyer, Adolf-Ernst. "Elfriede Jelinek im Gespräch mit Alfred-Ernst Meyer." In *Sturm und Zwang. Schreiben als Geschlechterkampf.* Hamburg: Klein, 1995, 9–74.
Miller, Norbert. "E. T. A. Hoffmann's doppelte Wirklichkeit. Zum Motiv der Schwellenüberschreitung in seinen Märchen." In *Literaturwissenschaft und Geschichtsphilosophie. Festschrift für Wilhelm Emrich.* Edited by Helmut Arntzen et al. Berlin: De Gruyter, 1975, 357–72.
Mitchell, W. J. T. *Landscape and Power.* Chicago: University of Chicago Press, 1995.
Mosès, Stéphane. "'Wege, auf denen die Sprache stimmhaft wird.' Paul Celans 'Gespräch im Gebirg'." In *Argumentum e silentio: International Paul Celan Symposium.* Edited by Amy Colin. Berlin: De Gruyter, 1987, 43–57.
Mülder-Bach, Inka. "Tiefe: Zur Dimension der Romantik." In *Räume der Romantik.* Edited by Inka Mülder-Bach and Gerhard Neumann. Würzburg: Königshausen & Neumann, 2007, 83–102.
Müller-Sievers, Helmut. *Desorientierung: Anatomie und Dichtung bei Georg Büchner.* Göttingen: Wallstein, 2003.
Niccolini, Elisabetta. *Der Spaziergang des Schriftstellers.* Stuttgart: Metzler, 2000.

Novalis. "Heinrich von Ofterdingen." In *Werke, Tagebücher und Briefe Friedrich von Hardenbergs*. Volume 1. Edited by Richard Samuel. München: Hanser Verlag, 1978, 237–383.

Oberlin, Johann Friedrich. "Herr L . . . . . ., (synoptischer Text)." In *Georg Büchner, Lenz, Georg Büchner: Sämtliche Werke und Schriften (Marburger Ausgabe)*. Volume 5. Edited by Burghard Dedner and Hubert Gersch. Darmstadt: Wissenschaftliche Buchgesellschaft, 2001, 219–41.

Ortner, Jessica. "Aspekte des Untoten in Elfriede Jelinek's Roman *Die Kinder der Toten*: Erinnerungsästhetische und narratologische Überlegungen." In *Jelinek[jahr]buch 2012*. Edited by Pia Janke. Wien: Praesens, 2012, 83–103.

Outhier, Réginald. *Journal d'un voyage au nord, en 1736 & 1737*. Amsterdam: H. G. Löhner, 1776.

Ovid. *Metamorphoses*. Translated by Frank Justus Miller. *The Loeb Classical Library*. Volume 42. Edited by Jeffrey Henderson. Cambridge, MA: Harvard University Press, 2004.

Ozturk, Anthony. "Geo-Poetics: The Alpine Sublime in Art and Literature, 1779–1860." In *Heights of Reflection: Mountains in the German Imagination from the Middle Ages to the Twenty-First Century*. Edited by Sean Ireton and Caroline Schaumann. Rochester, NY: Camden House, 2012, 77–97.

Pankow, Edgar. "Medienwechsel: Zur Konstellation von Literatur und Malerei in einigen Arbeiten E. T. A. Hoffmanns." *E. T. A. Hoffmann Jahrbuch* 10 (2002): 42–57.

Panofsky, Erwin. "Die Perspective als 'symbolische Form'." In *Vorträge der Bibliothek Warburg 1924–25*. Edited by Fritz Saxl. Berlin: Teubner, 258–330.

Paul, Jean. *Die unsichtbare Loge. Jean Pauls Sämtliche Werke, Historisch-kritische Ausgabe herausgegeben von der Preußischen Akademie der Wissenschaften*. Edited by Eduard Berend. Weimar: Herman Böhlaus Nachfolger, 1927.

Plato. "Sophist." Translated by F. M. Cornford. In *Plato: The Collected Dialogues including the Letters*. Edited by Edith Hamilton and Huntington Cairns. Princeton, NJ: Princeton University Press, 1989, 957–1017.

Pöggeler, Otto. *Spur des Wortes: Zur Lyrik Paul Celans*. Freiburg: K. Aber, 1986.

Poschmann, Henri. "Entstehung." In *Georg Büchner, Dichtungen, Sämtliche Werke, Briefe und Dokumente*. Volume 1. Edited by Henri Poschmann. Frankfurt/Main: Deutscher Klassiker Verlag, 1992, 798–802.

Poschmann, Henri. "Textgrundlage und Textgestaltung." In *Georg Büchner, Dichtungen, Sämtliche Werke, Briefe und Dokumente*. Volume 1. Edited by Henri Poschmann. Frankfurt/Main: Deutscher Klassiker Verlag, 1992, 791–8.

Ransmayr, Christoph. *Der Fliegende Berg*. Frankfurt/Main: Fischer, 2006.

Raymond, Petra. *Von der Landschaft im Kopf zur Landschaft aus Sprache: Die Romantisierung der Alpen und die Literarisierung des Gebirges in der Erzählprosa der Goethezeit*. Tübingen: Max Niemeyer, 1993.

Ritter, Joachim. "Landschaft: Zur Funktion des Ästhetischen in der modernen Gesellschaft." In *Subjektivität. Sechs Aufsätze*. Frankfurt/Main: Suhrkamp, 1974, 141–63.

Schaumann, Caroline. *Peak Pursuits: The Emergence of Mountaineering in the Nineteenth Century*. New Haven, CT: Yale University Press, 2020.

Schellenberger, Erika. "Von Gletschermühlen und Meermühlen: Geologische Motive in der Lyrik Paul Celans." *Wirkendes Wort* 38 (1988): 347–59.

Scheuchzer, Jakob. *Itinera per Helvetiae Alpinas Regiones Facta Annis 1702–1711*. n.p.p.: n.p., n.d.

Schiller, Friedrich. "Der Spaziergang." In *Sämtliche Werke in 5 Bänden*. Volume 1. Edited by Albert Meier. München: Carl Hanser Verlag, 2011, 228–34.
Schings, Hans-Jürgen. "Der mitleidigste Mensch ist der beste Mensch." In *Poetik des Mitleids von Lessing bis Büchner*. München: Beck Verlag, 1980, 68–84.
Schmeiser, Leonhard. "Das Gedächtnis des Bodens." *Tumult. Zeitschrift für Verkehrswissenschaft* 10 (1987): 38–56.
Schmidt, Harald. *Melancholie und Landschaft. Die psychotische und ästhetische Struktur der Naturschilderungen in Büchners "Lenz."* Opladen: Westdeutscher Verlag, 1994.
Schmidt, Harald. "Melancholie und Landschaft: Zur problematischen Differentialdiagnostik in Georg Büchners 'Lenz'." *Zeitschrift für deutsche Philologie* 117 (1998): 516–42.
Schnell, Ralf. "Stoffwechselprozesse. Oberfläche und Tiefe in Elfriede Jelineks Roman *Die Kinder der Toten*." In *Lob der Oberfläche. Zum Werk von Elfriede Jelinek*. Edited by Thomas Eder and Juliane Vogel. München: Wilhelm Fink, 2010, 169–79.
Schnyder, Peter. "Die Wiederkehr des Anderen: Ein Gang durch die Zeichenbergwerke zu Falun." In *Figur, Figura, Figuration: E. T. A: Hoffmann*. Edited by Daniel Müller Niebla et al. Würzburg: Königshausen & Neumann, 2011, 31–43.
Schöne, Albrecht. "Interpretationen zur dichterischen Gestaltung des Wahnsinns in der deutschen Literatur." Dissertation. Münster, 1952.
Schubert, Gotthilf Heinrich. *Ansichten von der Nachtseite der Naturwissenschaft*. Dresden: Arnoldsche Buchhandlung, 1808.
Schubert, Gotthilf Heinrich. "Fragmente aus einer Vorlesung." *Phöbus* 4–5 (1808): 67–8.
Schulz, Georg-Michael. "Individuation und Austauschbarkeit: Zu Paul Celans *Gespräch im Gebirg*." *Deutsche Vierteljahrschrift für Literaturwissenschaft und Geistesgeschichte* 53, no. 3 (1979): 463–77.
Schwann, Jürgen. *Georg Büchners implizite Ästhetik: Rekonstruierung und Situierung im ästhetischen Diskurs*. Tübingen: Gunter Narr, 1997.
Selbmann, Rolf. "Unverhofft kommt oft. Eine Leiche und die Folgen für die Literaturwissenschaft." *Euphorion* 94 (2000): 173–204.
Seling-Dietz, Carolin. "Büchners *Lenz* als Rekonstruktion eines Falls 'religiöser Melnacholie'." *Georg-Büchner-Jahrbuch* 9 (1995–9), 2000: 188–236.
Seng, Joachim. "'Die wahre Flaschenpost' Zur Beziehung zwischen Theodor W. Adorno und Paul Celan." In *Frankfurter Adorno Blätter VIII*. Edited by Rolf Tiedemann. München: edition text + kritik, 2003, 151–76.
Senn, Cathrin. *Framed Views and Dual Worlds: The Motif of the Window as a Narrative Device and Structural Metaphor in Prose Fiction*. Bern: Lang, 2001.
Shama, Simon. *Landscape and Memory*. New York: Knopf, 1996.
Sieber, Mirjam. *Paul Celans "Gespräch im Gebirg" Erinnerung und eine "versäumte Begegnung"*. Tübingen: Max Niemeyer Verlag, 2007.
Simmel, Georg. "Alpenreisen." In *Aufsätze und Abhandlungen 1894–1900, Gesamtausgabe in 24 Bänden*. Volume 5. Edited by Heinz-Jürgen Dahme and David P. Frisby. Frankfurt/Main: Suhrkamp, 1992, 91–5.
Simmel, Georg. "Die ästhetische Quantität." In *Aufsätze und Abhandlungen 1901–1908, Band 1, Gesamtausgabe in 24 Bänden*. Volume 7. Edited by Rüdiger Kramme et al. Frankfurt/Main: Suhrkamp, 1995, 190–200.

Simmel, Georg. "Über ästhetische Quantitäten." In *Aufsätze und Abhandlungen 1901–1908, Band 1, Gesamtausgabe in 24 Bänden.* Volume 7. Edited by Rüdiger Kramme et al. Frankfurt/Main: Suhrkamp, 1995, 184–9.

Simmel, Georg. "Zur Ästhetik der Alpen." In *Aufsätze und Abhandlungen 1909–1918, Band 1, Gesamtausgabe in 24 Bänden.* Volume 12. Edited by Rüdiger Kramme and Angelika Rammstedt. Frankfurt/Main: Suhrkamp, 2001, 162–9.

Stoichita, Victor I. *The Pygmalion Effect: From Ovid to Hitchcock.* Translated by Alison Anderson. Chicago: University of Chicago Press, 2008.

Stourzh, Gerald. *Einheit und Freiheit. Staatsvertrag, Neutralität und das Ende der Ost–West Besetzung Österreichs.* Wien: Böhlau, 1998, 607–8.

Sulzer, Johann Georg. "Verrückung." In *Allgemeine Theorie der schönen Künste* (1771). Volume 4. Leipzig: Weidmanns Erben und Reich, 1787, 551–2.

Szondi, Peter. "Durch die Enge geführt. Versuch über die Verständlichkeit des modernen Gedichts." In *Schriften.* Volume 2. Edited by Jean Bollack. Frankfurt/Main: Suhrkamp, 1978, 345–89.

Tate, Dennis "'Ewige deutsche Misere?' GDR Authors and Büchner's *Lenz.*" In *Culture and Society in the GDR.* Edited by Graham Bartram and Anthony Waine. GDR Monitor Special Series 2. Dundee: GDR Monitor, 1983, 85–99.

Tieck, Ludwig. "Leben und Tod des kleinen Rotkäppchens. Eine Tragödie." In *Phantasus. Schriften in zwölf Bänden.* Volume 6. Edited by Manfred Frank et al. Frankfurt/Main: Deutscher Klassiker Verlag, 1985, 362–93.

Tieck, Ludwig. "Runenberg." In *Phantasus. Schriften in zwölf Bänden.* Volume 6. Edited by Manfred Frank et al. Frankfurt/Main: Deutscher Klassiker Verlag, 1985, 184–209.

Tobias, Rochelle. "The Ground Gives Way: Intimations of the Sacred in Celan's 'Gespräch im Gebirg'." *MLN* 114 (1999): 567–89.

Tobias, Rochelle. *The Discourse of Nature in the Poetry of Paul Celan: The Unnatural World.* Baltimore, MD: Johns Hopkins University Press, 2006.

Treude, Sabine. *"Die Kinder der Toten* oder: Eine Verwicklung der Geschichten mit einer Geschichte, die fehlt." *Text+Kritik* 117 (2007): 100–9.

Turner, Victor. *The Ritual Process: Structure and Anti-Structure.* Ithaca, NY: Cornell University Press, 1969.

Uerlings, Herbert. "Novalis in Freiberg. Die Romantisierung des Bergbaus—Mit einem Blick auf Tiecks 'Runenberg' und E. T. A. Hoffmanns 'Bergwerke zu Falun'." *Aurora* 56 (1996): 57–77.

Valk, Thorsten. "Die Bergwerke zu Falun. Tiefenpsychologie aus dem Geist der romantischen Seelenkunde." In *E. T. A: Hoffmann: Romane und Erzählungen.* Edited by Günter Saße. Stuttgart: Reclam, 2004, 168–81.

Vogel, Juliane. "Elfriede Jelineks Kinder der Toten." *manuskripte* 132 (1996): 110–11.

Vogel, Juliane. "Wasser hinunter, wohin? Elfriede Jelineks Roman *Kinder der Toten*—ein Flüssigtext." In *"Other" Austrians: Post-1945 Austrian Women's Writing.* Edited and introduced by Allyson Fiddler. Bern: Lang, 1998, 235–42.

Vogel, Juliane. "'Keine Leere der Unterbrechung'—*Die Kinder der Toten* oder der Schrecken der Falte." *Modern Austrian Literature* 39, no. 3–4 (2006): 15–26.

Vranitzky, Franz. Stenographisches Protokoll. 35. Sitzung des Nationalrats der Republik Österreich. XVIII Gesetzgebungsperiode. Montag, 8., und Dienstag, 9.7.1991. 3268–408, 3282.

Werner, Uta. *Textgräber: Paul Celans geologische Lyrik.* München: Fink, 2002.

Whittow, John. *Dictionary of Physical Geography.* London: Penguin, 1984.

Wiese, Benno von. *Die deutsche Novelle von Goethe bis Kafka: Interpretationen.* Düsseldorf: August Bagel Verlag, 1956–62.

Will, Michael. *"Autopsie" und "reproductive Phantasie": Quellenstudien zu Georg Büchners Erzählung "Lenz."* Würzburg: Königshausen und Neumann, 2000.

Wilson, Ian. "Greeting the Holocaust's Dead? Narrative Strategies and the Undead in Elfriede Jelinek's *Die Kinder der Toten.*" *Modern Austrian Literature* 39, no. 3–4 (2006): 27–55.

Wiman, C. "Über neue und einige alte Leichenwachsfunde." *Bulletin of the Geogical Institution of the University of Upsala* 28 (1941): 141–55.

Wozniakowski, Jacek. *Die Wildnis. Zur Deutungsgeschichte des Berges in der europäischen Neuzeit.* Frankfurt/Main: Suhrkamp, 1974.

Zanetti, Sandro. "Orte/Worte—Erde/Rede. Celans Geopoetik." In *Geopoetiken: Geographische Entwürfe in den mittel- und osteuropäischen Literaturen.* Edited by Magdalena Marszalek and Sylvia Sasse. Berlin: Kulturverlag Kadmos, 2010, 115–31.

Ziolkowski, Theodore. *German Romanticism and its Institutions.* Princeton, NJ: Princeton University Press, 1989.

Index

Addison, Joseph 9, 10
aesthetics
   aesthetic philosophy 22
   Alpine aesthetic 3–34
   of disharmony and
      fragmentation 19
   of disinterred body 45–9
   of literary characters 87
   of madness 72, 73
   philosophy and aesthetic
      theory 31
Aiguebellette, Mount 10
Alberti, Leon Battista, *De pictura* 85
Allgemeine Theorie der schönen Künste See. Sulzer, Johann Georg
'Alpenreisen' [Alpine Journeys] (Simmel) 21
Alpine aesthetic 3–34
Alpine formation 25
Alpine landscape 140
Amelung, Franz *See.* Bird, Friedrich and Franz Amelung
Ansichten von der Nachtseite der Naturwissenschaft See. Schubert, Gotthilf Heinrich von
anthropomorphism *See.* human/humanity
Arnim, Achim von, *Des ersten Bergmanns ewige Jugend* 39, 55

art, artists
   Alberti, Leon Battista 85
   artistic knowledge 24
   artistic merit 87–8
   artistic space 84, 102
   Delécluse, Étienne 14
   difficulty in depicting
      mountains 15, 22–31, 34, 90, 169
   discussions about 87
   Hodler, Ferdinand 22
   and human existential
      condition 89
   illusion of stability 85
   lack of artistic intention 47
   Medusa's head as symbol of
      artistic aspiration 100
   mountain views 84
   photography 14
   Segantini, Giovanni 22
   'taking away' the mountains 167
astrology, and geological sciences 62
Austria
   and Holocaust *See.* Celan, Paul, *Gespräch im Gebirg*; Holocaust; Jelinek, Elfriede, *Die Kinder der Toten*
   modern literature of mountains 33–4
   postwar response to Nazism 145

tensions between 'German,'
'Austrian,' and 'Swiss'
literature 169

beauty
  death and 95
  existence of 96
  Kant's notion of 30
Beiträge zur Lehre von den Geisteswissenschaften See.
  Bird, Friedrich and Franz Amelung
Die Bergwerke zu Falun (Hoffmann) See. Hoffmann, E. T. A.
Bird, Friedrich and Franz Amelung, *Beiträge zur Lehre von den Geisteswissenschaften* 74
Brentano, Clemens von 39
Büchner, Georg, *Lenz*
  author's approach in current book 32
  Celan's *Gebirg* compared 112, 118
  displacement and disorientation as theme See. displacement and disorientation
  Lenz's arrival in the Vosges 71–83
  Lenz's distorted and shifted perspectives of his surroundings 83–9
  Lenz's return to the mountains 90–4
  madness as theme See. madness
  Medusa's head, meaning of 100–2
  perspectival shifts as substance of Lenz's madness 94–9
  Verrücktheit concept of madness 73–5
  Wahnsinn concept of madness 73
  See also. madness
Burke, Edmund, *A philosophical enquiry into the origin of our ideas of the sublime and the beautiful* 15
Burnet, Thomas 9, 154–5

Celan, Paul, *Gespräch im Gebirg* [Conversation in the Mountains] 103–34
  author's approach in current book 32–3
  Büchner's, *Lenz* compared 112, 118
  folded form as theme 32–3, 110–15, 117–18, 125–34, 165
  Hoffmann's *Bergwerke zu Falun* compared 112
  Holocaust and See. Holocaust
  inaccessibility of mountains to Jews as symbol of inaccessibility of German culture and language 32–3, 105–12
  and Jelinek's *Die Kinder der Toten* 141–2
  and Leibniz's *Monadologie* 112–16
  mountain landscapes as wordscapes of Nazi persecution 120–8
  vanished mountains as symbol of Nazi extermination of Jews 106, 108
  a walk through the mountains 116–20
chaos, order and 155
characters in literature, aesthetics of 87
Chateaubriand, François-René, vicomte de 14
coherence, order and 148

Index 187

conceptual stability 46
creation, death and 131
creativity and innovation
   current trends in fiction 169
   imaginative narrative 39
   literature as source of
      inspiration 8
   mountains as source of
      inspiration 33
   narrative experimentation 40
   new narrative techniques 15
cultural studies, geological
   sciences in 6

'Das Gedächtnis des Bodens'
   (Schmeiser) 137–8
death
   acknowledgment of 4
   beauty and 95
   creation and 131
   decay and 144
   dissolution of boundaries
      between life and death 32
   fecundity and 155
   images of 131
   individuation and 123
   as inversion, transformation
      and transition *See.* Falun
      iron ore mine incident
   mountain graves 137–42
   no to 158
   and the undead 148
   yes to 158
decay, death and 144
Delécluse, Étienne 14
Dennis, John 9–10
description, narrative 80
disorientation *See.* displacement
   and disorientation
displacement and disorientation
   of Jews 105–6
   madness and 72–3, 76
   music and 75
   spatial 72, 94–5

Verrückung concept of 32, 73–6,
   79, 82–3, 90–1, 96, 99
distance, stability and 81
documentary (form), fiction
   blended with 20
dragons, mountain sightings of
   8–9
drama, narrative as replacement
   for 20

emotion, narrative and 50
Enlightenment 40, 49, 139
Everest, Mount 165
existence, existential
   absence of 38
   aesthetic 45–9
   of beauty 96
   bringing into 33, 111
   burden of 99
   coexistence 31, 55, 71, 84, 115
   continuation of 99
   desire to end 56–7
   destruction of 155
   formless 28
   multiple states 32, 65
   non-existence 14, 109
   oppositional existences 31
   place of 165
   plight 89
   possibility of 97
   remembrance of 155
   reshaped 29
   semiotic 46
   singular 113–14
extraterrestrial order 27

fact, fiction and 20, 41, 45
Falun iron ore mine incident
   (1720)
   account of 42–5
   aesthetics of disinterred body
      45–9
   author's approach in current
      book 31–2

188 Index

discovery of miner's body 37–42
literary depictions of 39–40
mystery of body's identity and meaning 57–8
poetic treatments of 49–56
as story of inversion, transformation and transition 58–67
See also. Hoffmann, E. T. A., *Die Bergwerke zu Falun*
fecundity, death and 155
Fichtelgebirge 12–13
fiction
 current trends in 169
 documentary form blended with 20
 fact and 20, 41, 45
 mimesis and 47
 shifts within literary genres and forms 34
Der fliegende Berg (Ransmayr) 33–4
folded mountains *See.* Celan, Paul, *Gespräch im Gebirg*

geographical locations 107, 108–9
geographical sciences 6, 58
geological sciences
 aesthetic geology 6
 and anthropomorphic imagination 157
 astrology and 62
 beginning of 6
 in cultural and literary studies 6
 formation of mountain structures 110, 112, 113, 125
 geography and 58
 geological knowledge 6, 112
 geological time 152
 literary points of departure as geological ruptures 149
 norms 152
 taxonomies 126

German literature *See.* fiction; literature; poetry
Gespräch im Gebirg (Celan) *See.* Celan, Paul
Gessner, Konrad 7
Gessner, Solomon 105
Gestalt 24, 28
Glavinic, Thomas, *Das größere Wunder* 33–4
Goethe, Johann Wolfgang von 3–9, 13–14, 105
Grand Tour 9–10
Das größere Wunder (Glavinic) 33–4

Haller, Albrecht von, *In den Alpen* 11, 12
Hardenberg, Georg Philipp Friedrich Freiherr von (Novalis), *Heinrich von Ofterdingen* 58
harmony/disharmony, aesthetics of 19
Hausmann, Johann Ludwig, *Reise durch Skandinavien in den Jahren 1806 und 1807* 40, 61
Hebel, Johann Peter, 'Unverhofftes Wiedersehen' [Unexpected Reunion] 39, 55
Heinrich von Ofterdingen (Novalis) *See.* Hardenberg, Georg Philipp Friedrich Freiherr von (Novalis)
Henke, Adolph 73, 75–6
history
 historical vanishing-point within narrative 108
 mountains as literary historical forms 139
Hodler, Ferdinand 22
Hoffmann, E. T. A., *Die Bergwerke zu Falun* [The Mines of Falun] *See.* Falun iron ore mine incident

Hoffmannsthal, Hugo von 39
Holocaust
    Austria as necropolis 146–7, 152
    Austrian history of 143–50, 145
    author's approach in current book 32
    contamination of mountain literature tradition 108
    'erased' victims of 108, 153
    instability of post-Holocaust language 110
    literary representations of 139, 148
    transformation of Alpine landscape 137
human/humanity
    art and the human existential condition 89, 101–2
    death *See.* death
    displacement and disorientation, sense of *See.* displacement and disorientation
    emotion, narrative description of 50
    fecundity 155
    geological sciences and anthropomorphic imagination 157
    Kant's writings on mountains and the rational human mind 18–21, 32, 72
    madness *See.* madness
    man and mountain 23
    place within literary representations of mountains 106
    See also. death; existence, existential

Ich werde hier sein im Sonnenschein und im Schatten (Kracht) 33–4

illusion of stability 84
imagination, narrative and 39
In den Alpen (Haller) 11, 12
In den Alpen (play) *See.* Jelinek, Elfriede
inorganic (state) *See.* organic
inspiration, mountains as source of 33
instability *See.* stability/instability
Israelsson, Mathias, death and entombment of *See.* Falun iron ore mine incident; Hoffmann, E. T. A., *Die Bergwerke zu Falun*
Itinera per Helvetiae Alpinas Regiones Facta Annis 1702–1711 (Scheuchzer) 8

'Jean Paul' *See.* Richter, Friedrich
Jelinek, Elfriede, *Die Kinder der Toten* [The Children of the Dead]
    Alps as repository of Austria's Nazi past 33
    author's approach in current book 33–4, 135
    and Celan's *Gespräch im Gebirg* 141–2
    In den Alpen (play), and 142
    and history of Holocaust in Austria 143–50
    within mountain literature tradition 165, 168
    into the mountains 150–3
    Ovid's *Metamorphosis* 154–61
    Wolken. Heim [Clouds. Home] (play), and 137–8
Jews, Judaism
    displacement and disorientation of 105–6
    inaccessibility of mountains as symbol of inaccessibility of German culture and language 32–3

mountain landscapes as
  wordscapes of Nazi
  persecution 120–8
  See also. Holocaust
journalism 21, 37, 41, 55

Kant, Immanuel
  his emotional response to
    mountains 15–16
  his own experience of
    mountains 8
  his influence on contemporary
    authors 19, 29–30
  Kritik der Urteilskraft 8
  on mountains and the rational
    human mind 18–21, 32, 72
  his notion of beauty 30
  his notion of the sublime 15–21,
    29–30, 48, 72, 76–9, 160, 165
Die Kinder der Toten See. Celan,
  Paul
knowledge
  artistic 24
  conveying of 128
  geological 6, 112
  order of 41
  production of 41
Kracht, Christian, *Ich werde hier
  sein im Sonnenschein und im
  Schatten* [I'll be here in
  sunshine and in shadow]
  33–4
Kritik der Urteilskraft See. Kant,
  Immanuel

language
  accessibility/inaccessibility of
    107–8
  inaccessibility of mountains to
    Jews as symbol of
    inaccessibility of German
    culture and language 32–3
  instability of post-Holocaust
    language 110

mountain landscapes as
  wordscapes of Nazi
  persecution 120–8
  role of narrative voice within
    127–8
Leibniz, Gottfried Wilhelm,
  Monadologie 33, 110, 112–16
Lenz (Büchner) *See.* Büchner,
  Georg; madness
Lenz, Jakob Michael Reinhold 72,
  76, 77
Leyel, Adam, 'Narratio accurata
  de cadavere humano in
  fodina cuprimontana ante
  duos annos reperto'
  [Detailed account of a
  human corpse in a copper
  mine two years ago] 39,
  42–6, 55, 58, 65, 66
liminality 20, 27, 32, 57, 61, 67, 112,
  122, 157
literary characters *See.* characters
  in literature
literary studies, geological
  sciences in 6
literature
  discussions about 87
  humanity's place within 106
  interrogative role of 139
  literary points of departure as
    geological ruptures 149
  mountains as literary historical
    forms 139
  mountains as obsolete literary
    forms 139
  mountains as source of
    inspiration 33
  mountains as topos 105, 108
  mountains in literary
    imagination 169
  during Nazi era 107–8
  parameters of 108
  philosophy and literary theory
    31

representations of mountains 139
representations of the Holocaust 139
role of narrative voice within 127–8
roles of mountains within 108, 165, 168–9
shifts in forms of 31–4
shifts within genres and forms 34
as source of inspiration 8
and the sublime 102
tensions between 'German,' 'Austrian,' and 'Swiss' literature 169
use of historical material 20
lost in the mountains *See*. Büchner, Georg, *Lenz*
Luther, Martin 62

madness
  aesthetic of 72, 73
  and displacement and disorientation 72–3, 76
  Adolph Henke's description of 73–4
  perspective and 72, 87, 89, 94, 97–9
  and the sublime 72, 76–7
  as theme of Georg Büchner's *Lenz* 12, 32, 67, 71–4
  Verrücktheit concept 73–5
  Verrückung concept of 82
  Wahnsinn concept 73
Marti, Benedikt 7
Medusa's head in art 100–2
Metamorphosis (Ovid) 154–61
mimesis, fiction and 47
mind *See*. human/humanity
mines and mining *See*. Falun iron ore mine incident; Hoffmann, E. T. A., *Die Bergwerke zu Falun*

Mont Blanc 3–6, 8, 14, 168
More, Henry 9
mountain ranges
  folded structure *See*. Celan, Paul, *Gespräch im Gebirg*; xref Celan, Paul, *Gespräch im Gebirg*
  formation of mountain structures 110, 112, 113, 125
mountains
  author's approach in current book 7
  death and *See*. death; Falun iron ore mine incident
  depiction of *See*. art, artists
  folded *See*. Celan, Paul, *Gespräch im Gebirg*
  humanity's place within 106
  impact on literary imagination 3–15
  as literary historical forms 139
  in literary imagination 169
  literary representations of 139
  man and mountain 23
  mines and mining 37–66
  modern literature of 33–4
  narrative as generative means 31
  as obsolete literary forms 139
  origins (physical) of 154
  origins of concept of 6
  poetics of *See*. poetry
  resistance of 21–31
  roles within literature 139, 165, 168–9
  scholarly works on 6–7
  as source of inspiration 33
  as space 140, 148, 150, 153, 168
  in space 6, 9, 34, 40–1, 66–7, 82, 90–1
  and the sublime 15–21
  'taking away' by artists 169
  as topos 139

mountains and mountain ranges (individual)
  Aiguebellette 10
  Everest, Mount 165
  Fichtelgebirge 12–13
  Mont Blanc 3–6, 8, 14, 168
  Ochsenkopf 12
  Vosges 32, 71, 76
Mozart, Wolfgang Amadeus 148
music, displacement and 75
musical order 75–6
mutability and stability 113

'Narratio accurata de cadavere humano in fodina cuprimontana ante duos annos reperto' *See.* Leyel, Adam
narrative
  Alpine aesthetic 15, 20, 31–3
  backdrops 7
  coherence 120
  cohesion 38
  of constant change 160
  conventions 32
  description 80
  emotional 50
  evolution 144
  examples of 32, 41, 54–5, 101, 127
  experimentation 40
  form 111, 139
  as generative means 31
  historical vanishing-point 108
  imaginative 39
  linear 118
  movement 111
  narrative voice within literature and language 127–8
  new techniques 15
  norms 165
  official 145
  order 40
  possibilities 33
  production 41

  programme 166
  repeated 143
  replacement for drama 20
  stability 46
  of thresholds 63
  transition 58, 63–4
  voice 119, 127, 128, 140
Nazism
  Alps as repository of Austria's Nazi past 33, 141
  Austria's postwar response 145
  Holocaust *See.* Holocaust
  literature and language during Nazi era 107–8
  mountain landscapes as wordscapes of persecution 120–8
  victory over 137
news, newspapers *See.* journalism
Novalis *See.* Hardenberg, Georg Philipp Friedrich Freiherr von

Ochsenkopf, Mount 12
order (state of)
  bringing of 159
  chaos and 155
  coherence and 148
  destruction of 75
  different 127
  establishment 148
  extraterrestrial 27
  of knowledge 41
  of more than one 57
  musical 75–6
  narrative order 40
  new 27, 155
  realms of 41
  scenes of 87
  semantic 123
  social 41, 63
  spatial 76
  structure and 12
  symbolic 122
  taxonomic 58

temporal 28, 119
of transformation 60
universal 132
organic (state) *See.* inorganic
otherness
  becoming always other 48
  different order 127
  I and the other one 117, 131
  man and mountain 23
Ovid, *Metamorphosis* 44, 154–61

painting *See.* art
perspectival stability 93
perspective, madness and 72, 87, 89, 94, 97–9
Petrarca, Francesco (Petrarch) 7
A philosophical enquiry into the origin of our ideas of the sublime and the beautiful (Burke) 15
philosophy
  aesthetic philosophy 22
  and aesthetic theory 31
  Enlightenment 40, 49, 139
  Gestalt 24, 28
  and literary theory 31
  See also. . sublime
photography 14
physical stability 54
De pictura (Alberti) 85
plays *See.* theatre, plays
poetry
  difficulty in depicting mountains 3–7, 15
  experience of mountains 3–7, 12, 109
  forms of 20
  poetic transformation 41
  poetics of mountains 15, 32–4, 40–6, 63, 65–6, 100, 108–11, 115, 117, 120, 122–3, 133, 152, 154, 160, 170
  preference for 89
  task for 39, 49–58
psychology *See.* human/humanity

Ransmayr, Christoph, *Der fliegende Berg* [The Flying Mountain] 33–4
reason, rationalism *See.* human/humanity
Reise durch Skandinavien in den Jahren 1806 und 1807 (Hausmann) 40, 61
Richter, Friedrich ('Jean Paul'), *Die unsichtbare Loge* 12–13, 62
'Runenberg' *See.* Tieck, Ludwig

Scheuchzer, Johann Jakob, *Itinera per Helvetiae Alpinas Regiones Facta Annis 1702–1711* 8
Schiller, Friedrich (*Der Spaziergang*) 11–12
Schmeiser, Leonhard, 'Das Gedächtnis des Bodens' (essay) 137–8
Schneeberg, Mount 12–13
Schubert, Franz 148
Schubert, Gotthilf Heinrich von, *Ansichten von der Nachtseite der Naturwissenschaft* [Views from the dark side of science] 39, 40, 49–55, 57, 58, 66
science *See.* geographical sciences; geological sciences
semantic order 123
semantic stability 54
semiotics 117
Shaftsbury, Anthony 9
Simmel, Georg
  'Alpenreisen' [Alpine Journeys] (Simmel) 21
  on *Gestalt* 24, 28
  'Zur Ästhetik der Alpen' [On the Aesthetics of the Alps] 21–31, 34
social order 41, 63
Soulier, Charles 14, 168

space
  actual 109
  artistic 84, 102
  burial 157
  celestial 63
  characters within 119–20
  collapsing of 111
  concealment within 57
  for conversation 115
  cosmopolitan 169
  displacement *See.* displacement and disorientation
  dissolved boundaries of 141
  within dreams 59
  environmental 80
  fictional 58
  image space 80
  interior 93, 97
  inversion of 63
  liminal 112
  location and 77
  mountains as 140, 148, 150, 153, 168
  mountains within 6, 9, 34, 40–1, 66–7, 82, 90–1
  pictorial 85, 92, 98
  relationship to 76
  ruptures in 38
  spatial order 76
  and the sublime 67
  transition 51
  wild 82, 84
  without meaning 57
  between words 121
  See also. . time
Der Spaziergang (Schiller) 11–12
stability/instability
  conceptual 46
  distance and 81
  illusion of 84
  implicit instability 19
  moment of instability 64
  mutability and 113
  perspectival 93
  physical 54
  position of 89
  of post-Holocaust language 110
  quest for 63
  semantic 54
  strength of 40
  transition and instability 57
  of the word 141
structure, order and 12
sublime
  Kant's notion of 15–21, 29–30, 48, 72, 76–9, 160, 165
  literature and 102
  madness and 72, 76–7
  mountains and 15–21
Sulzer, Johann Georg, *Allgemeine Theorie der schönen Künste* [General theory of fine arts] 75–6
Switzerland
  modern literature of mountains 33–4
  tensions between 'German,' 'Austrian,' and 'Swiss' literature 169
symbolic order 122

taxonomies 58, 126
theatre, plays 39, 84, 137, 142
Tieck, Ludwig, 'Runenberg' 58, 66–7
time
  characters within 119–20
  collapsing of 111
  dissolved boundaries of 141
  ruptures in 38
  temporal order 28, 119
  transition 51
  See also. . space
topos, mountains as 139
Trakl, Georg 40
transformation, order of 60

transition and instability 57
travel writing 12–15

undead, death and 148
universal order 132
Die unsichtbare Loge See. Richter, Friedrich
'Unverhofftes Wiedersehen' *See.* Hebel, Johann Peter

Ventoux, Mont 7
Verrücktheit concept of madness 73–5

Verrückung See. displacement and disorientation
Vosges Mountains 32, 71, 76

Wagner, Richard 39
Wahnsinn concept of madness 73
Winkelmann, Johann Joachim 12
Wolken. Heim See. Jelinek, Elfriede
word, stability of the 141

'Zur Ästhetik der Alpen' [On the Aesthetics of the Alps] (Simmel) 21–31

Volumes in the series:

1. *Improvisation as Art: Conceptual Challenges, Historical Perspectives*
by Edgar Landgraf

2. *The German Pícaro and Modernity: Between Underdog and Shape-Shifter*
by Bernhard Malkmus

3. *Citation and Precedent: Conjunctions and Disjunctions of German Law and Literature*
by Thomas O. Beebee

4. *Beyond Discontent: 'Sublimation' from Goethe to Lacan*
by Eckart Goebel

5. *From Kafka to Sebald: Modernism and Narrative Form*
edited by Sabine Wilke

6. *Image in Outline: Reading Lou Andreas-Salomé*
by Gisela Brinker-Gabler

7. *Out of Place: German Realism, Displacement, and Modernity*
by John B. Lyon

8. *Thomas Mann in English: A Study in Literary Translation*
by David Horton

9. *The Tragedy of Fatherhood: King Laius and the Politics of Paternity in the West*
by Silke-Maria Weineck

10. *The Poet as Phenomenologist: Rilke and the* New Poems
by Luke Fischer

11. *The Laughter of the Thracian Woman: A Protohistory of Theory*
by Hans Blumenberg, translated by Spencer Hawkins

12. *Roma Voices in the German-Speaking World*
by Lorely French

13. *Vienna's Dreams of Europe: Culture and Identity beyond the Nation-State*
by Katherine Arens

14. *Thomas Mann and Shakespeare: Something Rich and Strange*
edited by Tobias Döring and Ewan Fernie

15. *Goethe's Families of the Heart*
by Susan E. Gustafson

16. *German Aesthetics: Fundamental Concepts from Baumgarten to Adorno*
edited by J. D. Mininger and Jason Michael Peck

17. *Figures of Natality: Reading the Political in the Age of Goethe*
by Joseph D. O'Neil

18. *Readings in the Anthropocene: The Environmental Humanities, German Studies, and Beyond*
edited by Sabine Wilke and Japhet Johnstone

19 *Building Socialism: Architecture and Urbanism in East German Literature, 1955–1973*
by Curtis Swope

20. *Ghostwriting: W. G. Sebald's Poetics of History*
by Richard T. Gray

21. *Stereotype and Destiny in Arthur Schnitzler's Prose: Five Psycho-Sociological Readings*
by Marie Kolkenbrock

22. *Sissi's World: The Empress Elisabeth in Memory and Myth*
edited by Maura E. Hametz and Heidi Schlipphacke

23. *Posthumanism in the Age of Humanism: Mind, Matter, and the Life Sciences after Kant*
edited by Edgar Landgraf, Gabriel Trop, and Leif Weatherby

24. *Staging West German Democracy: Governmental PR Films and the Democratic Imaginary, 1953–1963*
by Jan Uelzmann

25. *The Lever as Instrument of Reason: Technological Constructions of Knowledge around 1800*
by Jocelyn Holland

26. *The Fontane Workshop: Manufacturing Realism in the Industrial Age of Print*
by Petra McGillen

27. *Gender, Collaboration, and Authorship in German Culture: Literary Joint Ventures, 1750–1850*
edited by Laura Deiulio and John B. Lyon

28. *Kafka's Stereoscopes: The Political Function of a Literary Style*
by Isak Winkel Holm

29. *Ambiguous Aggression in German Realism and Beyond: Flirtation, Passive Aggression, Domestic Violence*
by Barbara N. Nagel

30. *Thomas Bernhard's Afterlives*
edited by Stephen Dowden, Gregor Thuswaldner, and Olaf Berwald

31. *Modernism in Trieste: The Habsburg Mediterranean and the Literary Invention of Europe, 1870–1945*
by Salvatore Pappalardo

32. *Grotesque Visions: The Science of Berlin Dada*
by Thomas O. Haakenson

33. *Theodor Fontane: Irony and Avowal in a Post-Truth Age*
by Brian Tucker

34. *Jane Eyre in German Lands: The Import of Romance, 1848–1918*
by Lynne Tatlock

35. *Weimar in Princeton: Thomas Mann and the Kahler Circle*
by Stanley Corngold

36. *Authors and the World: Modes and Models of Literary Authorship in 20th and 21st Century Germany*
by Rebecca Braun

37. *Germany from the Outside: Rethinking German Cultural History in an Age of Displacement*
edited by Laurie Johnson

38. *France/Kafka: An Author in Theory*
by John T. Hamilton

39. *Representing Social Precarity in German Literature and Film*
edited by Sophie Duvernoy, Karsten Olson, and Ulrich Plass

40. *The "German Illusion": Germany and Jewish-German Motifs in Hélène Cixous's Late Work*
by Olivier Morel

41. *Interwar Salzburg: Austrian Culture Beyond Vienna*
Edited by Robert Dassanowsky and Katherine Arens

42. *Writing the Mountains: The Alpine Form in German Fiction*
by Jens Klenner

www.ingramcontent.com/pod-product-compliance
Lightning Source LLC
Chambersburg PA
CBHW052043300426
44117CB00012B/1953